Coaching Defensive Football Successfully: Vol. 4—Secondary Play and Coverages

Denny M. Burdine

ISBN: 978-1-60679-130-1
Library of Congress Control Number: 2010937389
Cover design: Brenden Murphy
Book layout: Studio J Art & Design
Front cover photo: ©Romeo Guzman/Cal Sport Media/ZUMApress.com

Coaches Choice
P.O. Box 1828
Monterey, CA 93942
www.coacheschoice.com

Dedication

To my wife, Judy; thanks for being the perfect football coach's wife. To my mother for giving me the thirst for knowledge and my dad for teaching me that a man's work ethic makes all the difference. Thanks to Don Hubbard, my high school football coach, for introducing me to the great game of football.

Acknowledgments

Only a retired coach could have the passion to write such an in depth book about defensive football. When I decided to spend the time to write down my knowledge of defensive football in book format, I tried to account for every detail. The seven volumes of *Coaching Defensive Football Successfully,* are the result of thousands of hours of creating images, animation, and written information.

As I began to write, I quickly realized that what I know is a result of the hard work of others. I have spent my entire coaching career feeding off of the knowledge of other coaches. I applied what I saw others doing and modified it to suit my own situation. There are some great innovators in the game of football and their creations never remain a secret. Of course, from trial and error, I also developed my own defensive philosophy; however, I have invented nothing as it applies to defensive football. During my coaching career everyone that I came in contact with left an impression. As a coach moves through his coaching career it becomes very difficult to remember from whom his coaching knowledge was gained. I have taken no shortcuts in my efforts to honor those coaches who have had a profound influence on me.

As for me, I can quickly account for my knowledge of defensive football. It comes from three coaches.

My journey in football began with my high school coach, Don Hubbard. From him I learned in practice what the phrase, "Run it again!" meant. He was a die-hard for simplicity and fundamentals. We would run the same play over and over again until he was satisfied that it could be successful in a game situation. According to him, there was no need to have multiple plays if you could not run the basic plays correctly. He also showed me how important winning state championships was to the school and community, and most importantly, how it had an everlasting impact on the players. Much of my confidence in life was because of his influence on me and a belief that failure is not an option.

From John Thompson, former defensive coordinator at the University of Arkansas, I learned just about everything that I know about defensive football. Much of the defensive scheme found in this book came from Coach Thompson's ideas. The stack scheme with two-deep coverage was the foundation of my football knowledge. Coach Thompson's numbered blitz scheme, along with prowling and movement, taught me that modern day defensive football can be very unconventional, but very successful. I firmly believe that Coach Thompson is one of the best defensive minds that ever coached the game.

Special thanks to Richard Martin, who was my pipeline for defensive football information. He passed away at an early age, but he lived a full life for a football coach. Coach Martin had a great deal of passion for defense. He would be so intense about discussing new defensive ideas that you too would become enthusiastic.

Finally, to the players that I coached, thanks for the knowledge that I gained from your efforts. It was through your blood, sweat, and pain that I was able to experiment with various defensive schemes. I can only hope that I gave back all that I received.

Contents

Dedication 3

Acknowledgments 4

Preface 11

Introduction 13

Chapter 1: Secondary Basics 17

   Secondary Personnel
   Secondary Declaration
   Secondary Cardinal Rules
   Defensive Passing Zones
   Numbering Offensive Receivers
   Numbering Offensive Sets
     I Pro 21 Set
     Wishbone 11 Set
     I Twins 12 Set
     One-Back Tight-Trips 13 Set
     Empty Tight-Quads 14 Set
     One-Back Doubles 22 Set
     Empty Pro-Trips 23 Set
     One-Back Trips-Split 31 Set
     Empty Trips-Twins 32 Set
     Empty Quads-Split 41 Set

Chapter 2: Zone and Man Coverage Fundamentals 27

   Defensive Quarterback Reads
   Backpedal Techniques
   Man-to-Man Alignments
    Man-to-Man Alignment Adjustments
   Man-to-Man Stances
   Rules of Engagement (Attack Rules) for Man Coverage

Man-to-Man Coverage Techniques
    Man Cloud
    Man Sky
    Man Bail Sky
Man-Cloud Alignments and Techniques
    Ike
    Opie
    Marvin
Man-to-Man Ball Playing Techniques
Man Sky Coverage
Pass Coverages
    Man-to-Man Coverages
    Zone Coverages
    Combination Man and Zone Coverages
    Special Coverages

Chapter 3: Man Coverages 41
Cover 0
    Vs. a 21 Set
    Vs. a 12 Set
    Vs. a 13 Set
    Vs. a 14 Set
    Vs. a 22 Set
    Vs. a 23 Set
    Vs. a 31 Set
    Vs. a 32 Set
    Vs. a 41 Set
Cover 0 Lock
    Vs. a 21 Set
    Vs. a 12 Set
    Vs. a 13 Set
    Vs. a 14 Set
    Vs. a 22 Set
    Vs. a 23 Set
    Vs. a 31 Set
    Vs. a 32 Set
    Vs. a 41 Set
Cover 1
    Vs. a 21 Set
    Vs. a 12 Set
    Vs. a 13 Set

        Vs. a 14 Set

        Vs. a 22 Set

        Vs. a 23 Set

        Vs. a 31 Set

        Vs. a 32 Set

        Vs. a 41 Set

Chapter 4: Zone Coverages 79

    Advantages of Zone Coverage

    Zone Coverage Terminology

    Cover 2

        Vs. a 21 Set

        Vs. a 12 Set

        Vs. a 13 Set

        Vs. a 14 Set

        Vs. a 22 Set

        Vs. a 23 Set

        Vs. a 31 Set

        Vs. a 32 Set

        Vs. a 41 Set

        Crazy Horse Cover 2 vs. a 31 Set

    Cover 2 Half-Line Reads and Reactions

        Vs. Weakside X Fade

        Vs. Weakside X Slant

        Vs. Weakside Twins—X and Z Fades

        Vs. Weakside Twins—X Fade and Z Slant

        Vs. Weakside Twins—X Fade and Z Out

        Vs. Strongside Tight End (Y) Fade

        Vs. Strongside Pro Set—Z and Y Fades

        Vs. Strongside Pro Set—Z Fade and Y Out

        Vs. Strongside Pro Set—Z Slant

    Cover 3

        Vs. a 21 Set

        Vs. a 12 Set

        Vs. a 13 Set

        Vs. a 14 Set

        Vs. a 22 Set

        Vs. a 23 Set

        Vs. a 31 Set

        Vs. a 32 Set

        Vs. a 41 Set

Cover 3 Rhino
    Vs. a 21 Set
    Vs. a 22 Set
Cover 6
    Vs. a 21 Set
Cover 6 Snake
    Vs. a 21 Set

Chapter 5: Man/Zone Combination Coverages... 133
Toro
    Vs. a 21 Set
    Vs. a 12 Set
    Vs. a 13 Set
    Vs. a 14 Set
    Vs. a 22 Set
    Vs. a 23 Set
    Vs. a 31 Set
    Vs. a 32 Set
    Vs. a 41 Set
Cover 4
    Vs. a 21 Set
    Vs. a 12 Set
    Vs. a 13 Set
    Vs. a 14 Set
    Vs. a 22 Set
    Vs. a 23 Set
    Vs. a 31 Set
    Vs. a 32 Set
    Vs. a 41 Set
Cover 5
    Vs. a 21 Set
    Vs. a 12 Set
    Vs. a 13 Set
    Vs. a 14 Set
    Vs. a 22 Set
    Vs. a 23 Set
    Vs. a 31 Set
    Vs. a 32 Set
    Vs. a 41 Set

Zippo
    Vs. a 22 Set
    Zippo Quarterback vs. a 22 Set

Chapter 6: Special Coverages 185
    Cherokee Coverages
        Cover 2
        Cover 2 Scooter
        Cover 2 Sink
        Cover 2 Strike
        Cover 2 Whip
        Cover 2 Rhino
        Cover 2 Snake
        Zippo
        Cover 3
        Cover 3 Press
        Cover 3 Man
        Cover 1
        Cover 0
    Bracket Coverages
        Cover 0 "A"
        Cover 0 "C"
        Cover 0 "BC"

Chapter 7: Special Considerations 203
    Planning Coverages
    Coverage Modifications
        Calling and Checking Coverages
        Adjusting to Motion
    Special Man-to-Man Techniques
        Bump Technique
        Combo Technique
    Identifying Offensive Personnel

About the Author 206

Preface

Coaching Defensive Football Successfully consists of seven volumes that will help all coaches become better defensive coaches. It is for the young coach who is searching for a defensive package. It is also for the experienced coach who may be looking for new defensive ideas.

The following seven volumes are found in *Coaching Defensive Football Successfully:*
- Vol. 1—Philosophy and Fronts
- Vol. 2—Down Linemen
- Vol. 3—Linebackers
- Vol. 4—Secondary Play and Coverages
- Vol. 5—Blitz Package
- Vol. 6—Defending Offensive Schemes
- Vol. 7—Blocking and Returning Punts

The diagrammed plays found in most all books written about football use X's and O's to represent players. *Coaching Defensive Football Successfully* replaces the traditional X's and O's with drawn images of players to give the reader a more realistic view of diagrammed plays. Each book also includes a companion CD-ROM. The CDROM presents an animated PowerPoint® version of the play diagrams found in each book. By simply clicking a mouse, the reader can use a slide show presentation to see the diagrammed plays come to life as players move to defensive positioning. By using this sequence, the reader will acquire an in-depth understanding of each book.

A football coach must have a desire to acquire as much football knowledge as possible. Throughout his coaching career, he will always search for football information. He will buy books and videos and visit high school and college coaches, but the truth is, though, that no matter what he is searching for, he will get only bits and pieces of information. The worst feeling in the world is to see new defensive ideas, but have no way of learning the fine points. *Coaching Defensive Football Successfully* was written to give complete, detailed information from a coach's viewpoint.

Sometimes coaches work so hard using the same ideas that they become stale, much like a man with a dull saw. He is working hard, but is making very little progress. There comes a time when football coaches need to stop and sharpen their saws. A sharpened saw makes the job easier and more efficient. This defensive package will help to sharpen your defensive tools and make you a better football coach.

Each year, high school coaches see offenses that range from the Dead-T to the Spread, so coaches must have a package that is able to adapt to everything. *Coaching Defensive Football Successfully* provides a defensive package that allows you to make adjustments for all offensive schemes. It incorporates the Miami package, the 4-3 front, and all its adjustments. The Oklahoma package is the under 5-2 and all its adjustments. The Arizona package is made up of the 3-2, 3-3, 5-1, and the two-man fronts and all the adjustments from each. Secondary coverages are man-to-man, zone, and combination man and zone. Stemming, prowling, and movement are used extensively. Line stunts range from the simple one-man stunts to the complex four-man stunts. Finally, the blitz system involves using numbered blitzes and zone blitzes that are limited only by your imagination.

The defensive package described in this series is a proven defensive package. This package has won championships and produced major college players and NFL players.

If you are a new coach looking for defensive information, you will find it in this series. If you are a coach who already has a defensive scheme, you will gain information to build on what you already know.

Introduction

Congratulations for having chosen one of the most honorable professions known to man. The title "Coach" should be worn proudly, on and off the field. Your career choice of coaching also brings with it the title of teacher. To be given the ability and opportunity to teach others is a very honorable calling. As a football coach, you do much more than just coach and teach. You lead, you inspire, and you help to mold the lives of all those with whom you come in contact. The role of coach gives you the opportunity to teach character, discipline, leadership, and work ethics to your players. Knowing the impact you have on the lives of others is very sobering. Even on the bad days, be proud to tell people that you are a coach and a teacher. However, if you plan to continue to influence the lives of others, you must be able to win in the coaching profession. Unemployed coaches have very little impact on the lives of others. Being successful is a top priority.

Football is the greatest game that God ever allowed man to play. It is almost as if God said, "Let there be football so that all the young boys who play it can grow to become men, and all the men who coach it can always be boys."

Football coaches can be divided into three categories. The first type of coach is the "fundamentalist." He is very conservative in his thinking. He does not wear Tommy Hilfiger® shirts or Calvin Klein® pants. He does not brag about how much football he knows; he simply believes that in order to win, you must be fundamentally sound. He believes that blocking and tackling win football games. After all, Vince Lombardi said it, so it must be true. The fundamentalist works hard each day teaching basics. His team blocks and tackles and blocks and tackles. He has no interest in the spread offense or the zone blitz defense; he keeps everything simple.

When he walks off the field after each game, he cannot understand how he lost the game; after all, he worked fundamentals each day. A coach that is solely a fundamentalist is a dinosaur, and he is destined for extinction.

The second type of coach is the "theorist." He is very liberal in his thinking and wears the Tommy Hilfiger shirts and the Calvin Klein pants. He has a swagger in his walk, and he cannot end a conversation without letting one know how smart he is about the game of football. He spends all his time scheming how he can beat his opponents by outsmarting them. He believes that he wins the game on the chalkboard. His offensive scheme is very complex with formations, plays, and horizontal and vertical stretches. His defensive scheme is very complex with multiple fronts and coverages. He spends more time in practice working on alignments than he does working on fundamentals. Because he coaches a passive brand of football, his teams have a tendency to be soft when it comes to blocking and tackling.

When he walks off the field after each game, he cannot understand how he lost the game; after all, he is smarter than his opponents. This type of coach is not a dinosaur, but he also is destined for failure.

The third type of coach is the coach who understands that you win with fundamentals and modern-day offensive and defensive schemes. He is called the "theo-fundamentalist." He teaches fundamentals, but he also looks to gain the advantage by match-ups and alignments. His team works fundamentals each day from a scheme that gives them the best advantage to block and tackle. He understands that offensively a team must be multiple and stretch the defense both horizontally and vertically. He believes that a team must also be very multiple on defense and must use movement, blitzes, and multiple coverages to confuse and attack the offense. This type of coach has a great chance to be successful.

Each coach must develop a sound football philosophy. A defensive coach should have the philosophy that you play defense first, have a sound kicking game, and employ an offense that is exciting and moves the ball. The great coach Paul "Bear" Bryant once said, "Offense sells tickets, and defense wins championships." Nothing of greater truth has ever been said about the game of football. Defense comes first!

A good defensive package is one that allows the defenders to play in their natural state. The natural state for a defensive player is running to the ball and making tackles. All defensive schemes must allow the players to play in this manner. A coach must develop a defensive package that best allows this type of defense to occur. The natural state for a defender is to read and react while on the run, which means being aggressive when coming off the ball, attacking blockers, and pursuing the ballcarrier. To use this type of play against modern offenses, you must be multiple in your fronts and coverages. You must stunt, blitz, prowl, stem, and move both the fronts and coverages, thereby confusing the offense through disguises and illusions.

Most coaches will tell you that offense is assignment football, and defensive is reaction football. This saying may be true to a certain extent, but a defense must be a dictating type of defense, not just a reacting defense. Strike first and strike hard!

Place pressure on the offense and let them react to what you are doing on defense. Be simple enough to keep your players from being confused but complex enough to attack and confuse all offensive schemes.

When you think of defensive personnel, you must have a certain type of player in mind. You must look for players with great heart and aggressive personalities, who swarm to the ball. You do not want the "milk drinkers and cookie eaters" on your side of the ball. Instead, find the tough guys who will run to the ball and arrive in a very bad mood!

Football at any level from high school to the professional ranks is simply a good old-fashioned dogfight. Because it is a dogfight, you must bite the other dog harder and more often than he bites you. Show good sportsmanship but be aggressive. As the Mexicans proclaimed at the Battle of the Alamo, *"De Quello,"* which basically means, "Have no mercy and take no prisoners."

Placing your personnel in the proper positions is very important. Coaches must spend many hours in personnel meetings in order to get the best combination. The following ideas should be used when placing personnel into the proper positions:

- Corners are a must! Corners must be able to play man-to-man on an island. They must have good speed and jumping ability. The old cowboys out West used to say, "No hoof, no horse"; well in defensive football you can say, "No corners, no defense." When your corners can play on an island, your defensive scheme can become more complex and very dangerous to the offense. You must find your corners first.

- Safeties must be able to cover like corners and tackle like linebackers. They must be able to play in the box and also cover on an island. Safeties are your next priority after you have found the corners.

- Linebackers are the heart of the defense. They must be able to attack blockers, run to the ball, and tackle in the open field. They must be able to play both the pass and the run. Linebackers are a priority after you find corners and safeties.

- Linemen must be able to control the line of scrimmage. They are the "grunts," fighting it out in the trenches. They must defeat blockers and run to the ball. Most importantly, they must be able to rush the quarterback. Defensive ends must be a priority after you have found the secondary and linebackers. Defensive noses and tackles are the last, but not least, to be found.

Secondary Basics

Teams that win football games are the teams that do not beat themselves. Mistakes are the leading factors that equate to failure, and defensive mistakes can mean points for the opponents. The biggest mistake that a defense can make is giving up the quick touchdown through the air or the long run from scrimmage. It is the secondary that is ultimately responsible for stopping the long pass, long run, and preventing touchdowns. The secondary must be made up of special players who are physically skilled and mentally tough. They must understand the defensive scheme that they are playing, as well as the offensive scheme being used by their opponents.

Secondary Personnel

The secondary consist of four defensive backs in regular personnel: strong safety, Rover, field corner, and boundary corner. In the Arizona package, Geronimo comes in as the fifth defensive back and Tonto can be used as the sixth defensive back.

Secondary Declaration

The strong safety declares the secondary and aligns on the declared side. Rover aligns away from the declared side. The field corner aligns on the wide side of the field or to the left if the field is balanced. The boundary corner aligns away from the field corner. Geronimo's alignment depends on the coverage that is called. Tonto aligns to the declared side.

Secondary Cardinal Rules

Cardinal rules must exist for the secondary, so every player has a base understanding of what is expected from them.

- This scheme calls for a lot of man coverage. When playing man-to-man on an island, the offense will have success at times. However, the defensive back must be mentally tough and he must not have a letdown when bad things occur.
- The defender must know his responsibilities and the responsibilities of his teammates on each play.
- The defender must know where his coverage help is located and where the coverage weaknesses are located.
- Coaches create game plans that are based on the opponent's offensive tendencies. The secondary must know those offensive tendencies on each play.
- A good defensive back learns as much as possible about offensive passing schemes.
- The defensive back must use good footwork. He must have great balance and never leave his feet.
- When the ball is in the air, it belongs to the defense, so the defenders must go after the ball at its high point. The defenders must go to the ball when it is thrown and always expect a tipped ball.
- The sideline is the defensive back's best friend; he should always use it to restrict the offensive playing field.
- Defensive backs must read the quarterback for pass drops, which, in return, helps them to know the receivers' routes.
- Missed tackles in the secondary are a sin. Defenders must always tackle using good open field techniques. It is okay to give ground and force the ballcarrier into the sideline in order to get help from teammates.
- The secondary must communicate with each other at all times, using the following terminology:
  - ✓ They must call out the offensive formation by using numbers. The strong safety and Rover will call out the number of receivers on the strongside and the weakside. For example, versus a pro set, the strong safety calls out, "I've got two, I've got two!" Rover calls out, "I've got one, I've got one!" The strong safety then calls out, "Twenty-one, Twenty-one!" In doing so, the defense has identified the eligible receivers and the offensive set.
  - ✓ They must repeat the coverage calls by calling out coverage numbers and colors.

✓ All defensive backs must call out "Pass!" or "Run!" when they see it.

✓ The secondary must communicate by calling out pass routes, cracks, and reverses.

✓ Always yell "Ball!" when the ball is in the air and "Oskie!" when an interception occurs.

The modern day pass offenses, such as the spread offense, place a lot of pressure on the defense, even at the high school level. The defense must be very multiple to attack these offenses. This package uses several different coverages, such as man-to-man, zone, and man-zone combinations.

Defensive Passing Zones

Each defensive player must understand defensive pass terminology, which begins with a complete understanding of defensive passing zones. Basically, passing zones are areas located on a football field that divide the field into various zones. If everyone understands the location of defensive passing zones, they will not only know their responsibilities but also the location and responsibilities of their teammates. Defensive passing zones are shown in Figures 1-1 and 1-2.

When playing man-to-man pass coverage, the defense must be able to identify offensive sets as well as eligible pass receivers. To identify offensive set and receivers, numbers are used to identify receivers, thus also identifying the offensive formation.

Numbering Offensive Receivers

The numbering rules are used by the defense to number eligible receivers. Receivers are numbered on each side, from the sideline to the ball.

- The widest receiver is #1.
- The second widest receiver is #2.
- The third widest receiver is #3.
- The fourth widest receiver is #4.
- Backs are numbered depending on the formation and their release side. In an I pro formation, the first back to come to the strongside is #3. The first back to come to the weakside is #2. If both backs go to the strongside, the first back is #3 and the second back is #4. If both backs go to the weakside, the first back is #2 and the second back is #3. In one-back sets, the back can be #2, #3, or #4.
- Motion and receivers crossing will change the numbering of receivers.

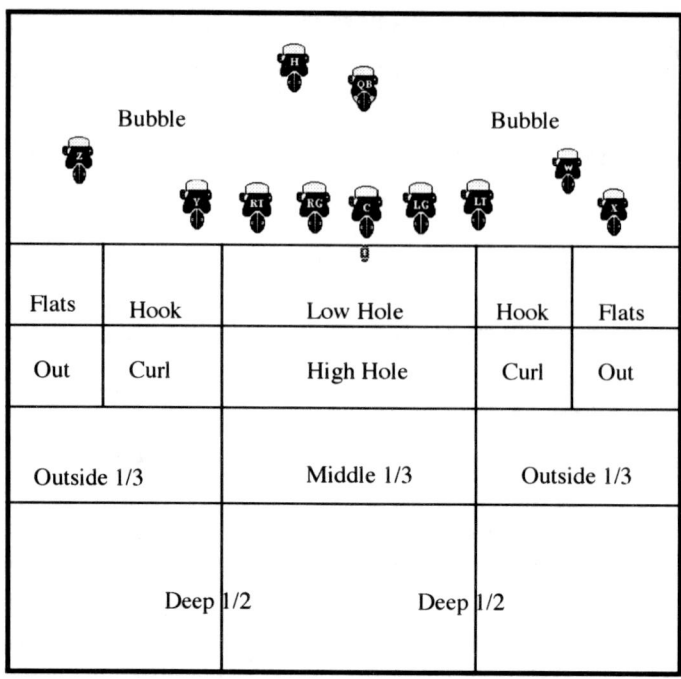

Figure 1-1. Defensive passing zones

Zone	Description
Bubble	An area behind the line of scrimmage from the ball to the sideline.
Flats	An area from the tight end to the sideline from six to eight yards deep.
Hook	An area over the tight end from 8 to 15 yards deep.
Low hole	An area from over the ball to a depth of six to eight yards.
Curl	An area inside a wideout from 8 to 15 yards deep and seven yards inside the receiver.
Out	An area outside a wideout extending to the sideline from 8 to 15 yards deep.
High hole	An area over the ball from 8 to 12 yards deep.
Outside 1/3	An area from the sideline to the hash from 12 yards deep to the goal line.
Middle 1/3	An area from hash-to-hash from 12 yards deep to the goal line.
Deep 1/2	An area from the sideline to the middle of the field from 12 yards deep to the goal line.

Figure 1-2. Description of defensive passing zones

Numbering Offensive Sets

After receivers have been numbered, the offensive set is then numbered based on the number of receivers to the strongside and weakside. For example, if two receivers are on the strongide and one receiver is on the weakside, it would be a 21 set. A pro set is a 21 set. However, it should also be noted that all 21 sets are not pro sets; split-twins would also be a 21 set.

I Pro 21 Set (Figure 1-3)

I Pro 21 set is an I backfield with two receivers to the strongside and one receiver to the weakside.

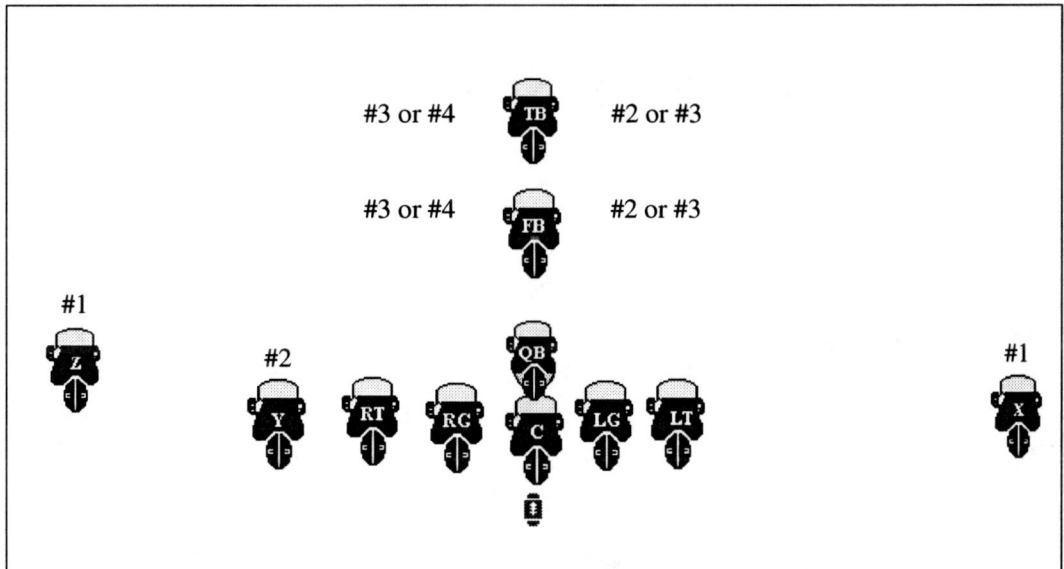

Figure 1-3. I pro 21 set

Wishbone 11 Set (Figure 1-4)

Wishbone 11 set is a three-back backfield with one receiver to the strongside and one receiver to the weakside.

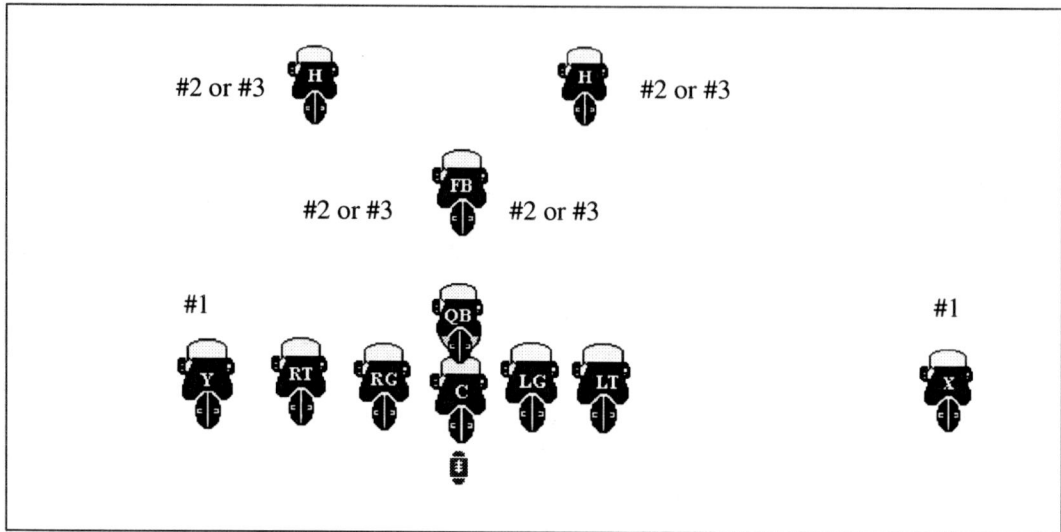

Figure 1-4. Wishbone 11 set

I Twins 12 Set (Figure 1-5)

I twins 12 set is an I backfield with one receiver to the strongside and two receivers to the weakside.

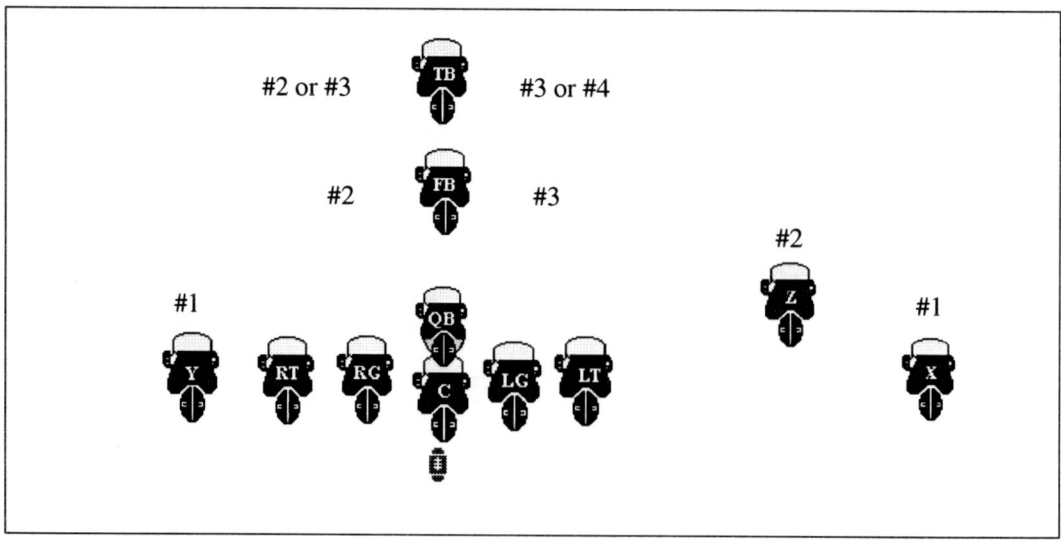

Figure 1-5. I twins 12 set

One-Back Tight-Trips 13 Set (Figure 1-6)

One-back tight-trips 13 set is a one-back backfield with one receiver to the strongside and three receivers to the weakside.

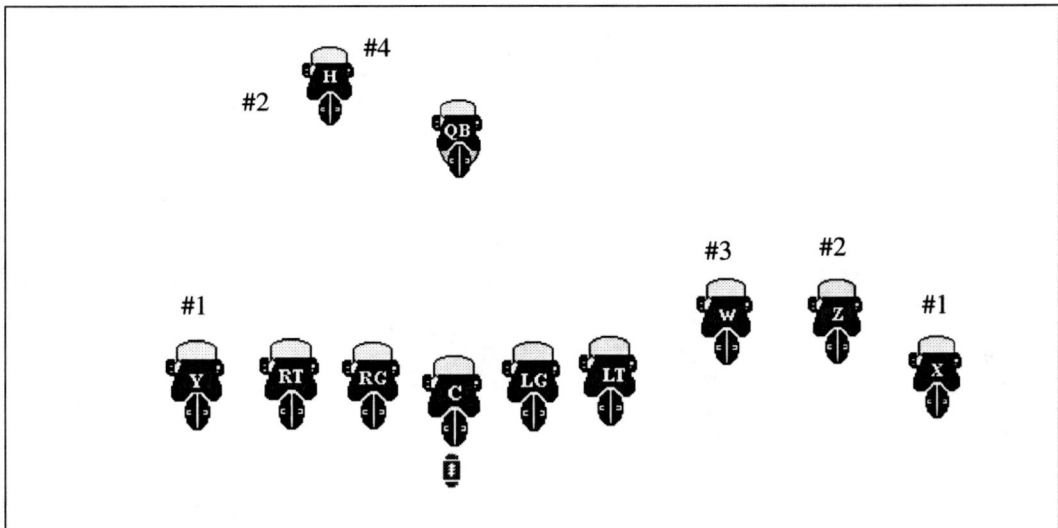

Figure 1-6. One-back tight-trips 13 set

Empty Tight-Quads 14 Set (Figure 1-7)

Empty tight-quads 14 set is an empty backfield with one receiver to the strongside and four receivers to the weakside.

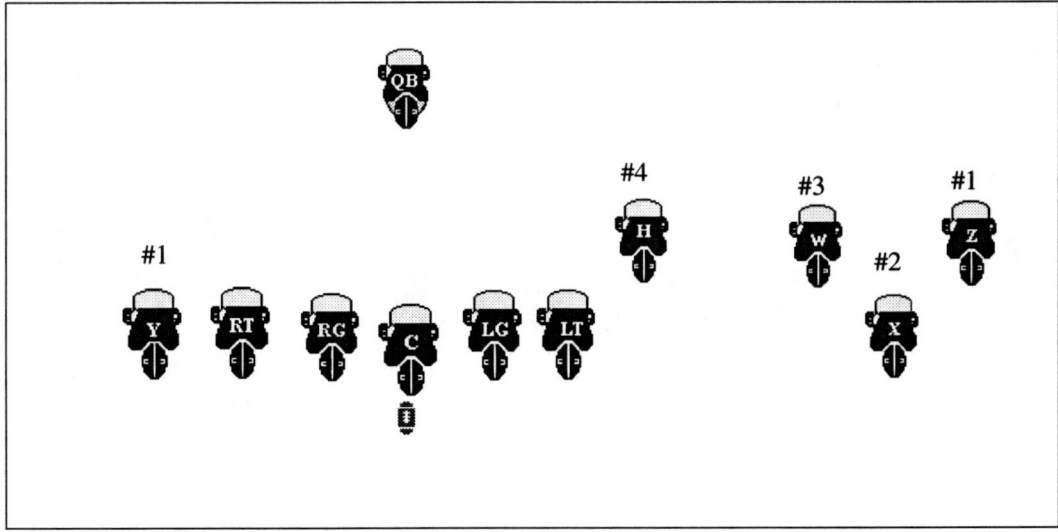

Figure 1-7. Empty tight-quads 14 set

One-Back Doubles 22 Set (Figure 1-8)

One-back doubles 22 set is a one-back backfield with two receivers to the strongside and two receivers to the weakside.

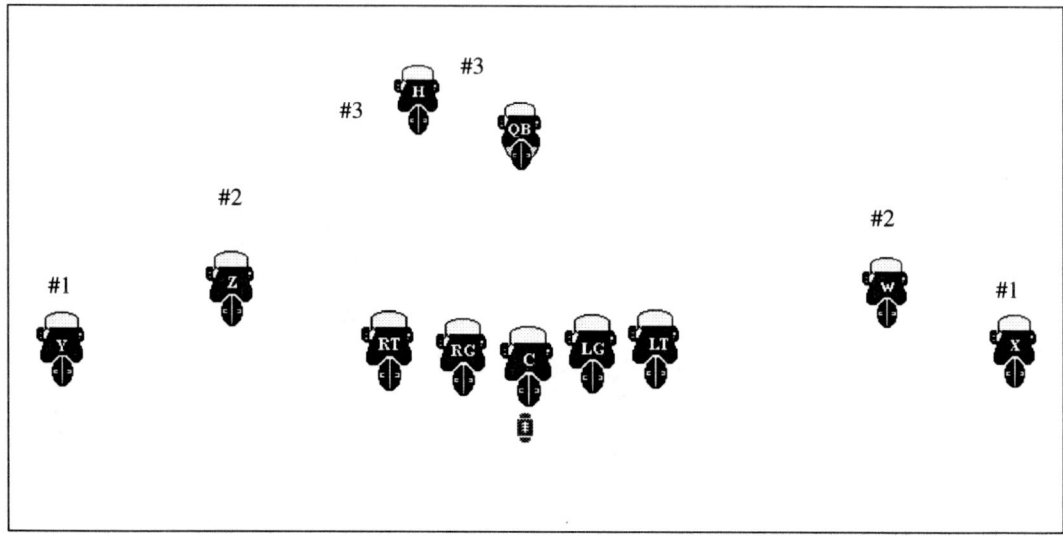

Figure 1-8. One-back doubles 22 set

Empty Pro-Trips 23 Set (Figure 1-9)

Empty pro-trips 23 set is an empty backfield with two receivers to the strongside and three receivers to the weakside.

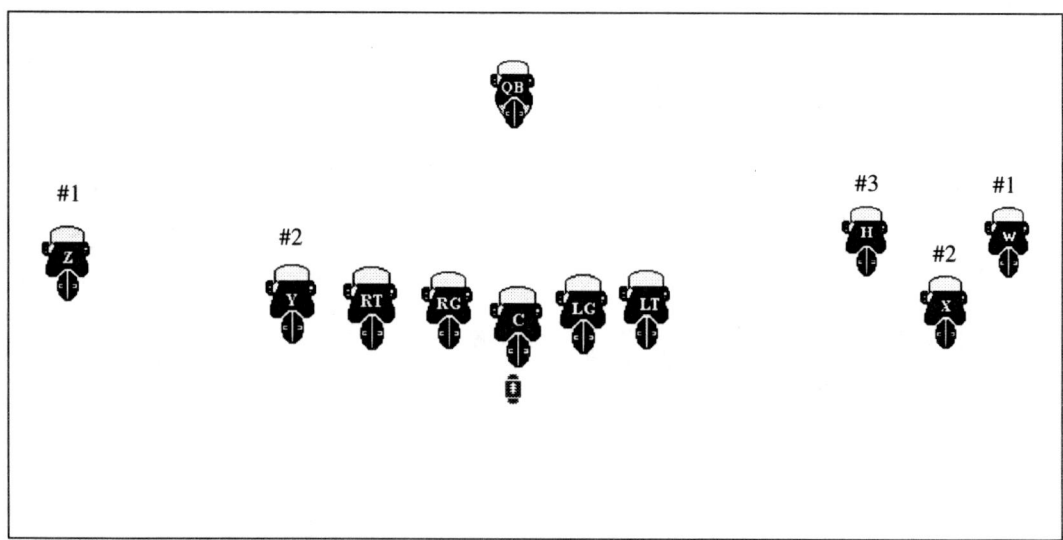

Figure 1-9. Empty pro-trips 23 set

One-Back Trips-Split 31 Set (Figure 1-10)

One-back trips-split 31 set is a one-back backfield with three receivers to the strongside and one receiver to the weakside.

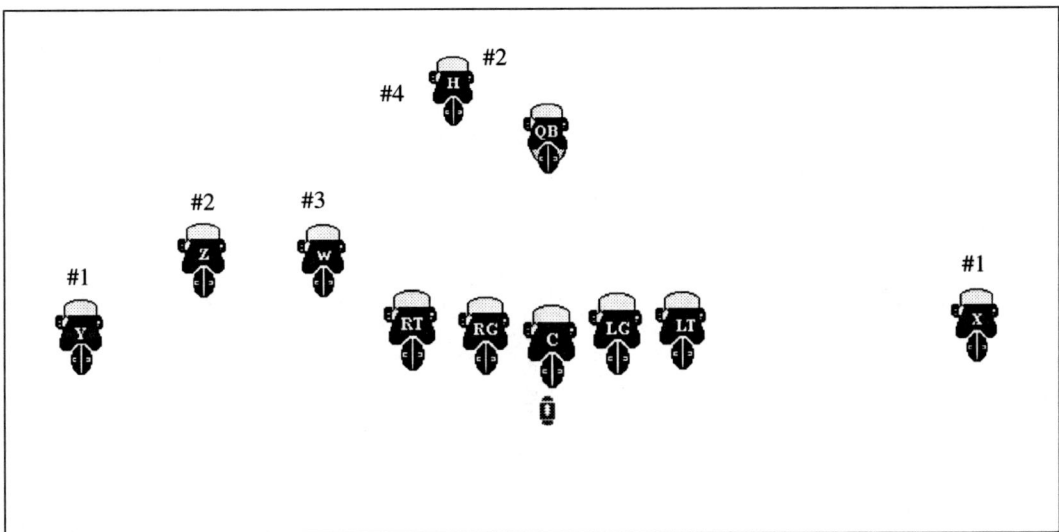

Figure 1-10. One-back trips-split 31 set

Empty Trips-Twins 32 Set (Figure 1-11)

Empty trips-twins 32 set is an empty backfield with three receivers to the strongside and two receivers to the weakside.

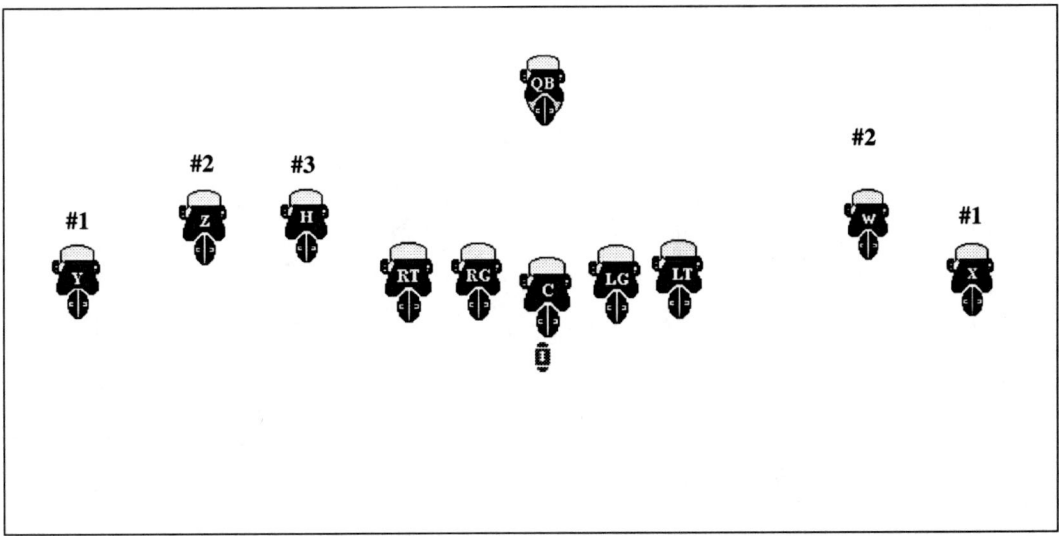

Figure 1-11. Empty trips-twins 32 set

Empty Quads-Split 41 Set (Figure 1-12)

Empty quads-split 41 set is an empty backfield with four receivers to the strongside and one receiver to the weakside.

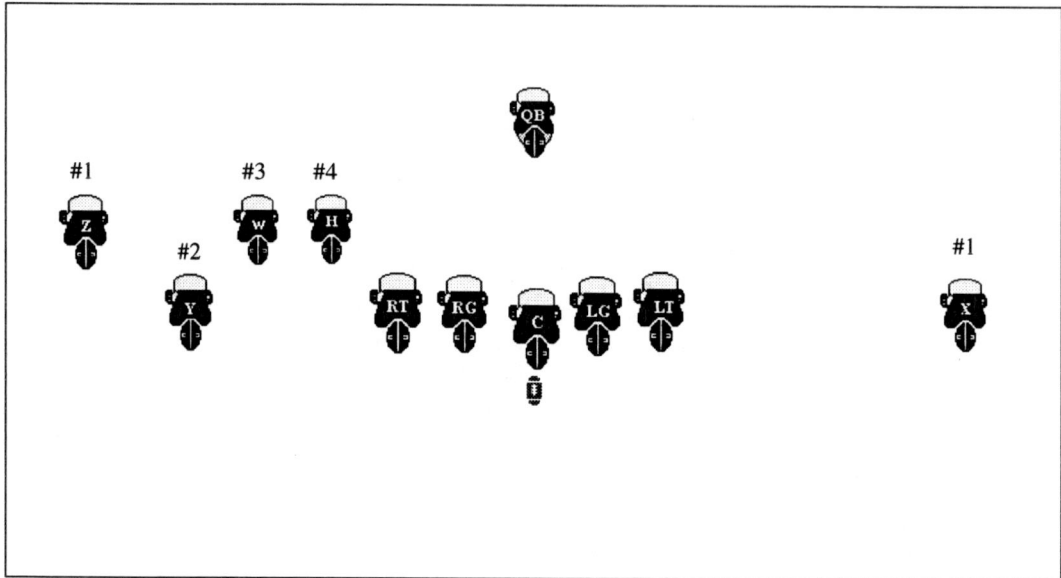

Figure 1-12. Empty quads-split 41 set

2

Zone and Man Coverage Fundamentals

When playing zone coverage, the defenders will drop to their assigned areas of responsibilities. For the secondary, this action means back pedaling, and for linebackers it means running on tilts. Defenders must get to their zones quickly and read the quarterback and receivers as they drop.

The quarterback tells the defender more about the play than any other factor. Defenders must learn to read the quarterback's throwing mechanics, as well as the routes of the receivers. A defensive back can get a great jump on the ball by reading the quarterback and knowing the location and routes of receivers.

Defensive Quarterback Reads

Defenders must be able to read the quarterback.

- The quarterback's head and eyes look to the receiver before he throws.
- He opens his shoulder in the direction that he will throw.
- He stands tall before he throws the ball.
- His guide hand comes off the football as he prepares to release the ball.
- His throwing arm is parallel to the ground as he prepares to throw the ball.
- He shifts his weight from his back foot to his front foot as he prepares to throw the ball.

- The defenders must always know if the quarterback is on or off the line of scrimmage. If the quarterback is off the line of scrimmage, it usually means pass. If the quarterback is on the line of scrimmage it usually means run or play action pass.
- A three-step quarterback drop usually means quick routes are being run.
- A five-step quarterback drop usually means medium to deep routes are being run.
- A seven-step quarterback drop usually means deep routes are being run.

A defensive back can never jump a receiver when he is playing zone coverage, unless he is certain no other threats exist to his coverage area. The defenders must never let an offensive receiver get behind them or lose their three-yard cushion on a receiver. The defenders must punish the receivers by gang tackling. The defenders must never break on short routes when they have deep coverage. Only after defenders are certain that the ball is being thrown, can they break on the short routes.

Backpedal Techniques

When playing zone coverage, the ability of defensive backs to backpedal is one of their most important weapons. Backpedal techniques must be mastered by all defensive backs.

- To begin a backpedal, the defensive back pushes off his front foot and reaches with his back foot.
- The feet are kept as close to the grass as possible when backpedaling; they should not be raised off the ground.
- The defensive back's chin is over his toes, not leaning too much forward or too much backward.
- The defensive back has a forward bend at the waist.
- His arms should move freely and smoothly in a back and forth motion.
- The elbows should be close to the hips as the arms swing back and forth.
- When the arms swing forward, the hands should be at eye level.
- When the arms swing backward, the hands should be at hip pocket level.
- When playing zone coverage, the defensive back keeps a three-yard cushion on the receiver as he reads the quarterback.

Today's modern pass offenses require that defenses play several different pass coverages. To be successful against modern offensives, defenders must become very sound in man-to-man coverage techniques.

In this package, the man-to-man pass coverages include pure man, man-free, and man with zone combinations. To play good man-to-man coverage, the defenders must master their man coverage techniques. They must have a sound understanding of what it takes to play man coverage and work hard each day in practice to develop these techniques.

Man-to-Man Alignments

When a defender aligns to play man-to-man, he aligns either inside, head-up, or outside of the offensive receiver. Three alignments are used when playing man coverage:

- Ike: The defender aligns with his outside foot on the receiver's inside foot.
- Opie: The defender aligns with his inside foot on the receiver's outside foot.
- Marvin: The defender aligns head-up on the receiver.

Man-to-Man Alignment Adjustments

The defender may be required to adjust his basic man-to-man alignment depending on a number of factors, including:

- The alignment of the receiver: If a receiver aligns close to the sideline, the defender must change from an Opie alignment to a Marvin or Ike alignment.
- The type of middle-of-the-field or over-the-top coverage: With middle-of-the-field help, the defender uses an Opie alignment. With no middle-of-the-field help, the defender uses an Ike alignment. Even with safety help, there may be times that the game plan calls for an Ike alignment in order to take away inside routes.
- The ability of the receiver: A receiver that possesses outstanding speed or ability may change the alignment and depth of the defender. He may have to play a little deep or farther inside or outside.

Man-to-Man Stances

The basic stance for playing man-to-man coverage includes several techniques:

- The defender aligns taking all-the-ball if man cloud is used.
- The defender aligns off the line of scrimmage if man sky is used.
- When playing man cloud coverage, the defender must look inside to be sure that he is onsides as he approaches the line of scrimmage.
- The defender's toes are parallel and pointed straight to the line of scrimmage.
- His feet are no wider than armpits-width apart.
- His weight is on the balls of the feet.

- He is bent at the waist and knees for explosion.
- The defender's arms are outside the knees and in an attack position; his hands are at shoulder level.
- The hands are in a ready position, with the fingers spread and the thumbs inside.
- He has a slight forward lean at the waist, with the back arched and the head up.
- The defender's eyes focus on the receiver's hip that is nearest the defender's shade alignment.
- From a sky alignment, the defender aligns off the line of scrimmage facing the quarterback at a 45-degree angle.

Rules of Engagement (Attack Rules) for Man Coverage

- The feet move first, determined by the direction of the receiver's release and the technique that is being played. The defender must avoid leaning or over playing the receiver's first move off the line of scrimmage.
- The hips must open to a 45-degree angle for two steps in order to jam the receiver. It is very important to open the hips in order to keep from getting beat off the line of scrimmage. Opening the hips also opens the shoulders and pulling with the elbow aids in opening the hips, which allows the defender to be able to run with the receiver.
- The hands are used to attack and reroute the receivers; rerouting the receivers destroys the timing of the quarterback and the receivers. The defender uses one or two hand jams. The defender must always lock his elbows, and never let a receiver get off the line of scrimmage in a straight upfield path.

Man-to-Man Coverage Techniques

In order to play sound man-to-man coverage, basic man-to-man techniques must be mastered.

Man Cloud

Man cloud coverage is an on-the-line bump and run coverage using several alignments and techniques. When using man cloud, the defender aligns taking all-the-ball and attacking the receiver when he comes off the line of scrimmage. He attacks and runs with the receiver using one of the following two techniques:

- High pocket is used when the defender has no safety help. This coverage is a high pocket position, close enough to the receiver to touch his front pocket.
- Low pocket is used when there is direct safety help. This coverage is a low pocket position, one yard behind the receiver, but near enough to touch his hip pocket.

Man Sky

When using man sky, the defender aligns seven yards deep off the receiver. This coverage is man-to-man from a sink position. The defender aligns in a 45-degree angle facing the quarterback.

Man Bail Sky

When using man bail sky, the defender aligns taking all-the-ball, then, just prior to the snap, bails to man sky coverage. The defender can also align in sky and spin down to man cloud coverage.

Man-Cloud Alignments and Techniques

Ike (Figure 2-1)

When playing an Ike alignment from a cloud position, the defender aligns taking all-the-ball with his outside foot on the receiver's inside foot.

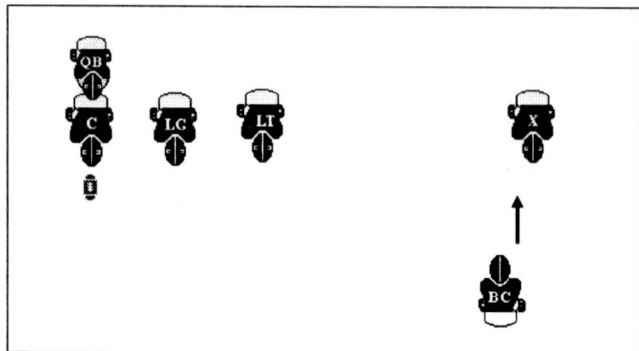

Figure 2-1. Ike alignment

Techniques
- The defender's eyes focus on the inside hip of the receiver.
- The defender must be patient and let the receiver take one step into his route- then attack his second step.
- Inside release—The defender contacts the receiver by driving his outside hand through the receiver's outside shoulder, and rides him down to the inside. The defender shuffles down inside of the receiver and cuts off his inside release.
- Outside release—The defender contacts the receiver by driving his inside hand through the receiver's inside shoulder; the defender pulls his outside elbow open, to help turn his hips.
- Inside to outside release—The receiver uses an inside release, then goes to an outside release. The defender uses his inside release techniques, then counter punches with the inside hand and plays his outside release techniques.
- Outside to inside release—The receiver uses an outside release, then goes to an inside release. The defender uses his outside release techniques, then counter punches with the outside hand and plays his inside release techniques.
- Track technique—When the receiver has established a parallel position, the defender uses his outside arm to ride the receiver into the sideline. The defender must make the ball be thrown over him. It is to his advantage to press the receiver into the sideline.
- Quick slants—If the defender loses inside leverage, he must close the cushion immediately. He must work to get his outside elbow in front of the receiver to create inside leverage.

Opie (Figure 2-2)

When playing an Opie alignment from a cloud position, the defender aligns taking all-the-ball with his inside foot on the receiver's outside foot.

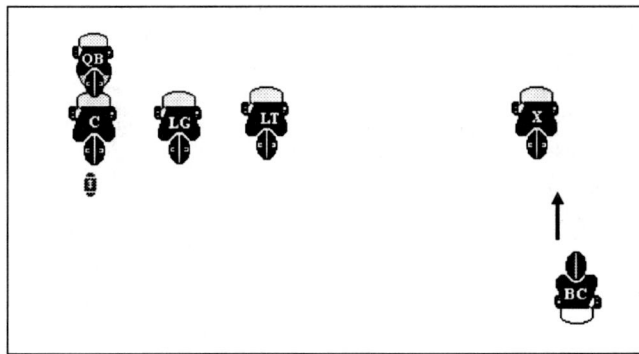

Figure 2-2. Opie alignment

Techniques
- The defender's eyes focus on the outside hip of the receiver.
- The defender must be patient and let the receiver take one step into his route, and then attack his second step.
- Inside release—The defender contacts the receiver by driving his outside hand through the receiver's outside shoulder, riding him down to the inside.
- Outside release—The defender contacts the receiver by driving his inside hand through the receiver's inside shoulder, and presses him to the outside.
- Inside to outside release—The receiver releases inside, then outside. The defender uses his inside release techniques, then counter punches with the inside hand and plays his outside release techniques.
- Outside to inside release—The receiver releases outside then inside. The defender uses his outside release techniques, then counter punches with the outside hand and plays his inside release techniques.

Marvin (Figure 2-3)

When playing a Marvin alignment from a cloud position, the defender aligns taking all-the-ball with his nose on the receiver's nose.

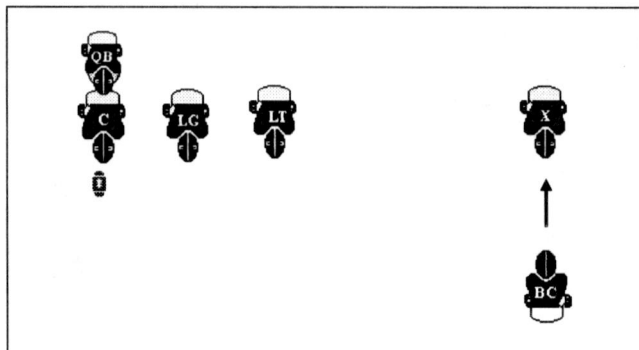

Figure 2-3. Marvin alignment

Techniques
- The defender's eyes focus on the belt buckle of the receiver.
- The defender must be patient and let the receiver take one step into his route, then attack his second step.
- Outside release—The defender contacts the receiver by driving his inside hand through the receiver's inside shoulder, pressing him to the outside.
- Inside release—The defender contacts the receiver by driving his outside hand through the receiver's outside shoulder, riding him down to the inside.
- Inside to outside release—The receiver releases inside, then outside. The defender uses his inside release techniques, then counter punches with the inside hand and plays his outside release techniques.
- Outside to inside release—The receiver releases outside, then inside. The defender uses his outside release techniques, then counter punches with the outside hand and plays his inside release techniques.

Man-to-Man Ball Playing Techniques

When playing the ball in man cloud coverage, the defender will use the following techniques:

- He always turns into the receiver on the long ball.
- He uses his long arm to break up passes.
- When he is beaten, he attacks the receiver's hands.
- He attacks the receiver's inside shoulder when going for routes in front of the defender, and attacks the outside shoulder when going for the tackle.
- In order to strip the ball, the defender attacks over the receiver's arms. He uses a long arm throwing motion with a violent rip at the end. His free arm grabs the receiver's opposite shoulder, in order to strip the ball.
  - ✓ He always attacks the elbow area when going for the strip.
  - ✓ He reads the receiver's eyes (they will get big when the ball is coming).
  - ✓ The receiver's hands reach for the ball when it arrives.
  - ✓ The receiver's head pushes away from the ball when the ball arrives.
  - ✓ The defender goes for the interception with two hands.

Coaching Points:

- There are only two types of releases by the offensive receiver—inside and outside.
- The defender stays on the line of scrimmage as long as the receiver is bouncing in place—be patient.
- The receiver's first move is rarely his last move.
- The defender must not be caught peeking at the quarterback; the receiver will tell him when the ball is coming.
- After 18 yards, the receiver is not going to run a route back to the quarterback.
- Once the receiver is set into his route, the defender matches his hips with the receiver's hips.
- The defender always looks up for the ball on fade routes, not back. He must not turn his shoulders.
- The defender reads the receiver's eyes (they will get big when the ball is coming).
- The defender never lets the receiver release straight upfield.
- The defender never chases to punch a receiver's release.
- The defender should not be overly aggressive when he attacks the receiver.
- The defender must match the receiver's angles when he breaks for his route. The defender should not disengage the receiver until the defender is hip-to-hip.
- The defender always breaks opposite the stick (plant spot). It is impossible for the receiver to break the same side that he sticks.

- The defender drives to the reception point in straight lines—no false steps.
- The defender keeps his eyes on the receiver's hips.
- The defender must learn to read the settling of the receiver's hips and the movement of his arms away from his body when he attempts to settle.

Man Sky Coverage

Man sky coverage is an over-the-top man-to-man coverage with the defenders having no deep help. The defender will align seven yards off the line of scrimmage as shown in Figure 2-4.

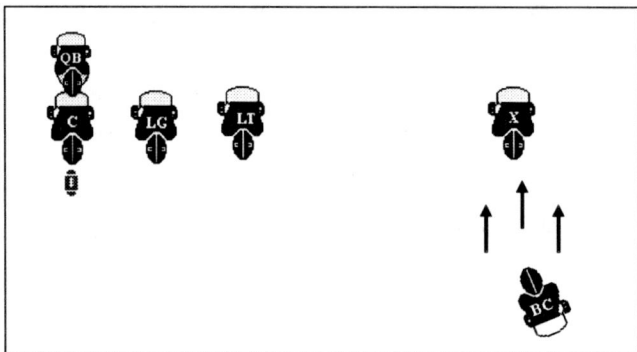

Figure 2-4. Man sky alignment

- The defender will use the following alignment rules when aligned in man sky:
  - ✓ Against a wideout or tight end, the defender aligns in an Ike, Opie, or Marvin alignment.
  - ✓ From sky, the defender aligns seven yards deep with his stance tilted at a 45-degree angle, facing the quarterback.
- The defender has a primary quarterback read when he plays man sky coverage. He uses the following rules for reading the quarterback's drops:
  - ✓ Three step drop—The defender must plant and attack the receiver's route immediately. The defender must think short routes and fades!
  - ✓ Five step drop—The defender backpedals, keeping over the top coverage on his receiver. The defender must think medium to deep routes!
  - ✓ Seven step drop—The defender backpedals, keeping over the top coverage. The defender must think deep routes!
- The defender uses the following rules when playing man sky coverage:
  - ✓ He must read the quarterback's drop in order to know the receiver's route.
  - ✓ He must backpedal, keeping a three-yard cushion as long as possible.

✓ The defender shuffles as long as he can, still keeping his cushion.

✓ The defender must stay over the top of the receiver, keeping him inside whenever possible.

✓ If the receiver gets an outside position, the defender must turn into the receiver and use the sideline for help, which is called a "speed turn." The receiver turns his back to the quarterback as he turns into the receiver.

Pass Coverages

The pass coverages used in this defensive package are divided into four categories: man-to-man, zone, combination man and zone, and special.

Man-to-Man Coverages

- *Cover 0:* Man-to-man coverage with no middle-of-the-field help. Each defender is playing on an island.
- *Cover 0 lock:* Man-to-man coverage with the strong safety and Rover playing the backs man-to-man.
- *Cover 1:* Man-to-man coverage with either the strong safety or Rover playing free in the middle of the field.

Zone Coverages

- *Cover 2*: A two-deep and five underneath read coverage.
- *Cover 2 super*: Used versus twins, trips, and quads. This coverage involves the flipping of a corner, so that both corners are playing on the same side of the field.
- *Cover 2 backer:* Used anytime a linebacker is forced to widen out of the box. This situation occurs against twins, trips, and quads. The corners will not super when cover 2 backer is called.
- *Cover 2 Raven:* Used versus twins, trips, and quads. This coverage involves a progression read on the routes of the #2 receiver.
- *Cover 3:* Three-deep zone coverage with a weakside pre-determined roll.
- *Cover 3 rhino:* Involves spinning Rover into the low hole. This coverage is usually used when the nickel back is in the game.
- *Cover 6:* Three-deep zone with a strongside pre-determined roll.
- *Cover 6 snake:* Involves spinning the strong safety into the low hole. This coverage is usually used when the nickel back is in the game.

Combination Man and Zone Coverages

- *Toro:* A combination man-to-man and zone coverage. Man-to-man coverage is played with zone coverage in the middle of the field and in the low hole.
- *Cover 4:* A combination of man-to-man and zone. This coverage is a two-deep zone with man coverage underneath.
- *Cover 5:* A combination of man-to-man and zone coverage. This coverage is a read progression that involves man-to-man and bracket man-to-man with zone coverage.

Special Coverages

- *Cherokee cover 2:* A form of cover 2 with Geronimo playing in the high hole.
- *Cherokee cover 2 scooter:* A form of cover 2 with Geronimo dropping from the high hole into the deep middle one-third.
- *Cherokee cover 2 sink:* A form of cover 2 with the corners, strong safety, and Rover sinking into quarter coverage. Geronimo aligns in the high hole.
- *Cherokee cover 2 strike:* A form of cover 2 with the strong safety spinning down to play the verticals on the strongside. Geronimo drops from the high hole to play the strongside deep half.
- *Cherokee cover 2 whip:* A form of cover 2 with the Rover spinning down to play the verticals on the weakside. Geronimo drops from the high hole to play the weakside deep half.
- *Cherokee cover 2 rhino:* A form of cover 2 with the Rover spinning down into the low hole and Geronimo dropping from the high hole to play the weakside deep half.
- *Cherokee cover 2 snake:* A form of cover 2 with the strong safety spinning down into the low hole and Geronimo dropping from the high hole to play the strongside deep half.
- *Cherokee zippo:* A form of zippo with Geronimo dropping from the high hole to play the deep middle one-third.
- *Cherokee cover 3:* A form of cover 3 with the strong safety and Rover spinning down to the wall-curl-flats and Geronimo dropping from the high hole to play the deep middle one-third.
- *Cherokee cover 3 press:* A form of cover 3 with the corners pressing the flats. The strong safety and Rover play the outside thirds. Geronimo drops from the high hole to play the middle one-third.
- *Cherokee cover 3 man:* Cover 3 with man coverage underneath.
- *Cherokee cover 1:* Man-to-man with Geronimo dropping from the high hole to play free in the middle of the field.

- *Cherokee cover 0:* Man-to-to-man coverage with Geronimo aligning in the high hole and playing the first back out man-to-man.
- *Bracket coverage:* Used to double cover certain receivers.

3

Man Coverages

Cover 0

Cover 0 vs. a 21 Set (Figure 3-1)

Cover 0 is pure man-to-man coverage with no middle-of-the field help. Each defender is playing on an island. The corners play man-to-man on the #1s and will play man-to-man on the #2s when they super over. The strong safety plays man-to-man on #2 strong. Rover plays man-to-man on #2 weak or drops free to the middle one-third. Sam is man-to-man on #3 strong or the first back out strong. Mike plays man-to-man on the second back out strong or drops to the low hole. Will plays man-to-man on #3 weak or the second back out weak.

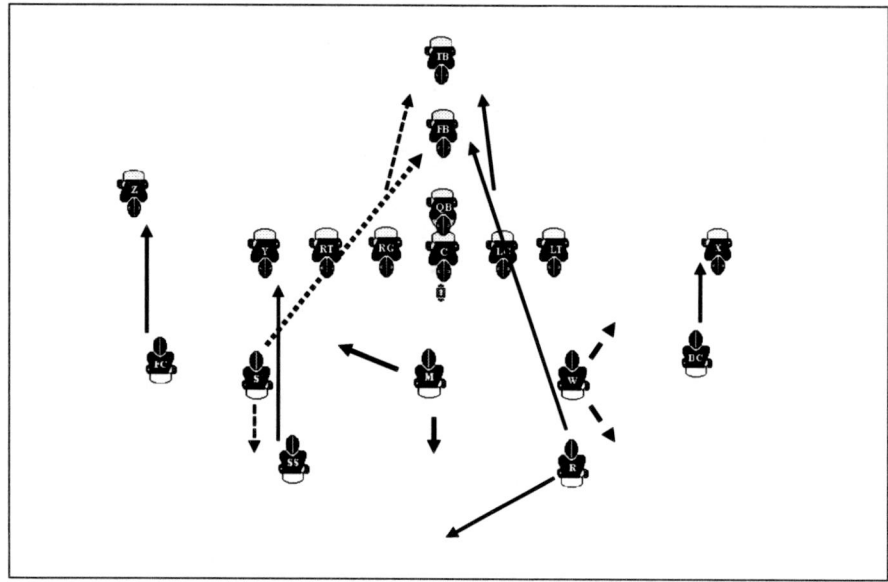

Figure 3-1. Cover 0 vs. a 21 set

Cover 0 Alignments, Stances, and Keys

❑ Field Corner

Alignment: The field corner aligns in his cover 2 shell, seven yards deep and one yard outside of #1. Just prior to the snap of the ball, he stems to man-to-man coverage on #1. He has no middle field help, so he must have inside alignment on #1. He can choose either man cloud or man sky alignment. If he chooses man cloud, he will align in an Ike alignment, on the line of scrimmage, with his outside foot on the inside foot of #1. If he uses man sky, he aligns seven yards deep and one yard inside of #1.

Stance: From an Ike alignment, he aligns in a square stance with his toes parallel to the line of scrimmage and pointing straight ahead. His feet are no wider than armpits-width apart with his weight on the balls of his feet. He is bent at the waist and knees for explosion. His arms are outside his knees and are relaxed and bent at the elbows. His hands are at shoulder-level with his fingers spread and his thumbs inside. His tail is down with his back arched. He has a slight forward lean at the waist. His head is up with his chin slightly over his toes. If he aligns in man sky, he tilts at a 45-degree angle facing the quarterback. His inside foot is back, and his outside foot is forward.

Keys: From an Ike alignment, he reads the inside hip of #1. From a sky alignment, he reads the quarterback's drop.
- Three-step drop: He attacks #1's route immediately, while thinking short routes and fade.
- Five-step drop: He backpedals, while keeping over-the-top coverage on #1 and thinking medium-to-deep routes.
- Seven-step drop: He backpedals, while keeping over-the-top coverage on #1 and thinking deep routes.

Responsibilities: He plays #1 man-to-man. He must not get beat deep. He supports the run late, only after the ball has crossed the line of scrimmage.

❑ Boundary Corner

Alignment: The boundary corner aligns in his cover 2 shell, seven yards deep and one yard outside of #1. Just prior to the snap of the ball, he stems to man-to-man coverage on #1. He has no middle field help, so he must have inside alignment on #1. He can choose either man cloud or man sky alignment. If he chooses man cloud, he aligns in an Ike alignment, on the line of scrimmage, with his outside foot on the inside foot of #1. If he uses man sky he aligns seven yards deep and one yard inside of #1.

Stance: From an Ike alignment, he aligns in a square stance with his toes parallel to the line of scrimmage and pointing straight ahead. His feet are no wider than armpit-width apart with his weight on the balls of his feet. He is bent at the waist and knees for explosion. His arms are outside his knees and are relaxed and bent at the elbows. His hands are at shoulder-level with his fingers spread his thumbs inside. His tail is down with his back arched. He has a slight forward lean at the waist. His head is up with his chin slightly over his toes. If he aligns in man sky, he tilts at a 45-degree angle facing the quarterback. His inside foot is back, and his outside foot is forward.

Keys: From an Ike alignment, he reads the inside hip of #1. From a sky alignment, he reads the quarterback's drop.

- Three-step drop: He attacks #1's route immediately, while thinking short routes and fade.
- Five-step drop: He backpedals, while keeping over-the-top coverage on #1 and thinking medium-to-deep routes.
- Seven-step drop: He backpedals, while keeping over-the-top coverage on #1 and thinking deep routes.

Responsibilities: He plays #1 man-to-man. He must not get beat deep. He supports the run late, only after the ball has crossed the line of scrimmage.

❏ Strong Safety

Alignment: The strong safety aligns in his cover 2 shell, 10 yards deep over a normal tight end alignment. Just prior to the snap of the ball, he stems to man-to-man coverage on #2. He has no middle field help, so he must have inside alignment on #2. He can choose either man cloud or man sky alignment. If he chooses man cloud, he aligns in an Ike alignment, on the line of scrimmage, with his outside foot on the inside foot of #2. If he uses man sky, he aligns seven yards deep and one yard inside of #2.

Stance: From an Ike alignment, he aligns in a square stance with his toes parallel to the line of scrimmage and pointing straight ahead. His feet are no wider than armpit-width apart, with his weight on the balls of his feet. He is bent at the waist and knees for explosion. His arms are outside his knees and are relaxed and bent at the elbows. His hands are at shoulder-level with his fingers spread and his thumbs inside. His tail is down with his back arched. He has a slight forward lean at the waist. His head is up with his chin slightly over his toes. If he aligns in man sky, he tilts at a 45-degree angle facing the quarterback. His inside foot is back, and his outside foot is forward.

Keys: From an Ike alignment, he reads the inside hip of #2. From a sky alignment, he reads the quarterback's drop.
- Three-step drop: He attacks #2's route immediately, while thinking short routes and fade.
- Five-step drop: He backpedals, while keeping over-the-top coverage on #2 and thinking medium-to-deep routes.
- Seven-step drop: He backpedals, while keeping over-the-top coverage on #2 and thinking deep routes.

Responsibilities: He has #2 man-to-man. He must not get beat deep. He supports the run late, only after the ball has crossed the line of scrimmage.

❏ Rover

Alignment: Rover aligns in his cover 2 shell, 10 yards deep over a normal tight end alignment. Just prior to the snap of the ball, he stems to man-to-man coverage on #2. He has no middle field help, so he must have inside alignment on #2. He can choose either man cloud or man sky alignment. If he chooses man cloud, he aligns in an Ike alignment, on the line of scrimmage, with his outside foot on the inside foot of #2. If he uses man sky, he aligns seven yards deep and one yard inside of #2.

Stance: From an Ike alignment, he aligns in a square stance with his toes parallel to the line of scrimmage and pointing straight ahead. His feet are no wider than armpits-width apart with his weight on the balls of his feet. He is bent at the waist and knees for explosion. His arms are outside his knees and are relaxed and bent at the elbows. His hands are at shoulder-level with his fingers spread and his thumbs inside. His tail is down with his back arched. His has a slight forward lean at the waist. His head is up with his chin slightly over his toes. If he aligns in man sky, he tilts at a 45-degree angle facing the quarterback. His inside foot is back, and his outside foot is forward.

Keys: From an Ike alignment, he reads the inside hip of #2. From a sky alignment, he reads the quarterback's drop.
  • Three-step drop: He attacks #2's route immediately, while thinking short routes and fade.
  • Five-step drop: He backpedals, while keeping over-the-top coverage on #2 and thinking medium-to-deep routes.
  • Seven-step drop: He backpedals, while keeping over-the-top coverage on #2 and thinking deep routes.

Responsibilities: He has #2 man-to-man. He must not get beat deep. He supports the run late, only after the ball has crossed the line of scrimmage.

❏ Sam

Alignment: Sam aligns in the defensive front that is called in the huddle.

Stance: He uses his normal linebacker stance, unless he is aligned on a wideout; he then aligns in an Ike or sky position. His stance and alignment are the same as those used by a corner or safety when playing Ike or sky coverage.

Keys: He uses his regular linebacker reads, unless he is aligned on a wideout; he then uses the same man cloud or man sky reads as a corner or safety. From man cloud, he uses an Ike alignment and reads the inside hip of #3. From sky, he reads the quarterback for a pass or run key.

- Three-step drop: He attacks #3's route immediately, while thinking short routes and fade.
- Five-step drop: He backpedals, while keeping over-the-top coverage on #3 and thinking medium-to-deep routes.
- Seven-step drop: He backpedals, while keeping over-the-top coverage on #3 and thinking deep routes.

Responsibilities: Sam has #3 strong or the second back out on the strongside man-to-man. If no #3 is present, he drops to the strongside hook/curl.

❑ Mike

Alignment: Mike aligns in the front that is called in the huddle.

Stance: He uses his normal linebacker stance.

Keys: He uses his normal linebacker keys.

Responsibilities: He has the second back out to the strongside. If no second back out exists, he drops to the low hole.

❏ Will

Alignment: Will aligns in the defensive front that is called in the huddle.

Stance: He uses his normal linebacker stance, unless he is aligned on a wideout; he then aligns in an Ike or sky position. His stance and alignment are the same as those used by a corner or safety when playing Ike or sky coverage.

Keys: He uses his regular linebacker reads unless he is aligned on a wide-out; he then uses the same man cloud or man sky reads as a corner or safety. From man cloud, he uses an Ike alignment and reads the inside hip of #3. From sky, he reads the quarterback for a pass or run key.

- Three-step drop: He attacks #3's route immediately, while thinking short routes and fade.
- Five-step drop: He backpedals, while keeping over-the-top coverage on #3 and thinking medium-to-deep routes.
- Seven-step drop: He backpedals, while keeping over-the-top coverage on #3 and thinking deep routes.

Responsibilities: He has #3 weak or the second back out on the weakside man-to-man. If no #3 is present, he drops to the weakside hook/curl.

Cover 0 vs. a 12 Set (Figures 3-2 and 3-3)

The field corner supers over and aligns in a Marvin (sky) alignment on #2. The boundary corner aligns in an Ike alignment on #1. The strong safety aligns in a sky alignment on the tight end. Rover aligns in his Cover 2 Shell. All linebackers align in their normal linebacker alignments.

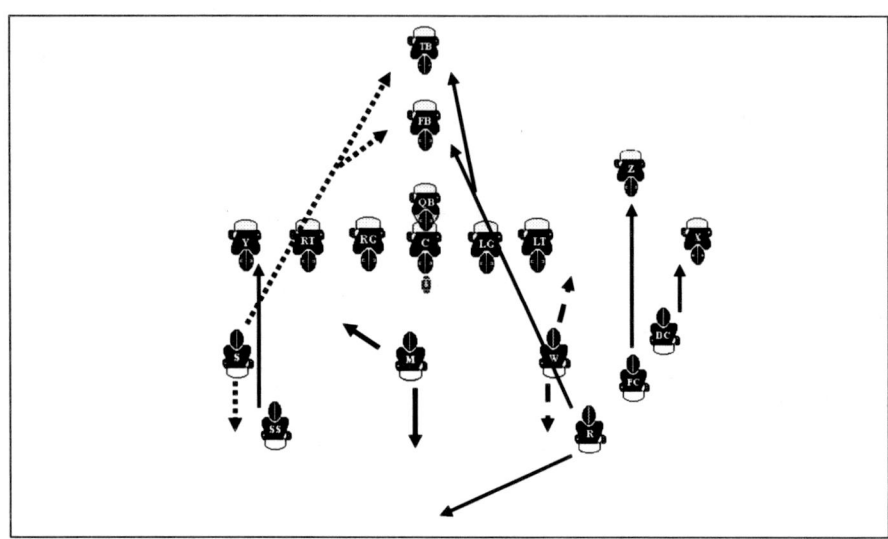

Figure 3-2. Cover 0 vs. a 12 set

Position	Pass responsibility
Sam	Plays the first back out strong man-to-man or drops to the strongside hook.
Mike	Plays man-to-man on the second back out strong or drops to the low hole.
Will	Plays man-to-man on the second back out weak or drops to the weak hook.
Strong safety	Plays man-to-man on the tight end.
Rover	Plays man-to-man on the first back out to the weakside or drops free to the middle one-third.
Field corner	Supers over and plays #2 man-to-man; if the twins are to the wideside, he plays #1 man-to-man.
Boundary corner	Plays man-to-man on #1; if the twins are to the wideside, he supers over and plays #2 man-to-man.

Figure 3-3. Position and pass responsibility for cover 0 vs. a 12 set

Cover 0 vs. a 13 Set (Figures 3-4 and 3-5)

The field corner supers over and aligns in a Marvin alignment on #2. The boundary corner aligns in a sky alignment on #1. The strong safety aligns in a sky alignment on the tight end. Rover aligns in a sky alignment on #3. All linebackers align in their normal linebacker alignments.

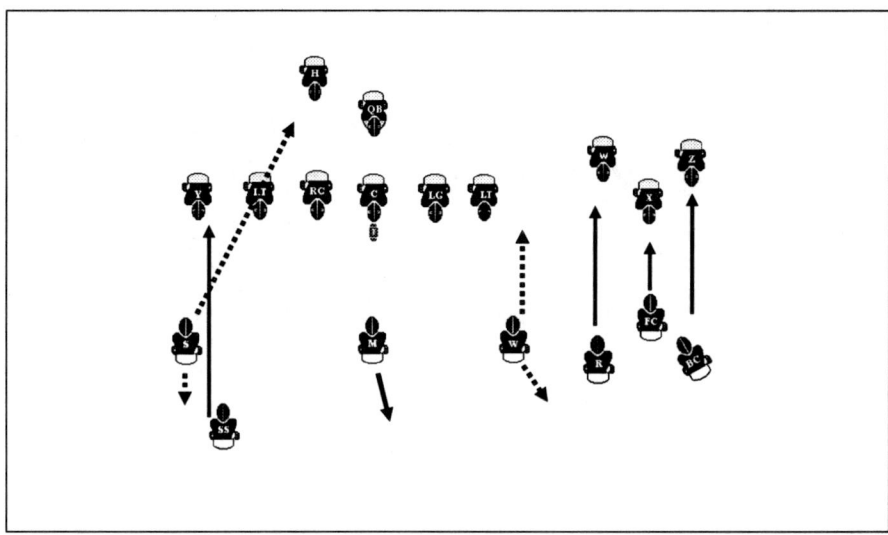

Figure 3-4. Cover 0 vs. a 13 set

Position	Pass responsibility
Sam	Plays the first back out to the strongside man-to-man or drops to the strongside hook.
Mike	Drops to the low hole and mirrors the quarterback.
Will	Plays man-to-man on the second back out weak or drops to the weak hook.
Strong safety	Plays the tight end man-to-man.
Rover	Plays #3 man-to-man.
Field corner	Supers over and plays #2 man-to-man; if the trips are to the wideside, he plays #1 man-to-man.
Boundary corner	Plays man-to-man on #1; if the trips are to the wideside, he supers over and plays #2 man-to-man.

Figure 3-5. Position and pass responsibility for cover 0 vs. a 13 set

Cover 0 vs. a 14 Set (Figures 3-6 and 3-7)

The field corner supers over and aligns in a Marvin alignment on #2. The boundary corner aligns in a sky alignment on #1. The strong safety aligns in a sky alignment on the tight end. Rover aligns in a sky alignment on #3. Will aligns in a sky alignment on #4. Sam and Mike align in their normal linebacker alignments.

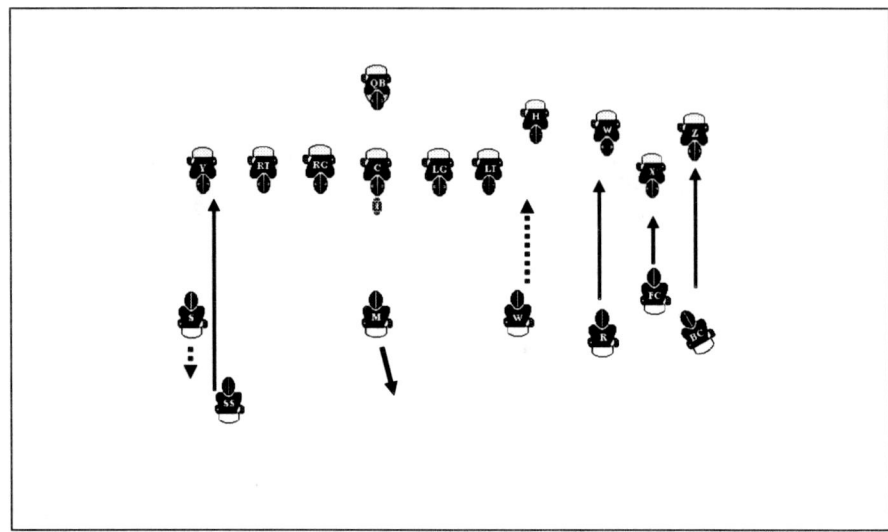

Figure 3-6. Cover 0 vs. a 14 set

Position	Pass responsibility
Sam	Drops to the strongside hook and mirrors the quarterback.
Mike	Drops to the low hole and mirrors the quarterback.
Will	Plays #4 man-to-man.
Strong safety	Plays the tight end man-to-man.
Rover	Plays #3 man-to-man.
Field corner	Supers over and plays #2 man-to-man; if the quads are to the wideside, he plays #1 man-to-man.
Boundary corner	Plays man-to-man on #1; if the quads are to the wideside, he supers over and plays #2 man-to-man.

Figure 3-7. Position and pass responsibility for cover 0 vs. a 14 set

Cover 0 vs. a 22 Set (Figures 3-8 and 3-9)

The corners align in an Ike alignment on the #1s. The strong safety aligns in a sky alignment on the tight end. Rover aligns in a sky alignment on #2. The linebackers align in their normal linebacker alignments.

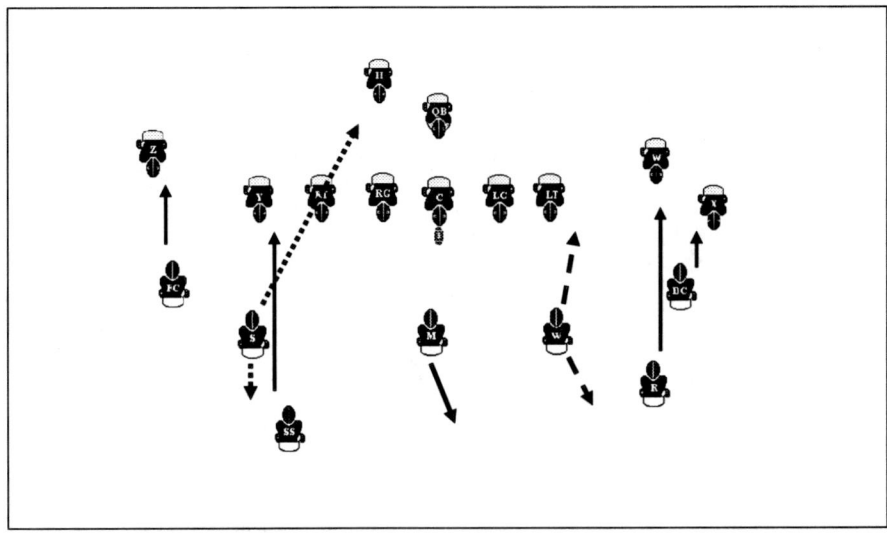

Figure 3-8. Cover 0 vs. a 22 set

Position	Pass responsibility
Sam	Plays the first back out to the strongside man-to-man or drops to the strongside hook.
Mike	Drops to the low hole and mirrors the quarterback.
Will	Plays man-to-man on the first back out to the weakside or drops to the weakside hook.
Strong safety	Plays the tight end man-to-man.
Rover	Plays #2 man-to-man.
Field corner	Plays #1 man-to-man.
Boundary corner	Plays #1 man-to-man.

Figure 3-9. Position and pass responsibility for cover 0 vs. a 22 set

Cover 0 vs. a 23 Set (Figures 3-10 and 3-11)

The corners align in an Ike alignment on the #1s. The strong safety aligns in a sky alignment on the tight end. Rover aligns in a sky alignment on #2. Sam and Mike align in their normal linebacker alignments. Will aligns in a sky alignment on #3.

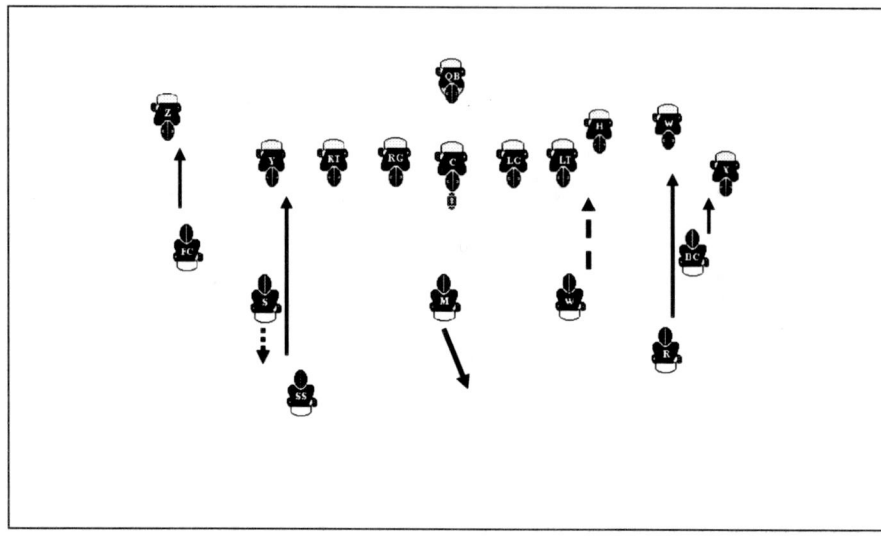

Figure 3-10. Cover 0 vs. a 23 set

Position	Pass responsibility
Sam	Drops to the strongside hook and mirrors the quarterback.
Mike	Drops to the low hole and mirrors the quarterback.
Will	Plays #3 man-to-man.
Strong safety	Plays the tight end man-to-man.
Rover	Plays #2 man-to-man.
Field corner	Plays #1 man-to-man.
Boundary corner	Plays #1 man-to-man.

Figure 3-11. Position and pass responsibility for cover 0 vs. a 23 set

Cover 0 vs. a 31 Set (Figures 3-12 and 3-13)

The corners align in an Ike alignment on the #1s. The strong safety aligns in a Marvin (sky) alignment on #2. Rover aligns in his cover 2 shell. All linebackers align in their normal linebacker alignments.

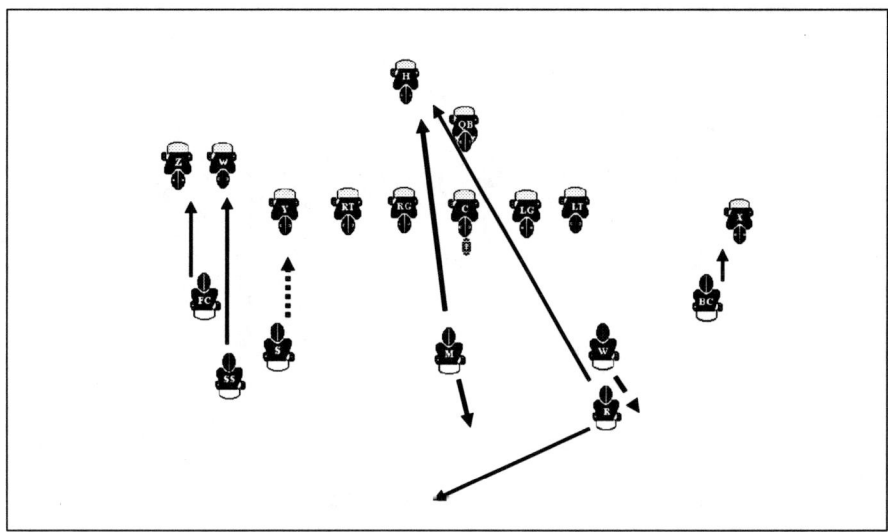

Figure 3-12. Cover 0 vs. a 31 set

Position	Pass responsibility
Sam	Plays the tight end man-to-man.
Mike	Plays the first back out to the strongside man-to-man or drops to the low hole and mirrors the quarterback.
Will	Drops to the weakside hook and mirrors the quarterback.
Strong safety	Plays #2 man-to-man.
Rover	Plays the first back out to the weakside man-to-man or drops free to the middle one-third.
Field corner	Plays #1 man-to-man.
Boundary corner	Plays #1 man-to-man.

Figure 3-13. Position and pass responsibility for cover 0 vs. a 31 set

Cover 0 vs. a 32 Set (Figures 3-14 and 3-15)

The corners align in an Ike alignment on the #1s. The strong safety aligns in a sky alignment on #2. Rover aligns in a sky alignment on #2. All linebackers align in their normal linebacker alignments.

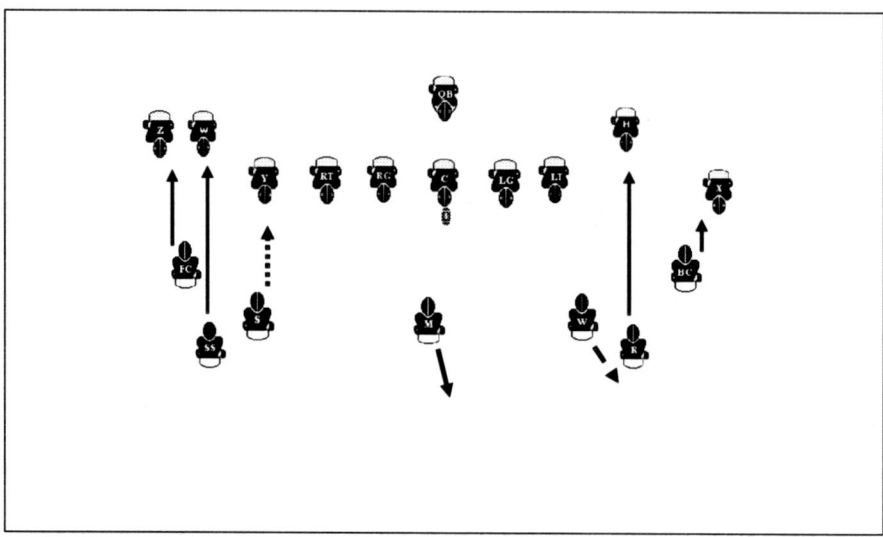

Figure 3-14. Cover 0 vs. a 32 set

Position	Pass responsibility
Sam	Plays the tight end man-to-man.
Mike	Drops to the low hole and mirrors the quarterback.
Will	Drops to the weakside hook and mirrors the quarterback.
Strong safety	Plays #2 man-to-man.
Rover	Plays #2 man-to-man.
Field corner	Plays #1 man-to-man.
Boundary corner	Plays #1 man-to-man.

Figure 3-15. Position and pass responsibility for cover 0 vs. a 32 set

Cover 0 vs. a 41 Set (Figures 3-16 and 3-17)

The field corner aligns in a sky alignment on the #1. The boundary aligns in an Ike alignment on #1. The strong safety aligns in a Marvin alignment on #2. Rover aligns in a sky alignment on #3 strong. All linebackers align in their normal linebacker alignments.

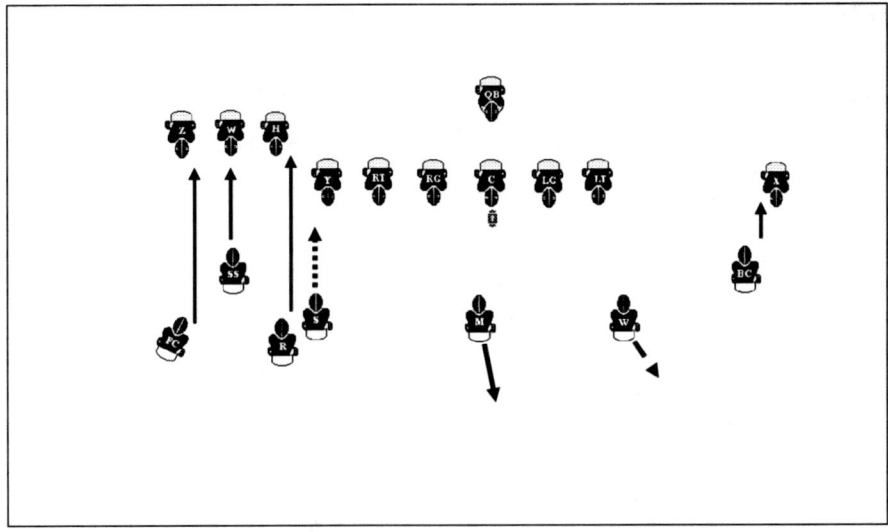

Figure 3-16. Cover 0 vs. a 41 set

Position	Pass responsibility
Sam	Plays the tight end man-to-man.
Mike	Drops to the low hole and mirrors the quarterback.
Will	Drops to the weakside hook and mirrors the quarterback.
Strong safety	Plays #2 man-to-man.
Rover	Plays #3 strong man-to-man.
Field corner	Plays #1 man-to-man.
Boundary corner	Plays #1 man-to-man.

Figure 3-17. Position and pass responsibility for cover 0 vs. a 41 set

Cover 0 Lock

Cover 0 lock is pure man-to-man coverage with the strong safety and Rover playing the backs man-to-man. The corners play the #1s man-to-man. Sam has #2 strong man-to-man and Mike and Will are free and take care of the low hole and weak hook.

Cover 0 Lock vs. a 21 Set (Figures 3-18 and 3-19)

The corners align in an Ike alignment on the #1s. The strong safety and Rover align in their cover 2 shell. All linebackers align in their normal linebacker alignments.

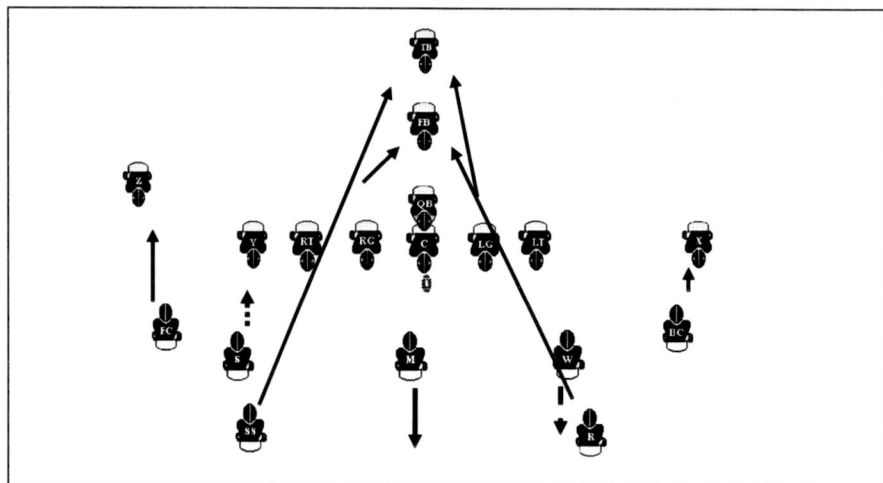

Figure 3-18. Cover 0 lock vs. a 21 set

Position	Pass responsibility
Sam	Plays the tight end man-to-man.
Mike	Drops to the low hole and mirrors the quarterback.
Will	Drops to the weakside hook and mirrors the quarterback.
Strong safety	Plays the first back out to the strongside man-to-man or the second back out to the weakside man-to-man.
Rover	Plays the first back out to the weakside man-to-man or the second back out to the strongside man-to-man.
Field corner	Plays #1 man-to-man.
Boundary corner	Plays #1 man-to-man.

Figure 3-19. Position and pass responsibility for cover 0 lock vs. a 21 set

Cover 0 Lock vs. a 12 Set (Figures 3-20 and 3-21)

The field corner supers over and aligns in a sky alignment on #2. The boundary corner aligns in an Ike alignment on #1. The strong safety and Rover align in their cover 2 shell. All linebackers align in their normal linebacker alignments.

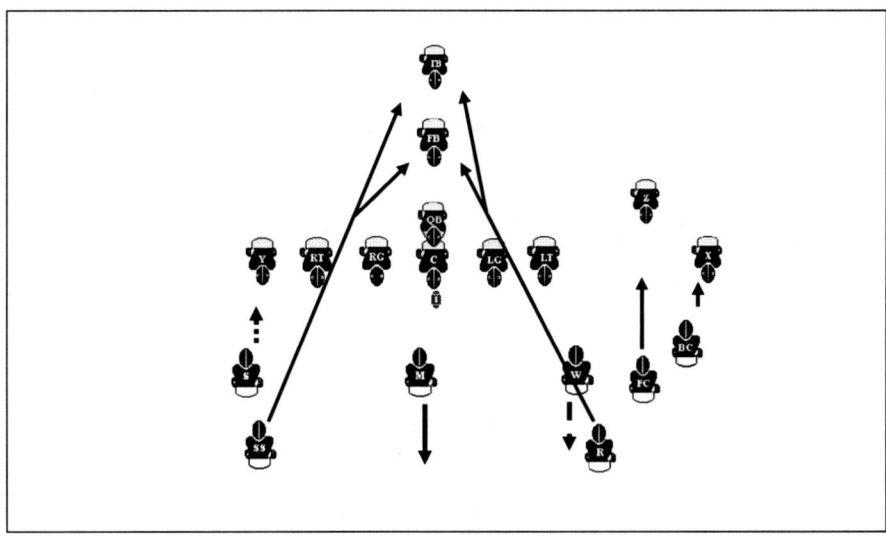

Figure 3-20. Cover 0 lock vs. a 12 set

Position	Pass responsibility
Sam	Plays the tight end man-to-man.
Mike	Drops to the low hole and mirrors the quarterback.
Will	Drops to the weakside hook and mirrors the quarterback.
Strong safety	Plays the first back out to the strongside man-to-man or the second back out to the weakside man-to-man.
Rover	Plays the first back out to the weakside man-to-man or the second back out to the strongside man-to-man.
Field corner	Supers over and plays #2 man-to-man; if the twins are to the wideside, he plays #1 man-to-man.
Boundary corner	Plays man-to-man on #1; if the twins are to the wideside, he supers over and plays #2 man-to-man.

Figure 3-21. Position and pass responsibility for cover 0 lock vs. a 12 set

Cover 0 Lock vs. a 13 Set (Figures 3-22 and 3-23)

The field corner supers over and aligns in a Marvin alignment on #2. The boundary corner aligns in a sky alignment on #1. The strong safety aligns in his cover 2 shell. Rover aligns in a sky alignment on #3. All linebackers align in their normal linebacker alignments.

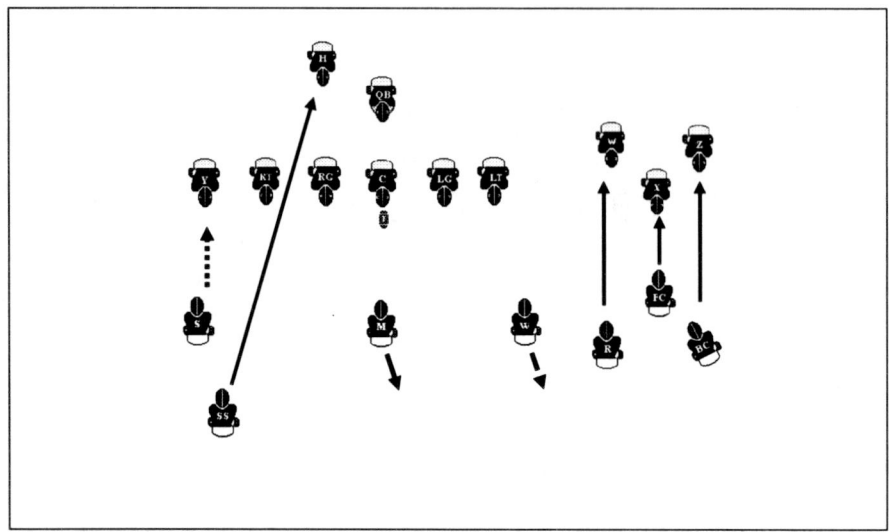

Figure 3-22. Cover 0 lock vs. a 13 set

Position	Pass responsibility
Sam	Plays the tight end man-to-man.
Mike	Drops to the low hole and mirrors the quarterback.
Will	Drops to the weakside hook and mirrors the quarterback.
Strong safety	Plays the back out either side man-to-man.
Rover	Plays #3 man-to-man.
Field corner	Supers over and plays #2 man-to-man; if the trips are to the wideside, he plays #1 man-to-man.
Boundary corner	Plays man-to-man on #1; if the trips are to the wideside, he supers over and plays #2 man-to-man.

Figure 3-23. Position and pass responsibility for cover 0 lock vs. a 13 set

Cover 0 Lock vs. a 14 Set (Figures 3-24 and 3-25)

The field corner supers over and aligns in a Marvin alignment on #2. The boundary corner aligns in a sky alignment on #1. The strong safety aligns in a sky alignment over #4. Rover aligns in a sky alignment on #3. All linebackers align in their normal linebacker alignments.

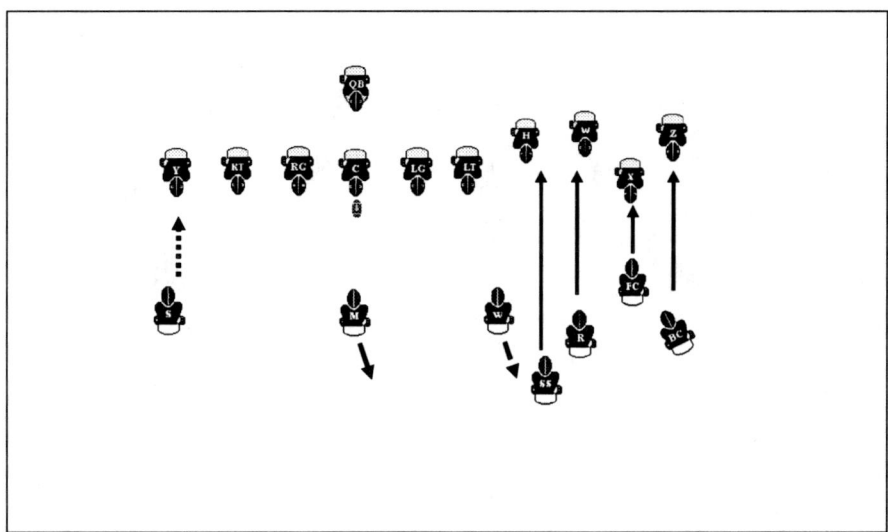

Figure 3-24. Cover 0 lock vs. a 14 set

Position	Pass responsibility
Sam	Plays the tight end man-to-man.
Mike	Drops to the low hole and mirrors the quarterback.
Will	Drops to the weakside hook and mirrors the quarterback.
Strong safety	Plays #4 man-to-man.
Rover	Plays #3 man-to-man.
Field corner	Supers over and plays #2 man-to-man; if the quads are to the wideside, he plays #1 man-to-man.
Boundary corner	Plays man-to-man on #1; if the quads are to the wideside, he supers over and plays #2 man-to-man.

Figure 3-25. Position and pass responsibility for cover 0 lock vs. a 14 set

Cover 0 Lock vs. a 22 Set (Figures 3-26 and 3-27)

The corners align in an Ike alignment on the #1s. The strong safety aligns in his cover 2 shell. Rover aligns in a sky alignment on #2. All linebackers align in their normal linebacker alignments.

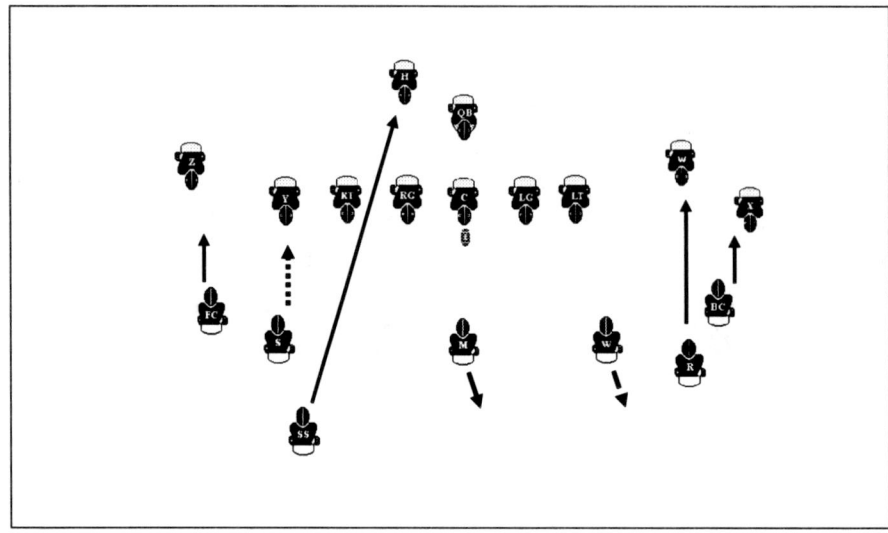

Figure 3-26. Cover 0 lock vs. a 22 set

Position	Pass responsibility
Sam	Plays the tight end man-to-man.
Mike	Drops to the low hole and mirrors the quarterback.
Will	Drops to the weakside hook and mirrors the quarterback.
Strong safety	Plays the back man-to-man to either side he releases.
Rover	Plays #2 man-to-man.
Field corner	Plays #1 man-to-man.
Boundary corner	Plays #1 man-to-man.

Figure 3-27. Position and pass responsibility for cover 0 lock vs. a 22 set

Cover 0 Lock vs. a 23 Set (Figures 3-28 and 3-29)

The field corner aligns in an Ike alignment on #1. The boundary corner aligns in a sky alignment on #1. The strong safety aligns in a sky alignment on #3. The Rover aligns in a Marvin alignment on #2. All linebackers align in their normal linebacker alignments.

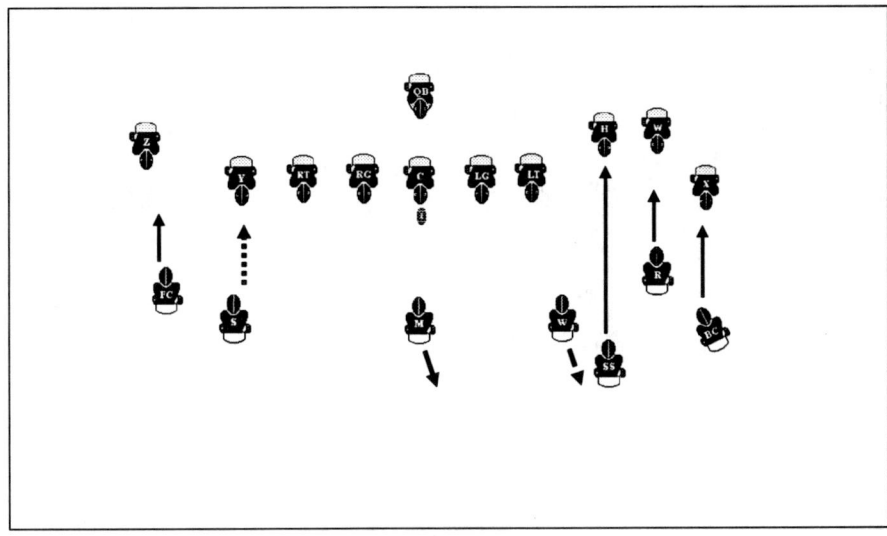

Figure 3-28. Cover 0 lock vs. a 23 set

Position	Pass responsibility
Sam	Plays the tight end man-to-man.
Mike	Drops to the low hole and mirrors the quarterback.
Will	Drops to the weakside hook and mirrors the quarterback.
Strong safety	Plays #3 man-to-man to the weakside.
Rover	Plays #2 man-to-man.
Field corner	Plays #1 man-to-man.
Boundary corner	Plays #1 man-to-man.

Figure 3-29. Position and pass responsibility for cover 0 lock vs. a 23 set

Cover 0 Lock vs. a 31 Set (Figures 3-30 and 3-31)

The field corner aligns in a sky alignment on #1. The boundary corner aligns in an Ike alignment on #1. The strong safety aligns in a Mavin alignment on #2. Rover aligns on the H back. All linebackers align in their normal linebacker alignments.

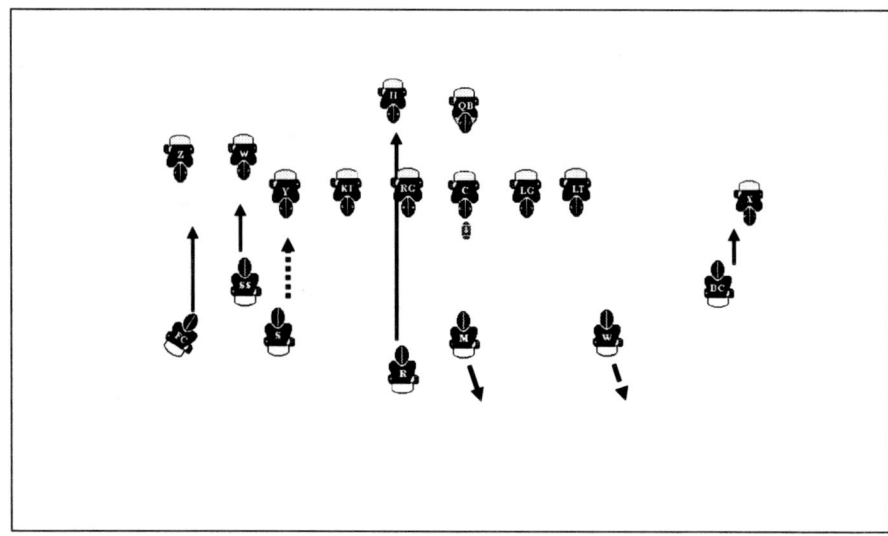

Figure 3-30. Cover 0 lock vs. a 31 set

Position	Pass responsibility
Sam	Plays the tight end man-to-man.
Mike	Drops to the low hole and mirrors the quarterback.
Will	Drops to the weakside hook and mirrors the quarterback.
Strong safety	Plays #2 man-to-man.
Rover	Plays the back man-to-man to either side he releases.
Field corner	Plays #1 man-to-man.
Boundary corner	Plays #1 man-to-man.

Figure 3-31. Position and pass responsibility for cover 0 lock vs. a 31 set

Cover 0 Lock vs. a 32 Set (Figures 3-32 and 3-33)

The corners align in an Ike alignment on the #1s. The strong safety aligns in a sky alignment on #2. Rover aligns in a sky alignment on #2. All linebackers align in their normal linebacker alignments.

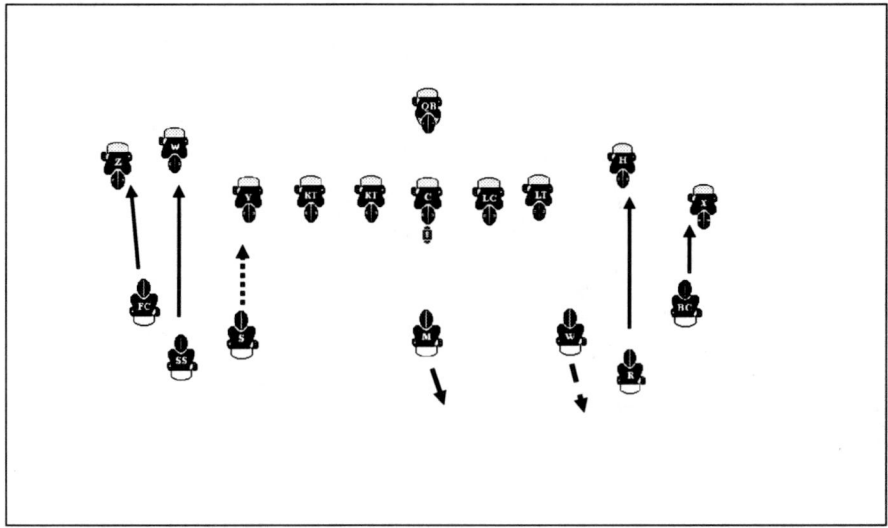

Figure 3-32. Cover 0 lock vs. a 32 set

Position	Pass responsibility
Sam	Plays the tight end man-to-man.
Mike	Drops to the low hole and mirrors the quarterback.
Will	Drops to the weakside hook and mirrors the quarterback.
Strong safety	Plays #2 man-to-man.
Rover	Plays #2 man-to-man.
Field corner	Plays #1 man-to-man.
Boundary corner	Plays #1 man-to-man.

Figure 3-33. Position and pass responsibility for cover 0 lock vs. a 32 set

Cover 0 Lock vs. a 41 Set (Figures 3-34 and 3-35)

The field corner aligns in a sky alignment on #1. The boundary corner aligns in an Ike alignment on #1. The strong safety aligns in a Marvin alignment on #2. Rover aligns in a sky alignment on #3 strong. All linebackers align in their normal linebacker alignments.

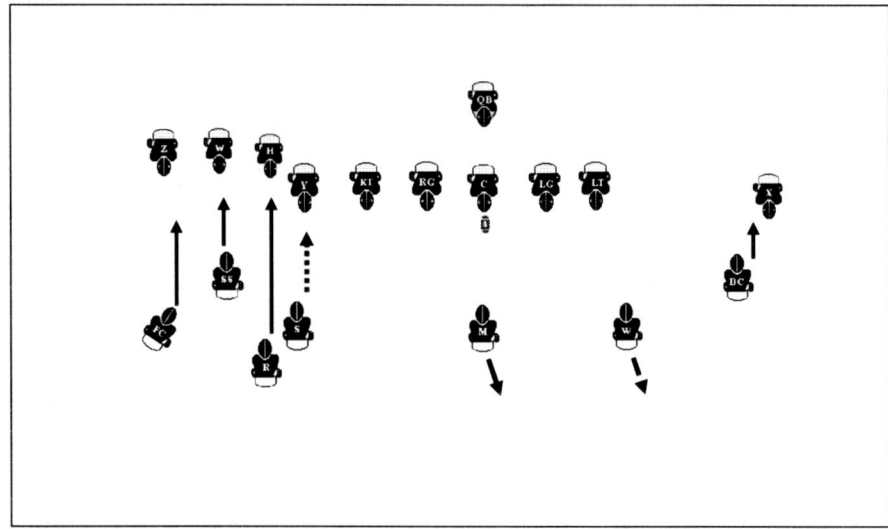

Figure 3-34. Cover 0 lock vs. a 41 set

Position	Pass responsibility
Sam	Plays the tight man-to-man.
Mike	Drops to the low hole and mirrors the quarterback.
Will	Drops to the weakside hook and mirrors the quarterback.
Strong safety	Plays #2 man-to-man.
Rover	Plays #3 strong man-to-man.
Field corner	Plays #1 man-to-man.
Boundary corner	Plays #1 man-to-man.

Figure 3-35. Position and pass responsibility for cover 0 lock vs. a 41 set

Cover 1

Cover 1 vs. a 21 Set (Figure 3-36)

Cover 1 is man coverage with a free safety playing the middle of the field. The corners play the #1s man-to-man. The strong safety or Rover are free in the middle of the field or play man-to-man on #2 on their side. Sam and Will have the first backs out to their side man-to-man and Mike has the second back out either side man-to-man.

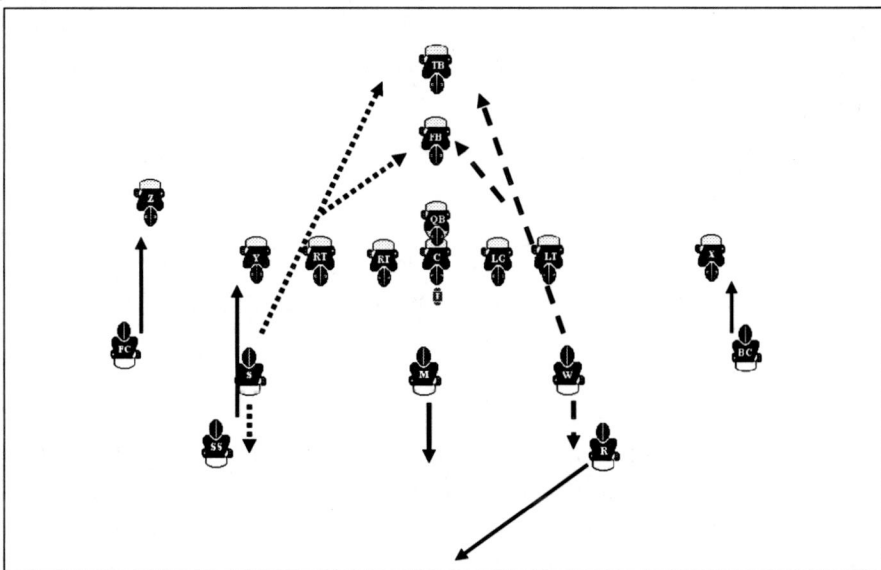

Figure 3-36. Cover 1 vs. a 21 set

Cover 0 Alignments, Stances, and Keys

❑ Field Corner

Alignment: The field corner aligns in his cover 2 shell, seven yards deep and one yard outside of #1. Just prior to the snap of the ball, he stems to man-to-man coverage on #1. He has middle field help, so he plays an outside alignment on #1. He can choose either man cloud or man sky alignment. If he chooses man cloud, he aligns in an Opie alignment, on the line of scrimmage, with his inside foot on the outside foot of #1. If he uses man sky, he aligns seven yards deep and one yard outside of #1.

Stance: From an Opie alignment, he aligns in a square stance with his toes parallel to the line of scrimmage and pointing straight ahead. His feet are no wider than armpits-width apart with his weight on the balls of his feet. He is bent at the waist and knees for explosion. His arms are outside his knees and are relaxed and bent at the elbows. His hands are at shoulder-level, with his fingers spread and his thumbs inside. His tail is down with his back arched. He has a slight forward lean at the waist. His head is up with his chin slightly over his toes. If he aligns in man sky, he tilts at a 45-degree angle facing the quarterback. His inside foot is back, and his outside foot is forward.

Keys: From an Opie alignment, he reads the outside hip of #1. From a sky alignment, he reads the quarterback's drop.
- Three-step drop: He attacks #1's route immediately, while thinking short routes and fade.
- Five-step drop: He backpedals, while keeping over-the-top coverage on #1 and thinking medium-to-deep routes.
- Seven-step drop: He backpedals, while keeping over-the-top coverage on #1 and thinking deep routes.

Responsibilities: He plays #1 man-to-man. He must not get beat deep. He supports the run late, only after the ball has crossed the line of scrimmage.

❏ Boundary Corner

Alignment: The boundary corner aligns in his cover 2 shell, seven yards deep and one yard outside of #1. Just prior to the snap of the ball, he stems to man-to-man coverage on #1. He has middle field help, so he plays an outside alignment on #1. He can choose either man cloud or man sky alignment. If he chooses man cloud, he aligns in an Opie alignment, on the line of scrimmage, with his inside foot on the outside foot of #1. If he uses man sky, he aligns seven yards deep and one yard outside of #1.

Stance: From an Opie alignment, he aligns in a square stance with his toes parallel to the line of scrimmage and pointing straight ahead. His feet are no wider than armpits-width apart with his weight on the balls of his feet. He is bent at the waist and knees for explosion. His arms are outside his knees and are relaxed and bent at the elbows. His hands are at shoulder-level with his fingers spread and his thumbs inside. His tail is down with his back arched. He has a slight forward lean at the waist. His head is up with his chin slightly over his toes. If he aligns in man sky, he tilts at a 45-degree angle facing the quarterback. His inside foot is back, and his outside foot is forward.

Keys: From an Opie alignment, he reads the outside hip of #1. From a sky alignment, he reads the quarterback's drop.
- Three-step drop: He attacks #1's route immediately, while thinking short routes and fade.

- Five-step drop: He backpedals, while keeping over-the-top coverage on #1 and thinking medium-to-deep routes.
- Seven-step drop: He backpedals, while keeping over-the-top coverage on #1 and thinking deep routes.

Responsibilities: He plays #1 man-to-man. He must not get beat deep. He supports the run late, only after the ball has crossed the line of scrimmage.

❑ Strong Safety

Alignment: The strong safety aligns in his cover 2 shell, 10 yards deep over a normal tight end alignment. Just prior to the snap of the ball, he stems to man-to-man coverage on #2. He has middle field help, so he plays an outside alignment on #2. He can choose either man cloud or man sky alignment. If he chooses man cloud, he aligns in an Opie alignment, on the line of scrimmage, with his inside foot on the outside foot of #2. If he uses man sky, he aligns seven yards deep and one yard outside of #2.

Stance: From an Opie alignment, he aligns in a square stance with his toes parallel to the line of scrimmage and pointing straight ahead. His feet are no wider than armpits-width apart with his weight on the balls of his feet. He is bent at the waist and knees for explosion. His arms are outside his knees and are relaxed and bent at the elbows. His hands are at shoulder-level with his fingers spread and his thumbs inside. His tail is down with his back arched. His has a slight forward lean at the waist. His head is up with his chin slightly over his toes. If he aligns in man sky, he tilts at a 45-degree angle facing the quarterback. His inside foot is back, and his outside foot is forward. If he has middle-of-the-field responsibilities, he aligns in a square stance at a depth of 12 yards. His width depends on the position of the ball. If the ball is in the middle of the field, he aligns over the ball. If the ball is into the boundary, he slides over the guard-tackle area to the wideside of the field.

Keys: From an Opie alignment, he reads the outside hip of #2. From the middle-of-the-field alignment, he keys the quarterback for a pass or run read. He must read uncovered linemen for a high-hat read. He must also stay deeper than all middle-of-the field routes. He must listen for route calls from his teammates and read receiver routes as he backpedals. From sky, he reads the quarterback for a pass or run keys.
- Three-step drop: He attacks #2's route immediately, while thinking short routes and fade.
- Five-step drop: He backpedals, while keeping over-the-top coverage on #2 and thinking medium-to-deep routes.
- Seven-step drop: He backpedals, while keeping over-the-top coverage on #2 and thinking deep routes.

Responsibilities: He has #2 man-to-man. He must not get beat deep. He supports the run late, only after the ball has crossed the line of scrimmage. If he has the deep middle of the field, he must keep all passes in front of him and not get beat deep. He must fit where help is needed from the inside out on all runs. He basically fits from seam-to-seam or plays #2 man-to-man.

❏ Rover

Alignment: Rover aligns in his cover 2 shell, 10 yards deep over a normal tight end alignment. Just prior to the snap of the ball, he stems to man-to-man coverage on #2. He has middle field help, so he will play an outside alignment on #2. He can choose either man cloud or man sky alignment. If he chooses man cloud, he will align in an Opie alignment, on the line of scrimmage, with his inside foot on the outside foot of #2. If he uses man sky, he aligns seven yards deep and one yard outside of #2.

Stance: From an Opie alignment, he aligns in a square stance with his toes parallel to the line of scrimmage and pointing straight ahead. His feet are no wider than armpits-width apart with his weight on the balls of his feet. He is bent at the waist and knees for explosion. His arms are outside his knees and are relaxed and bent at the elbows. His hands are at shoulder-level with his fingers spread and his thumbs inside. His tail is down with his back arched. His has a slight forward lean at the waist. His head is up with his chin slightly over his toes. If he aligns in man sky, he tilts at a 45-degree angle facing the quarterback. His inside foot is back, and his outside foot is forward. If he has middle-of-the-field responsibilities, he aligns in a square stance at a depth of 12 yards. His width depends on the position of the ball. If the ball is in the middle of the field, he aligns over the ball. If the ball is into the boundary, he slides over the guard-tackle area to the wideside of the field.

Keys: From an Opie alignment, he reads the outside hip of #2. From the middle-of-the-field alignment, he keys the quarterback for a pass or run read. He must read uncovered linemen for a high-hat read. He must also stay deeper than all middle-of-the field routes. He must listen for route calls from his teammates and read receiver routes as he backpedals. From sky, he reads the quarterback for a pass or run keys.
- Three-step drop: He attacks #2's route immediately, while thinking short routes and fade.
- Five-step drop: He backpedals, while keeping over-the-top coverage on #2 and thinking medium-to-deep routes.
- Seven-step drop: He backpedals, while keeping over-the-top coverage on #2 and thinking deep routes.

Responsibilities: He has #2 man-to-man. He must not get beat deep. He supports the run late, only after the ball has crossed the line of scrimmage. If he has the deep middle of the field, he must keep all passes in front of him and not get beat deep. He must fit where help is needed from the inside out on all runs. He basically fits from seam-to-seam or plays #2 man-to-man.

❑ Sam

Alignment: Sam uses his normal linebacker stance, unless he is aligned on a wideout; he then aligns in an Opie or sky position. His stance and alignment are the same as those used by a corner or safety when playing Opie or sky coverage.

Keys: He uses his regular linebacker reads unless he is aligned on a wideout; he then uses the same man cloud or man sky reads as a corner or safety. From man cloud, he uses an Opie alignment and reads the outside hip of #3. From sky, he reads the quarterback for a pass or run key.
- Three-step drop: He attacks #3's route immediately, while thinking short routes and fade.
- Five-step drop: He backpedals, while keeping over-the-top coverage on #3 and thinking medium-to-deep routes.
- Seven-step drop: He backpedals, while keeping over-the-top coverage on #3 and thinking deep routes.

Responsibilities: He has #3 strong or the second back out to the strongside man-to-man. If no #3 exists, he drops to the strongside hook/curl.

❑ Mike

Alignment: Mike aligns in the front that is called in the huddle.

Stance: He uses his normal linebacker stance.

Keys: He uses his normal linebacker keys.

Responsibilities: He has the second back to the strongside man-to-man. If no second back is out, he drops to the low hole.

❑ Will

Alignment: Will uses his normal linebacker stance, unless he is aligned on a wideout; he then aligns in an Opie or sky position. His stance and alignment are the same as those used by a corner or safety when playing Opie or sky coverage.

Keys: He uses his regular linebacker reads, unless he is aligned on a wideout; he then uses the same man cloud or man sky reads as a corner or safety. From man cloud, he uses an Opie alignment and reads the outside hip of #3. From sky, he reads the quarterback for a pass or run key.

- Three-step drop: He attacks #3's route immediately, while thinking short routes and fade.
- Five-step drop: He backpedals, while keeping over-the-top coverage on #3 and thinking medium-to-deep routes.
- Seven-step drop: He backpedals, while keeping over-the-top coverage on #3 and thinking deep routes.

Responsibilities: He has #3 man-to-man or the first back out on the weakside. If no #3 is present, he drops to the weakside hook/curl.

Cover 1 vs. a 12 Set (Figures 3-37 and 3-38)

Cover 1 vs. a 12 set is a man-free coverage. The field corner aligns in a sky alignment on #1. The boundary corner aligns in an Opie alignment on #1. The strong safety aligns in his cover 2 shell. Rover aligns in a sky alignment on #2. All linebackers align in their normal linebacker alignments.

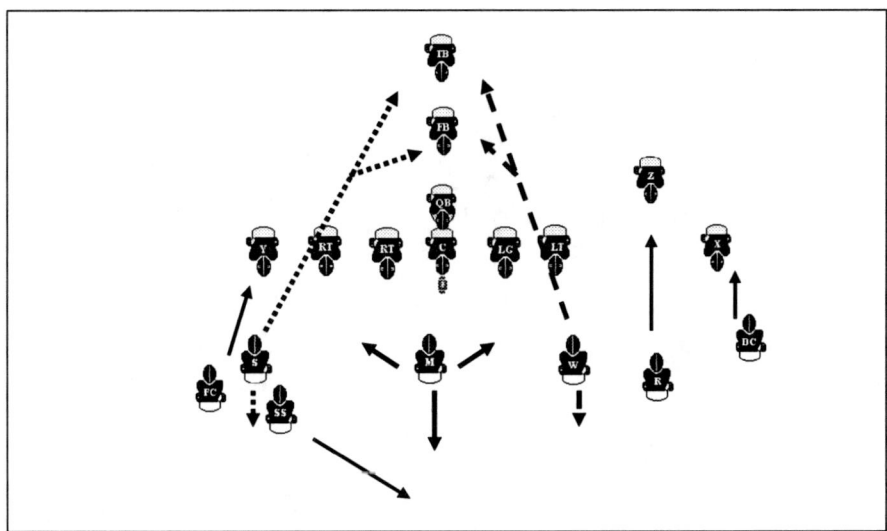

Figure 3-37. Cover 1 vs. a 12 set

Position	Pass responsibility
Sam	Plays the first back out to the strongside man-to-man or drops to the strongside hook.
Mike	Plays the second back out to either side man-to-man or drops to the low hole.
Will	Plays the first back out to the weakside man-to-man or drops to the weakside hook.
Strong safety	Plays free in the middle one-third.
Rover	Plays #2 man-to-man.
Field corner	Plays the tight end man-to-man.
Boundary corner	Plays #1 man-to-man.

Figure 3-38. Position and pass responsibility for cover 1 vs. a 12 set

Cover 1 vs. a 13 Set (Figures 3-39 and 3-40)

Cover 1 vs. a 13 set is a Toro check (see Toro coverage in Chapter 5). Rover plays a sky alignment on #3. The strong safety is free in the middle one-third. The field corner supers to play #2 from a Marvin alignment. The boundary aligns in an Opie (sky) alignment over #1. Sam has the tight end man-to-man. Mike and Will align in their normal linebacker alignment.

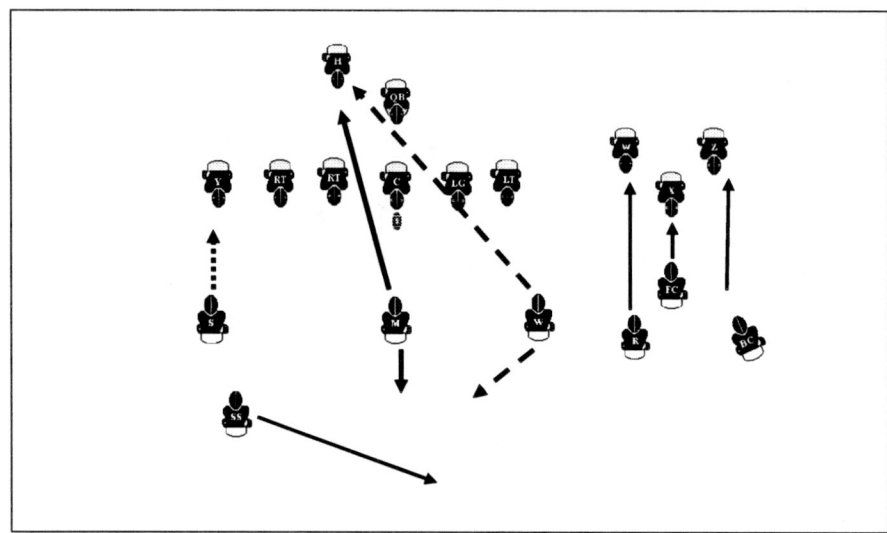

Figure 3-39. Cover 1 vs. a 13 set

Position	Pass responsibility
Sam	Plays the tight end man-to-man.
Mike	Plays his Toro rules.
Will	Plays his Toro rules.
Strong safety	Plays free in the middle one-third.
Rover	Plays #3 man-to-man.
Field corner	Supers over and plays #2 man-to-man; if the trips have been to the field, he plays #1 man-to-man.
Boundary corner	Plays man-to-man on #1; if the trips have been to the field, he supers over and plays #2 man-to-man.

Figure 3-40. Position and pass responsibility for cover 1 vs. a 13 set

Cover 1 vs. a 14 Set (Figures 3-41 and 3-42)

Cover 1 vs. a 14 set is a Toro check (see Toro coverage in Chapter 5). Rover plays a sky alignment on #3. The strong safety is free in the middle one-third. The field corner supers over to play #2 from a Marvin alignment. The boundary corner aligns in an Opie (sky) alignment over #1. Sam has the tight end man-to-man. Mike aligns in his normal linebacker alignment. Will aligns in a sky alignment over #4.

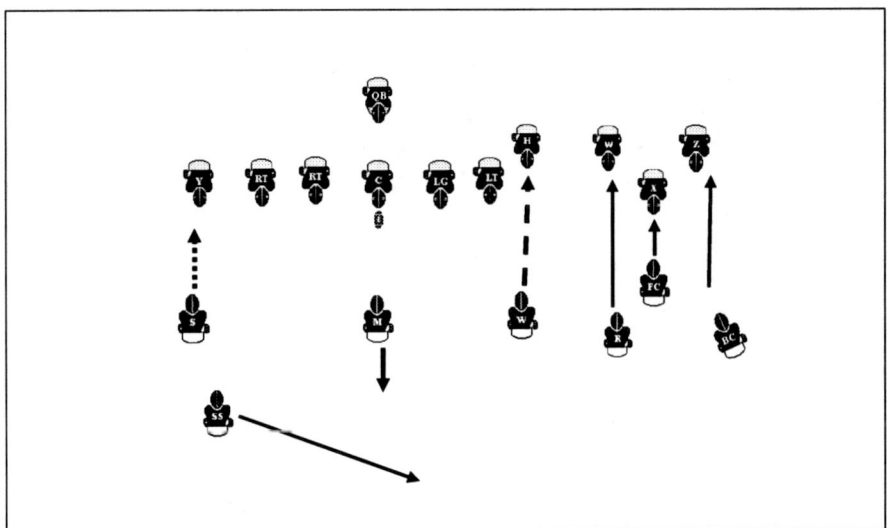

Figure 3-41. Cover 1 vs. a 14 set

Position	Pass responsibility
Sam	Plays the tight end man-to-man.
Mike	Drops to the low hole and mirrors the quarterback.
Will	Plays #4 man-to-man.
Strong safety	Plays free in the middle one-third.
Rover	Plays #3 man-to-man.
Field corner	Supers over and plays #2 man-to-man; if the trips have been to the field, he plays #1 man-to-man.
Boundary corner	Plays man-to-man on #1; if the trips have been to the field, he supers over and plays #2 man-to-man.

Figure 3-42. Position and pass responsibility for cover 1 vs. a 14 set

Cover 1 vs. a 22 Set (Figures 3-43 and 3-44)

Cover 1 vs. a 22 set is a Toro check (see Toro coverage in Chapter 5). Rover plays a sky alignment on #2. The strong safety is free in the middle one-third. The corners play an Opie alignment on the #1s. Sam has the tight end man-to-man. Mike and Will align in their normal linebacker alignments.

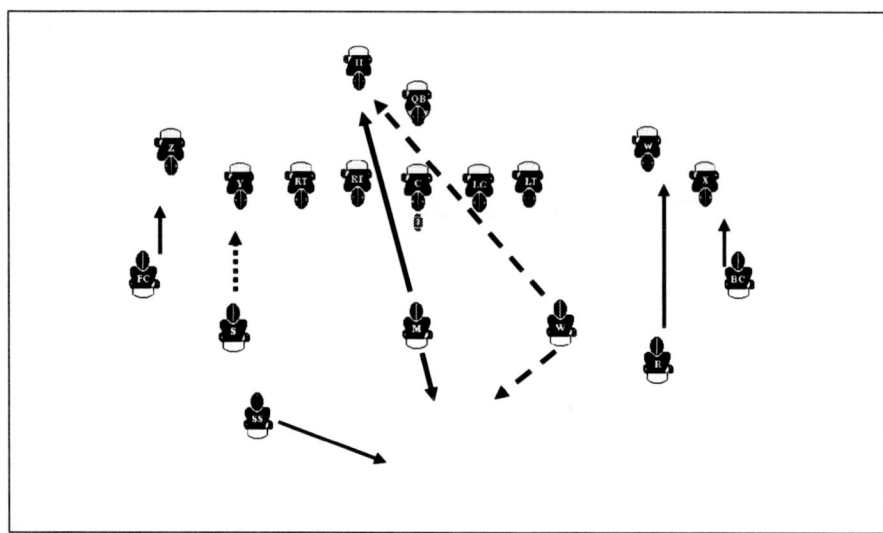

Figure 3-43. Cover 1 vs. a 22 set

Position	Pass responsibility
Sam	Plays the tight man-to-man.
Mike	Plays his Toro rules.
Will	Plays his Toro rules.
Strong safety	Plays free in the middle one-third.
Rover	Plays #2 man-to-man.
Field corner	Plays #1 man-to-man.
Boundary corner	Plays #1 man-to-man.

Figure 3-44. Position and pass responsibility for cover 1 vs. a 22 set

Cover 1 vs. a 23 Set (Figures 3-45 and 3-46)

Cover 1 vs. a 23 set is a Toro check (see Toro coverage in Chapter 5). Rover plays a sky alignment on #2. The strong safety is free in the middle one-third. The corners play an Opie alignment on the #1s. Sam has the tight end man-to-man. Mike aligns in his normal linebacker alignment. Will plays a sky alignment over #3.

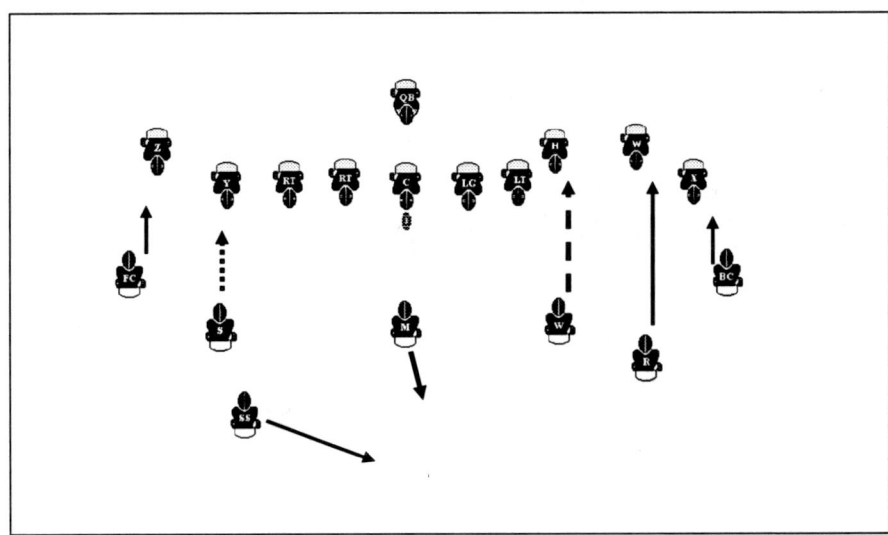

Figure 3-45. Cover 1 vs. a 23 set

Position	Pass responsibility
Sam	Plays the tight end man-to-man.
Mike	Drops to the low hole and mirrors the quarterback.
Will	Plays #3 man-to-man.
Strong safety	Plays free in the middle one-third.
Rover	Plays #2 man-to-man.
Field corner	Plays #1 man-to-man.
Boundary corner	Plays #1 man-to-man.

Figure 3-46. Position and pass responsibility for cover 1 vs. a 23 set

Cover 1 vs. a 31 Set (Figures 3-47 and 3-48)

Cover 1 vs. a 31 set is a Toro check (see Toro coverage in Chapter 5). Rover is free in the middle one-third. The strong safety plays a Marvin alignment on #2. The field corner plays a sky alignment on #1. The boundary corner plays an Opie alignment on #1. Sam has the tight end man-to-man. Mike and Will align in their normal linebacker alignments.

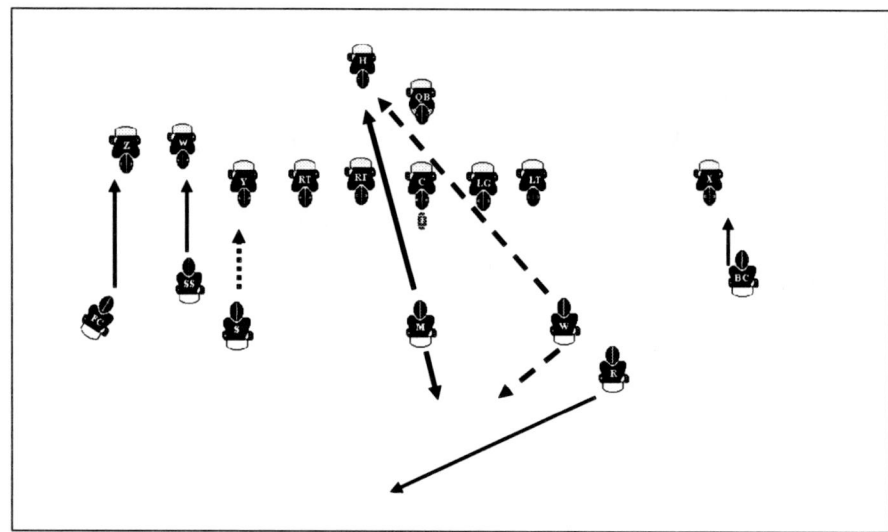

Figure 3-47. Cover 1 vs. a 31 set

Position	Pass responsibility
Sam	Plays the tight end man-to-man.
Mike	Plays his Toro rules.
Will	Plays his Toro rules.
Strong safety	Plays #2 man-to-man.
Rover	Plays free in the middle one-third.
Field corner	Plays #1 man-to-man.
Boundary corner	Plays #1 man-to-man.

Figure 3-48. Position and pass responsibility for cover 1 vs. a 31 set

Cover 1 vs. a 32 Set (Figures 3-49 and 3-50)

Cover 1 vs. a 32 set is a Toro check (see Toro coverage in Chapter 5). Rover is free in the middle one-third. The strong safety plays a Marvin alignment on #2. The field corner plays a sky alignment on #1. The boundary corner plays an Opie alignment on #1. Sam has the tight end man-to-man. Mike aligns in his normal linebacker alignment. Will aligns in a sky alignment on #2.

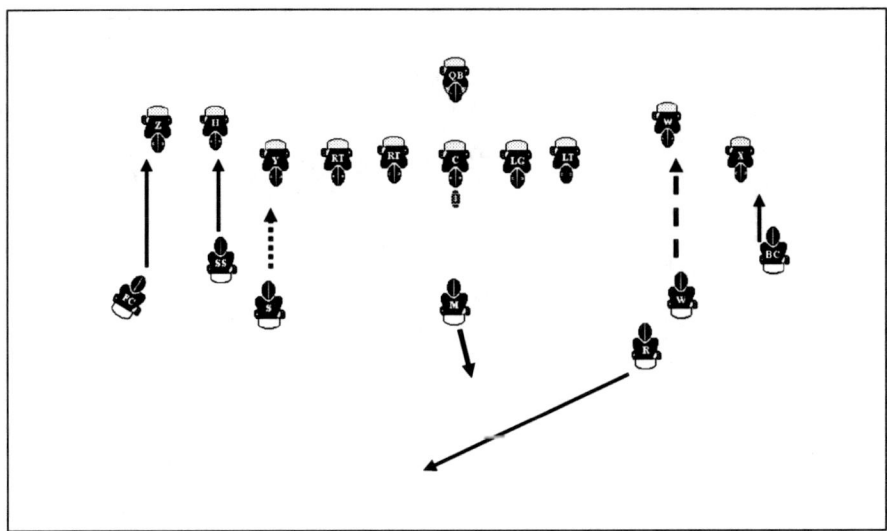

Figure 3-49. Cover 1 vs. a 32 set

Position	Pass responsibility
Sam	Plays the tight end man-to-man.
Mike	Drops to the low hole and mirrors the quarterback.
Will	Plays #2 man-to-man.
Strong safety	Plays #2 man-to-man.
Rover	Plays free in the middle one-third.
Field corner	Plays #1 man-to-man.
Boundary corner	Plays #1 man-to-man.

Figure 3-50. Position and pass responsibility for cover 1 vs. a 32 set

Cover 1 vs. a 41 Set (Figures 3-51 and 3-52)

Cover 1 vs. a 41 set is a Toro check (see Toro coverage in Chapter 5). Rover is free in the middle one-third. The strong safety plays a Marvin alignment on #2. The field corner plays a sky alignment on #1. The boundary corner plays an Opie alignment on #1. Sam has the tight end man-to-man. Mike aligns in his normal linebacker alignment. Will aligns in a sky alignment on #3 to the strongside.

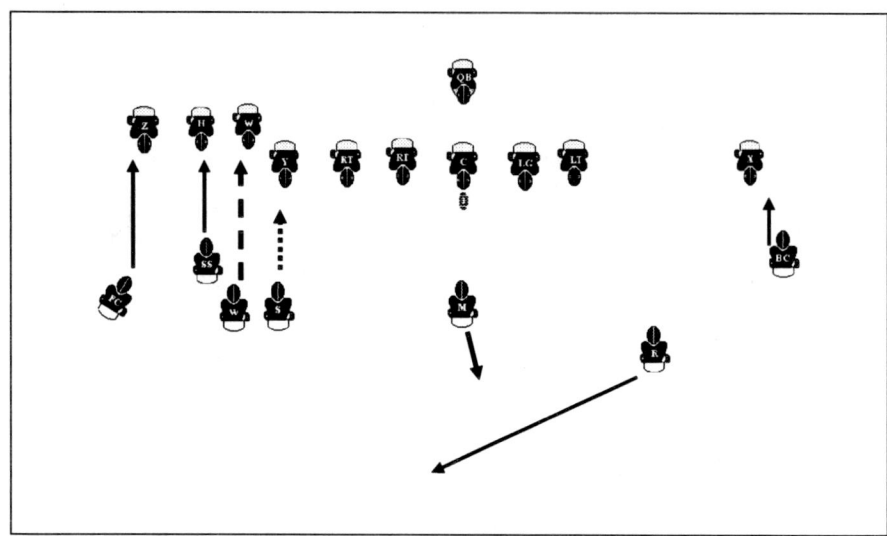

Figure 3-51. Cover 1 vs. a 41 set

Position	Pass responsibility
Sam	Plays the tight end man-to-man.
Mike	Drops to the low hole and mirrors the quarterback.
Will	Plays #3 strong man-to-man.
Strong safety	Plays #2 man-to-man.
Rover	Plays free in the middle one-third.
Field corner	Plays #1 man-to-man.
Boundary corner	Plays #1 man-to-man.

Figure 3-52. Position and pass responsibility for cover 1 vs. a 41 set

4

Zone Coverages

Chapter 3 presented a detailed look at the techniques of playing man-to-man coverage. Some individuals may ask, "Why not just play man-to-man coverage entirely?" To answer that question, it must be understood that the first golden rule of playing defense is to stop the run and make the offense throw the ball. Knowledgeable coaches know that modern day offensive schemes use one-back and no-back formations to spread the defense both horizontally and vertically. These schemes give the illusion that the offense is interested in passing the ball but, in reality, they also spread the field in order to run the ball. To stop the running game, the defense must be able to play great zone coverage, which allows the defensive players to read the offense as they drop to their area of pass responsibility.

Advantages of Zone Coverage

- Commits more players to stop the run
- Allows for more eyes on the ball
- Better gang tackling
- Allows the defense to better defend screens, draws, bubbles, and the short passing game

- Gives the defense more flexibility to stem and prowl on the fringes of the box in order to confuse the offense, which keeps the offensive thinking about who (defensively) is committed to the run and who is committed to the pass.
- Allows the defense to blitz and stunt without having to adjust to multiple offensive formations and motion
- Safer pass coverage to protect certain areas of the field

The discussion of zone coverage begins with an in-depth look at cover 2. This coverage is the base coverage from which all other zone and man/zone combinations will evolve. The defensive players must be confident in their ability to play cover 2 against all offensive formations.

Zone Coverage Terminology

In order to understand zone coverage, zone coverage terminology must be understood.

- *Cover 2 shell*: The pre-snap alignment of the defensive secondary. The corners align seven yards deep over the wideouts. The strong safety and Rover align 10 yards deep over the tight end area. Aligning in a cover 2 shell helps to disguise coverages.
- *Backer call*: A call made by a linebacker anytime he must widen to the outside in order to be able to cover the wall-curl-pull. This move is usually about a three-step lateral.
- *Wall-curl-pull*: Tells defenders to wall any inside route by an outside receiver. If no wall coverage is needed, he then moves to the curl. If no curl coverage is needed, he pulls to any back, crossing his face from the inside to the outside.
- *Five-yard highway*: An area five yards deep and in front of a wide receiver. The defender works laterally in this area as he attacks the upfield routes of receivers.
- *Over the top*: Tells defenders that they must keep deep coverage over the top of receivers and cannot let anyone get behind them. He must keep at least a three-yard cushion on the receiver.
- *Rally*: Tells defenders to break late on receivers who are running short routes.
- *Rerouting receivers*: When defenders attack offensive receivers as they come off the line of scrimmage, which reroutes the receiver, taking him out of his pass pattern, and disrupts the timing between the quarterback and the receiver.
- *Super call*: A call made by a corner telling the defense that he is moving to the other side of the defense in order to cover receivers.

- *Speed turn*: A backpedal turn made by a pass defender that allows him to turn his back on the quarterback and run to a receiver. The purpose of a speed turn is to enable him to use speed in order to turn and cover a receiver.

Cover 2

Cover 2 vs. a 21 Set (Figure 4-1)

Cover 2 is a two-deep and five underneath zone coverage. Several theories exist about alignments and keys when playing two-deep coverage. Some schemes are true zone coverage with the safeties reading the quarterback's drop, as well as his eyes. Other schemes, such as this scheme, call for pattern reads to determine individual coverage, instead of just dropping to zone areas. As in all coverages, the secondary aligns in a cover 2 shell. The corners reroute the #1s and read the #2s in order to know if they should sink or rally to the flats, depending on the release of #2. The strong safety and Rover bail to the hashes and read the quarterback to #2 for their run or pass responsibility. Sam and Will have wall-curl-pull responsibilities. Mike stays over the top of #3.

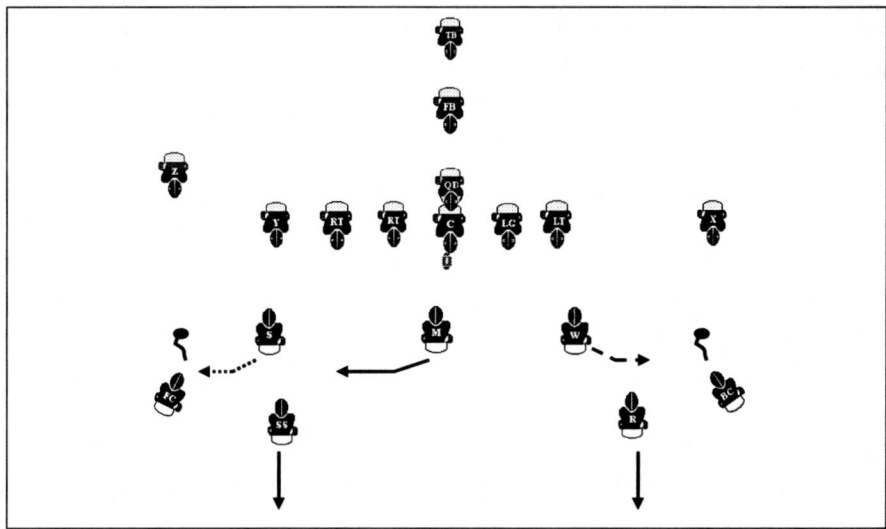

Figure 4-1. Cover 2 vs. a 21 set

Cover 2 Alignments, Stances, and Keys

❑ Field Corner

Alignment: The field corner aligns in his cover 2 shell at seven yards deep and one yard outside of a normal wideout. He then stems to five yards deep and one yard inside of #1. If a twin or trip set is to his side, he plays five yards deep and one yard outside of #1. If only a tight end is on his side, he aligns three yards by three yards off the tight end.

Stance: He aligns in a square stance with his toes pointing straight ahead. His feet are no more than armpits-width apart. His weight should be on the balls of his feet. He is bent at the waist and knees for explosion. His tail is down and his back is arched. His head is up with his chin slightly forward over his toes. His arms are outside his knees and relaxed and bent at the elbows. His hands are at shoulder level. His fingers are open with his thumbs inside. His eyes are looking to the inside for his read keys.

Keys: He reads the quarterback through #2 for his run or pass key. He should also be aware of high-hat by the offensive line, especially the end man on the line of scrimmage.

Responsibilities: He moves from a cover 2 shell to a five-yard highway position. As he moves forward, he reads the quarterback to #2. All movement by the corner is to collision #1 and shuffle laterally on the five-yard highway.

- Flow toward: He reroutes #1 by using the proper hand-shiver techniques. He has primary contain and cannot let anything get outside of him.
- Flow away: He reroutes #1 and sinks, turning his knees to the inside as he looks for any cutback or reverse to his side. The corner is the last man in pursuit to prevent a touchdown; therefore, his angle must be deep.
- Pass: He reads the quarterback and the release of #2 to determine his responsibilities. If #2 is vertical or inside, the corner reroutes #1 and sinks with #1 on all upfield routes. If #2 is flat, he reroutes #1 and sinks with #1 as he reads the quarterback. If the quarterback is under center, his drop depth will tell the corner what type of routes are being run by the receivers. A three-step quarterback drop tells the defender to look for the receiver to be running a fade, slant, or out route. A five-step quarterback drop tells the defender to look for the receiver to be running medium depth routes. A seven-step quarterback drop tells the defender to look for the receiver to be running deep routes. On all passes, he reroutes, sinks, and then rallies back to all short routes.

❑ Boundary Corner

Alignment: The boundary corner aligns in his cover 2 shell at seven yards deep and one yard outside of a normal wideout. He then stems to five yards deep and one yard inside of #1. If a twin or trip set is to his side, he plays five yards deep and one yard outside of #1. If only a tight end is on his side, he aligns three yards by three yards off the tight end.

Stance: He aligns in a square stance with his toes pointing straight ahead. His feet are no more than armpits-width apart. His weight should be on the balls of his feet. He is bent at the waist and knees for explosion. His tail is down and his back is arched. His head is up with his chin slightly forward over his toes. His arms are outside his knees and relaxed and bent at the elbows. His hands are at shoulder level. His fingers are open with his thumbs inside. His eyes are looking to the inside for his read keys.

Keys: He reads the quarterback through #2 for his run or pass key. He should also be aware of high-hat by the offensive line, especially the end man on the line of scrimmage.

Responsibilities: He moves from a cover 2 shell to a five-yard highway (an area five yards off the wide receiver) position. As he moves forward, he reads the quarterback to #2. All movement by the corner is to collision #1 and shuffle laterally on the five-yard highway.
- Flow toward: He reroutes #1 by using the proper hand-shiver techniques. He has primary contain and cannot let anything get outside of him.
- Flow away: He reroutes #1 and sinks, turning his knees to the inside as he looks for any cutback or reverse to his side. The corner is the last man in pursuit to prevent a touchdown; therefore, his angle must be deep.
- Pass: He reads the quarterback and the release of #2 to determine his responsibilities. If #2 is vertical or inside, the corner reroutes #1 and sinks with #1 on all upfield routes. If #2 is flat, the corner reroutes #1 and sinks with #1 as he reads the quarterback. If the quarterback is under center, his drop depth will tell the corner what type of routes are being run by the receivers. A three-step quarterback drop tells the defender to look for the receiver to be running a fade, slant, or out route. A five-step quarterback drop tells the defender to look for the receiver to be running medium depth routes. A seven-step quarterback drop tells the defender to look for the receiver to be running deep routes. On all passes, he reroutes, sinks, and then rallies back to all short routes.

❑ Strong Safety

Alignment: The strong safety aligns in a cover 2 shell at 10 yards deep over the tight end area. Just prior to the snap, he bails 12 to 14 yards deep on the strong hash. If only a tight end is on his side, he aligns at eight yards deep.

Stance: He aligns with his toes parallel to the line of scrimmage. His outside foot is staggered back in a toe-to-heel relationship with his inside foot. His feet are no more than armpits-width apart. His weight should be on the balls of his feet. He is bent at the waist and knees for explosion. His tail is down and his back is arched. His head is up with his chin slightly forward over his toes. His arms are outside his knees and relaxed and bent at the elbows. His eyes are looking to the quarterback for his read keys.

Keys: He keys the quarterback to #2 to #1.

Responsibilities: He thinks pass first and run second. He bails to the hash and reads the quarterback. He weaves in his backpedal in the direction that the quarterback's eyes are looking. He also reads #2 to #1 for receiver routes.
- Flow toward: He drops to the deep strongside half until no threat of a pass occurs; he then fits where he is needed.
- Flow away: He drops to the deep strongside half, and then takes a flat pursuit angle looking for cutbacks. He fits where he is needed, playing the ball from the inside out.
- Pass: He must read the quarterback's drop and eyes. He then weaves in the direction that the quarterback is looking. A three-step drop makes the safety think slant or fade. A five-step drop makes him think medium-to-deep routes. A seven-step drop makes him think deep routes. In addition, the release of #2 helps the safety get a jump on the ball. If #2 is inside or vertical, he sinks over the top of #2. If #2 is flat, he widens and sinks over the top of #1. If no #2 is on his side, he reads the quarterback's drops and eyes for his reaction.

❏ Rover

Alignment: Rover aligns in a cover 2 shell at 10 yards deep over the tight end area. Just prior to the snap, he bails 12 to 14 yards deep on the weak hash. If only a tight end is on his side, he aligns at eight yards deep.

Stance: He aligns with his toes parallel to the line of scrimmage. His outside foot is staggered back in a toe-to-heel relationship with his inside foot. His feet are no more than armpits-width apart. His weight should be on the balls of his feet. He is bent at the waist and knees for explosion. His tail is down and his back is arched. His head is up with his chin slightly forward over his toes. His arms are outside his knees and relaxed and bent at the elbows. His hands are at shoulder level. His eyes are looking to the quarterback for his read keys.

Keys: Rover keys the quarterback to #2 to #1.

Responsibilities: He thinks pass first and run second. Rover bails to the hash and reads the quarterback. He weaves in his backpedal in the direction that the quarterback's eyes are looking. He also reads #2 to #1 for receiver routes.

- Flow toward: He drops to the deep weakside deep half until no threat of a pass occurs; he then fits where he is needed.
- Flow away: He drops to the deep weakside half, and then takes a flat pursuit angle looking for cutbacks. He fits where he is needed, playing the ball from the inside out.
- Pass: He must read the quarterback's drop and eyes. He then weaves in the direction that the quarterback is looking. A three-step drop makes Rover think slant or fade. A five-step drop makes him think medium-to-deep routes. A seven-step-drop makes him think deep routes. In addition, the release of #2 helps him to get a jump on the ball. If #2 is inside or vertical, he sinks over the top of #2. If #2 is flat, he widens and sinks over the top of #1. If no #2 is on his side, the strong safety reads the quarterback's drops and eyes for his reaction.

❏ Sam

Alignment: Sam aligns in the front that is called in the huddle.

Stance: He uses his normal linebacker stance.

Keys: He uses his normal linebacker keys.

Responsibilities: If he reads pass, he opens to the outside, at a 45-degree angle and works width for three steps, as he drops to his wall-curl-pull responsibilities. He walls the first outside receiver, forcing him outside; he then settles in the curl. He plays late pull on any route that crosses his face from the inside.

❏ Mike

Alignment: Mike aligns in the front that is called in the huddle.

Stance: He uses his normal linebacker stance.

Keys: He uses his normal linebacker keys.

Responsibilities: If he reads pass, he must stay over the top of #3. He opens to the release of #3 and reads #2 to #3. If the tight end is vertical, he runs with him. If the tight end is outside, he stays on the top of #3. Mike must understand that when #3 and #2 cross, #2 becomes #3.

❑ Will

Alignment: Will aligns in the front called in the huddle.

Stance: He uses his normal linebacker stance.

Keys: He uses his normal linebacker keys.

Responsibilities: If he reads pass, he opens to the outside, at a 45-degree angle and works width for three steps, as he drops to his wall-curl-pull responsibilities. He walls the first outside receiver, forcing him outside. He then settles in the curl. He plays late pull on any route that crosses his face from the inside.

Cover 2 vs. a 12 Set (Figures 4-2 and 4-3)

Because of the twin set, a backer or super call must be made. In Figure 4-2, Will makes a backer call, and widens enough to be able to wall #2. When he hears a backer call, Mike moves three steps to the weakside, but must still be able to defend his strongside A gap. When Sam hears the backer call he slides three steps to the inside. The field corner aligns three yards by three yards off of the tight end. The boundary corner aligns five yards deep and one yard outside of #1. The strong safety aligns eight yards deep over the tight end. Rover aligns 12 to 14 yards deep on the weakside hash.

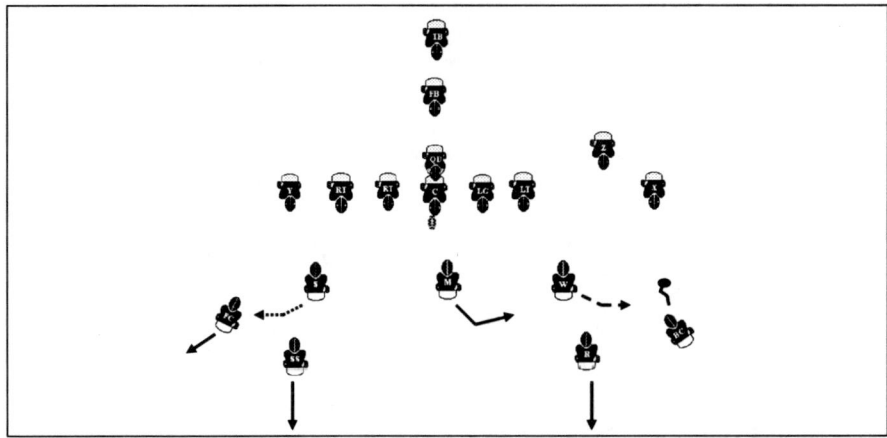

Figure 4-2. Cover 2 vs. a 12 set

Position	Pass responsibility
Sam	Drops to the strongside hook and walls the tight end. He also plays pull on the first back out to the strongside.
Mike	Opens to #3 and reads the release of #3 for his responsibility.
Will	Drops to the weakside wall-curl-pull and reads #2 for his responsibilities.
Strong safety	Drops to the deep strongside hash and reads the quarterback to #1 for his responsibilities.
Rover	Drops on the deep weakside hash and reads the quarterback to #2 for his responsibilities.
Field corner	Reads the quarterback through the tight end, as he drops to the outside at a 45-degree angle. He plays the strongside flats.
Boundary corner	Reads the quarterback to #2 for his responsibilities.

Figure 4-3. Position and pass responsibility for cover 2 vs. a 12 set

Cover 2 vs. a 13 Set (Figures 4-4 and 4-5)

A backer or super call must be made. In Figure 4-4, Will makes a backer call, and widens enough to be able to wall #2. When he hears a backer call, Mike moves three steps to the weakside, but must still be able to defend his strongside A gap. When Sam hears the backer call, he slides three steps to the inside. The field corner aligns three yards by three yards off of the tight end. The boundary corner aligns five yards deep and one yard outside of #1. The strong safety aligns eight yards deep over the tight end. Rover aligns 12 to 14 yards deep on the weakside hash.

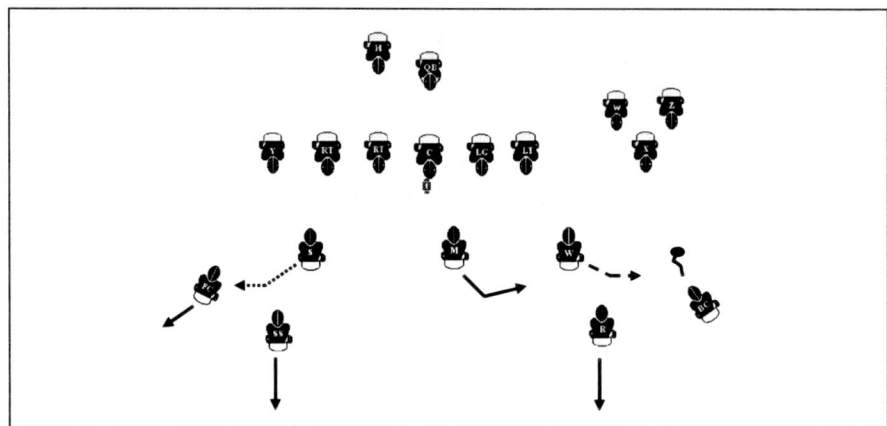

Figure 4-4. Cover 2 vs. a 13 set

Position	Pass responsibility
Sam	Drops to the strongside hook and walls the tight end. He also plays pull on the first back out to the strongside.
Mike	Opens to #3 and reads the release of #3 for his responsibilities.
Will	Drops to the weakside wall-curl-pull and reads #2 for his responsibilities.
Strong safety	Drops to the deep strongside hash and reads the quarterback to #1 for his responsibilities.
Rover	Drops on the deep weakside hash and reads the quarterback to #2 for his responsibilities.
Field corner	Reads the quarterback through the tight end, as he drops to the outside at a 45-degree angle. He plays the strongside flats.
Boundary corner	Reads the quarterback to #2 for his responsibilities.

Figure 4-5. Position and pass responsibility for cover 2 vs. a 13 set

Cover 2 vs. a 14 Set (Figures 4-6 and 4-7)

A backer or super call must be made. In Figure 4-6, the field corner makes a super call and moves to the other side of the field and aligns four yards deep and one yard inside of #2. The boundary corner aligns five yards deep and one yard outside of #1. The strong safety aligns eight yards deep over the tight end. Rover aligns 12 to 14 yards deep on the weakside hash. Mike slides over the center. Sam aligns in a normal alignment. Will aligns over #4 to the weakside.

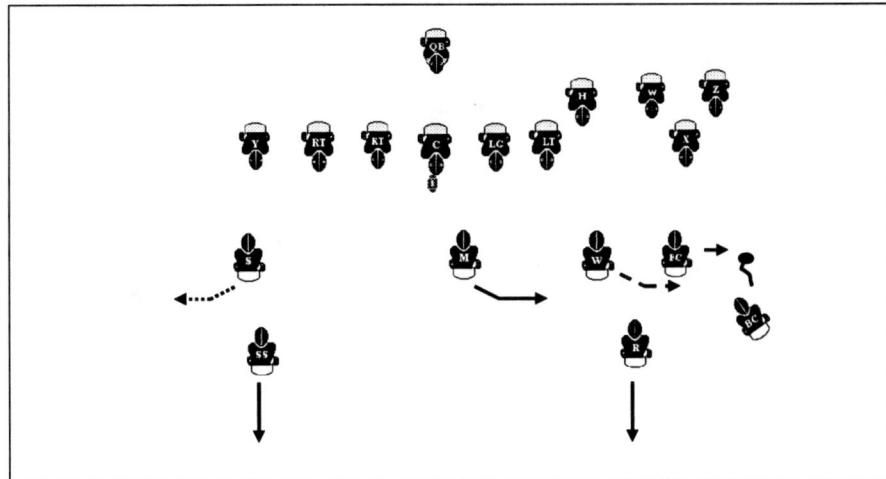

Figure 4-6. Cover 2 vs. a 14 set

Position	Pass responsibility
Sam	Walls the tight end or drops to the strongside flats.
Mike	Opens to #4 and reads the release of #4 for his responsibilities.
Will	Drops to the weakside wall-curl-pull and reads #3 for his responsibilities.
Strong safety	Drops to the deep strongside hash and reads the quarterback to #1 for his responsibilities.
Rover	Drops on the deep weakside hash and reads the quarterback to #2 for his responsibilities.
Field corner	Supers to the weakside and reads the quarterback to #2 for his responsibilities.
Boundary corner	Reads the quarterback to #2 for his responsibilities.

Figure 4-7. Position and pass responsibility for cover 2 vs. a 14 set

Cover 2 vs. a 22 Set (Figures 4-8 and 4-9)

Sam aligns in his normal alignment. If #2 is split out, Sam widens three steps to the outside. Mike aligns over the center and opens to the release of #3. Will widens enough to be able to wall #2. The field corner aligns five yards deep and one yard inside of #1. The boundary corner aligns five yards deep and one yard outside of #1. The strong safety and Rover align 12 to 14 yards deep on the hashes.

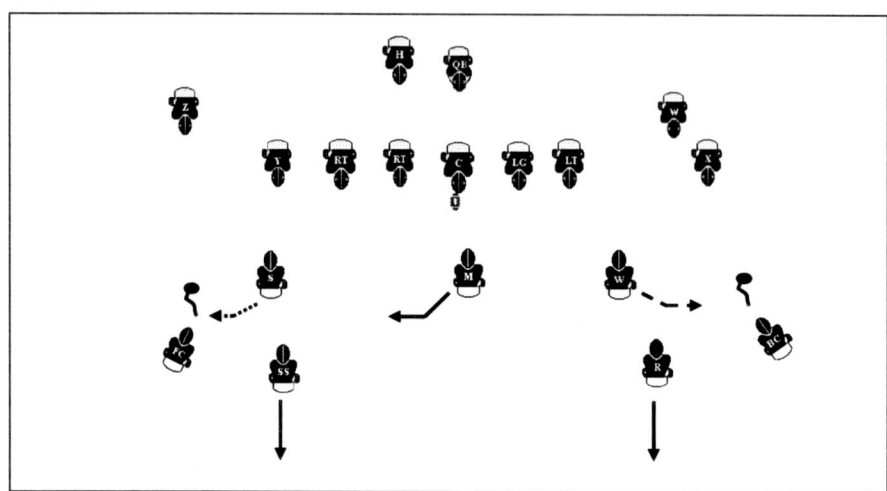

Figure 4-8. Cover 2 vs. a 22 set

Position	Pass responsibility
Sam	Drops to the strongside wall-curl-pull.
Mike	Drops over the top of #3's release.
Will	Drops to the weakside wall-curl-pull and reads #2 for his responsibilities.
Strong safety	Drops to the strongside hash and reads the quarterback to #2 for his responsibilities.
Rover	Drops to the weakside hash and reads the quarterback to #2 for his responsibilities.
Field corner	Reads the quarterback through #2 for his responsibilities.
Boundary corner	Reads the quarterback through #2 for his responsibilities.

Figure 4-9. Position and pass responsibility for cover 2 vs. a 22 set

Cover 2 vs. a 23 Set (Figures 4-10 and 4-11)

Sam aligns in his normal linebacker alignment. Will widens enough to be able to wall #2. Mike aligns over the center. The field corner aligns five yards deep and one yard inside of #1. The boundary corner aligns five yards deep and one yard outside of #1. The strong safety and Rover align 12 to 14 yards deep on the hashes.

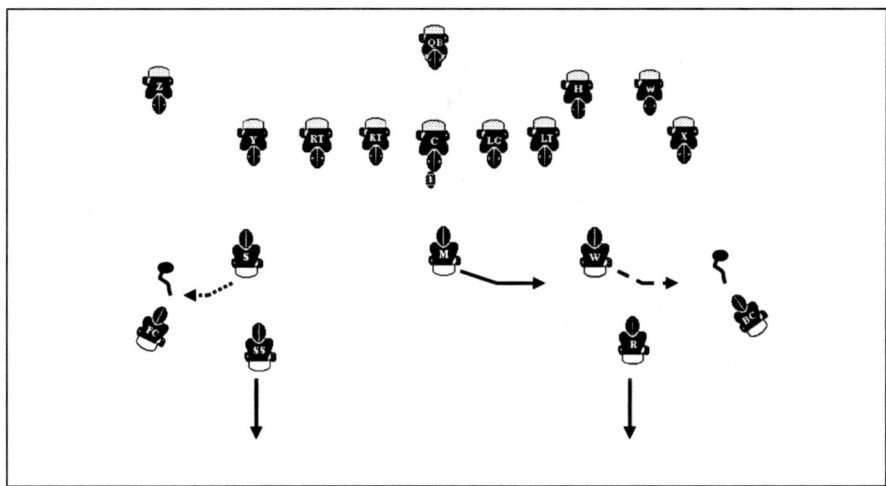

Figure 4-10. Cover 2 vs. a 23 set

Position	Pass responsibility
Sam	Drops to the strongside wall-curl-pull and reads #2 for his responsibilities.
Mike	Drops over the top of #3's release.
Will	Drops to the weakside wall-curl-pull and reads #2 for his responsibilities.
Strong safety	Drops to the strongside hash and reads the quarterback to #2 for his responsibilities.
Rover	Drops to the weakside hash and reads the quarterback to #2 for his responsibilities.
Field corner	Reads the quarterback through #2 for his responsibilities.
Boundary corner	Reads the quarterback through #2 for his responsibilities.

Figure 4-11. Position and pass responsibility for cover 2 vs. a 23 set

Cover 2 vs. a 31 Set (Figures 4-12 and 4-13)

Sam makes a backer call and widens enough to be able to wall #2. When Mike hears the backer call, he moves three steps to the strongside. When Will hears the backer call he slides three steps to the inside. The field corner aligns five yards deep and one yard outside of #1. The boundary corner aligns five yards deep and one yard inside of #1. The strong safety and Rover align 12 to 14 yards deep on the hashes.

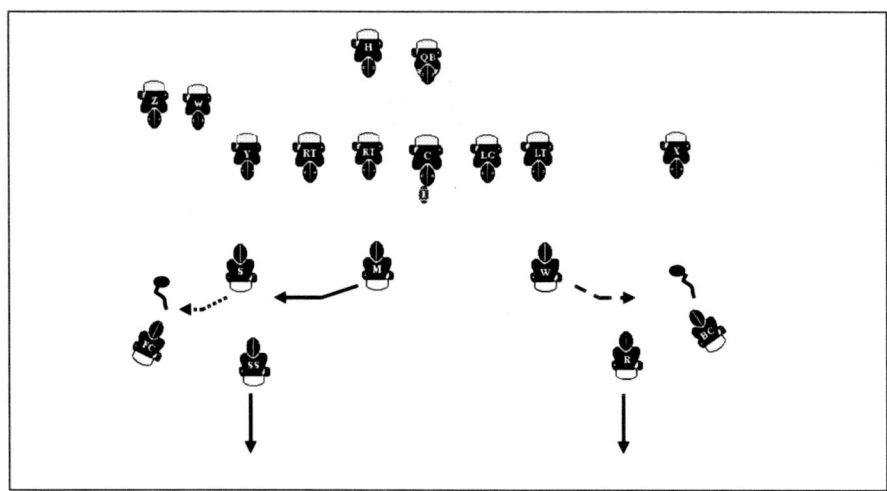

Figure 4-12. Cover 2 vs. a 31 set

Position	Pass responsibility
Sam	Drops to the strongside wall-curl-pull and reads #2 for his responsibilities.
Mike	Opens and drops over the top of #3's release.
Will	Drops to the weakside wall-curl-pull. He walls #1 and reads the back for his pull responsibilities.
Strong safety	Drops to the strongside hash and reads the quarterback and #2 for his responsibilities.
Rover	Drops to the weakside hash and reads the quarterback and #1 for his responsibilities.
Field corner	Reads the quarterback through #2 for his responsibilities.
Boundary corner	Reads the quarterback and #2 for his responsibilities.

Figure 4-13. Position and pass responsibility for cover 2 vs. a 31 set

Cover 2 vs. a 32 Set (Figures 4-14 and 4-15)

Sam and Will widen enough to be able to wall the #2s. Mike slides to the strongside and drops over the top of #3. The field corner aligns 5 yards deep and 1 yard outside of #1. The boundary corner aligns 5 yards deep and 1 yard outside of #1. The strong safety and Rover align 12 to 14 yards deep on the hashes.

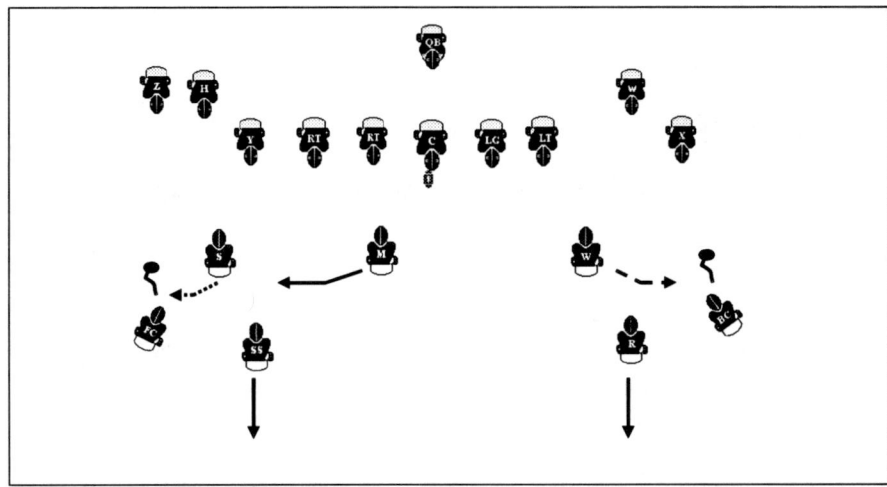

Figure 4-14. Cover 2 vs. a 32 set

Position	Pass responsibility
Sam	Drops to the strongside wall-curl-pull and reads #2 for his responsibilities.
Mike	Opens and drops over the top of #3's release.
Will	Drops to the weakside wall-curl-pull and reads #2 for his responsibilities.
Strong safety	Drops to the strongside hash and reads the quarterback to #2 for his responsibilities.
Rover	Drops on the weakside hash and reads the quarterback to #2 for his responsibilities.
Field corner	Reads the quarterback to #2 for his responsibilities.
Boundary corner	Reads the quarterback to #2 for his responsibilities.

Figure 4-15. Position and pass responsibility for cover 2 vs. a 32 set

Cover 2 vs. a 41 Set (Figures 4-16 and 4-17)

Sam makes a backer call and widens enough to be able to wall #2. When Mike hears the backer call, he slides three steps to the strongside. When Will hears the backer call, he slides three steps to the inside. The field corner aligns five yards deep and one yard outside of #1. The boundary corner aligns five yards deep and one yard inside of #1.The strong safety and Rover align 12 to 14 yards deep on the hashes.

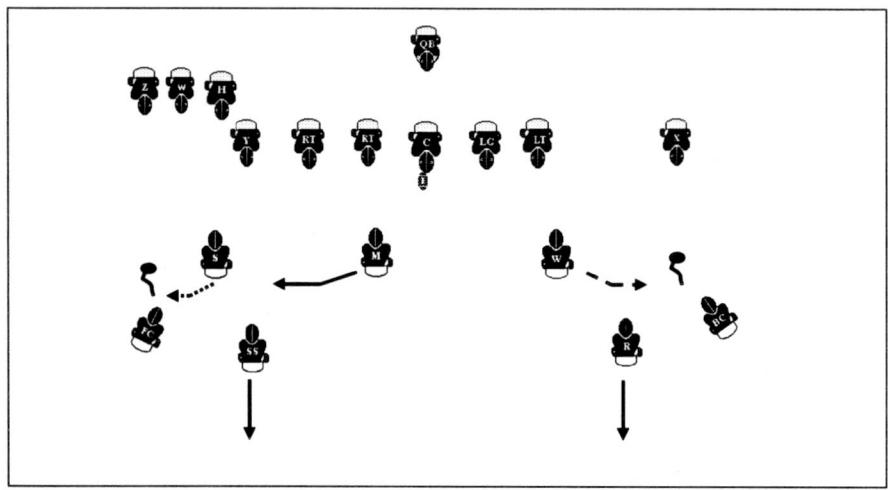

Figure 4-16. Cover 2 vs. a 41 set

Position	Pass responsibility
Sam	Drops to the strongside wall-curl-pull and reads #2 for his responsibilities.
Mike	Opens and drops over the top of #4's release.
Will	Drops to the weakside wall-curl-pull, walls #1, and reads the back for his pull responsibilities.
Strong safety	Drops to the strongside hash and reads the quarterback to #2 for his responsibilities.
Rover	Drops on the weakside hash and reads the quarterback to #1 for his responsibilities.
Field corner	Reads the quarterback to #2 for his responsibilities.
Boundary corner	Reads the quarterback to #2 for his responsibilities.

Figure 4-17. Position and pass responsibility for cover 2 vs. a 41 set

Crazy Horse Cover 2 vs. a 31 Set (Figures 4-18 and 4-19)

If you are seeing a lot of one-back and no-back sets, you will want to bring in the Arizona personnel, which helps cover 2 by giving you an extra defensive back in the game. Crazy Horse cover 2 vs. a 31 set is a two-deep zone read coverage. Sam drops to the strongside wall-curl-pull. Mike drops over the top of #3's release. Will drops to the weakside wall-curl-pull. The strong safety and Rover align 12 to 14 yards deep on the hashes. The field corner aligns five yards deep and one yard outside of #1. The boundary corner aligns five yards deep and one yard inside of #1. Geronimo aligns four yards deep and one yard inside of #2.

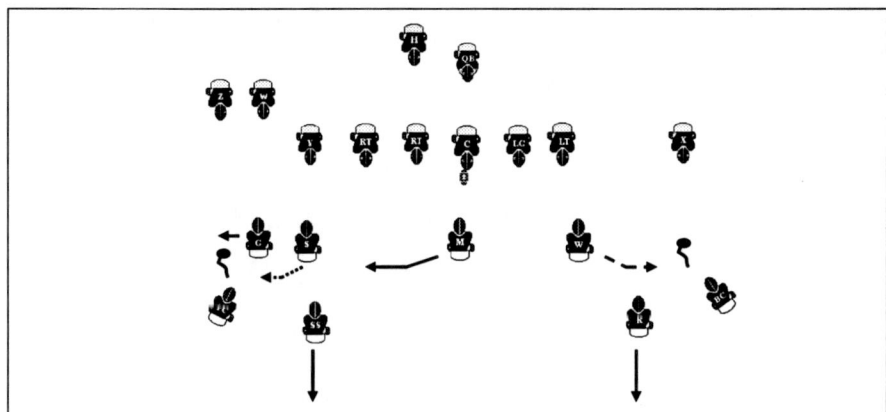

Figure 4-18. Crazy Horse cover 2 vs. a 31 set

Position	Pass responsibility
Sam	Drops to the strongside wall-curl-pull and reads the release of #2 for his responsibilities.
Mike	Opens and drops over the top of the #3's release.
Will	Drops to the weakside wall-curl-pull, walls #1, and reads the back for his pull responsibilities.
Strong safety	Drops to the strongside hash and reads the quarterback to #2 for his responsibilities.
Rover	Drops on the weakside hash and reads the quarterback to #1 for his responsibilities.
Field corner	Reads the quarterback to #2 for his responsibilities.
Boundary corner	Reads the quarterback to #2 for his responsibilities.
Geronimo	Drops to the wall-curl-pull and reads #2 for his responsibilities.

Figure 4-19. Position and pass responsibility for Crazy Horse cover 2 vs. a 31 set

Cover 2 Half-Line Reads and Reactions

Because cover 2 is such an important coverage and the base from which all other coverages evolve, a more detailed study should be taken of cover 2.

Cover 2 vs. Weakside X Fade (Figure 4-20)

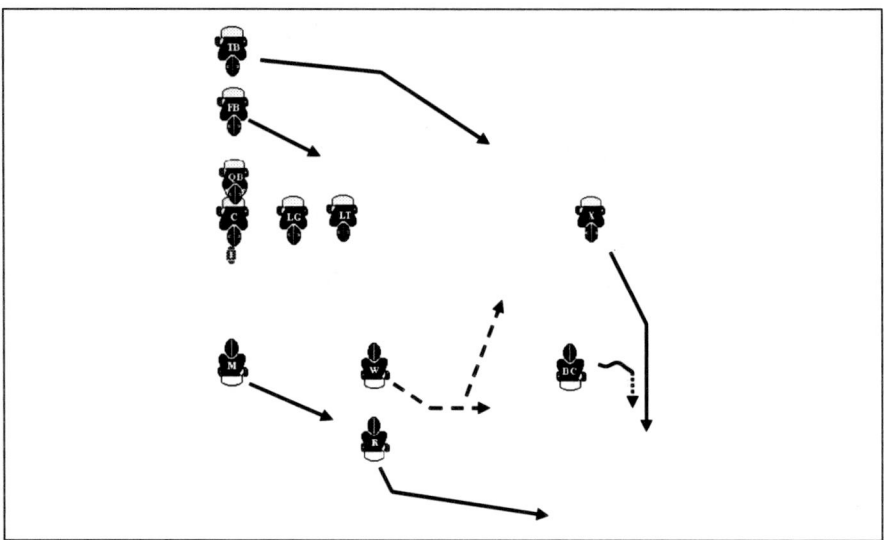

Figure 4-20. Cover 2 vs. weakside X fade

❑ Corner

Alignment: The corner stems to five yards deep and one yard inside of #1.

Keys: He keys the quarterback through the offensive tackle as he reroutes #1.

Responsibility: He shuffles outside for no more that three steps. He then makes a "speed turn" and runs with #1 on the vertical, which is a trail technique.

Coaching Point: The corner can run with #1 because there is no immediate threat to the flats.

❑ Will

Alignment: Will aligns in the defense that is called in the huddle.

Keys: He uses his normal linebacker keys.

Responsibility: When Will reads pass, he drops three steps at a 45-degree angle and levels outside to the wall-curl-pull.

Coaching Points: He has no one to wall and no one in the curl, so he pulls late on the back, flaring out of the backfield.

❑ Rover

Alignment: Rover aligns 10 yards deep then bails 12 to 14 yards on the hash. He then slow shuffles two to three yards outside the hash.

Keys: He keys the quarterback and the release of #1.

Responsibility: He comes off the hash and works over the top of #1.

Coaching Point: Rover can come off the hash and move over the top of #1 *only* if the quarterback's eyes are focused on the #1 receiver. He cannot come off the hash if the quarterback's eyes are focused on the strongside receivers.

❑ Mike

Alignment: Mike aligns in the defense that is called in the huddle.

Keys: He uses his normal linebacker keys.

Responsibility: He opens and works to the outside staying over the top of #3.

Coaching Point: He stays over the top of #3 thinking that #3 may run a vertical route.

Cover 2 vs. Weakside X Slant (Figure 4-21)

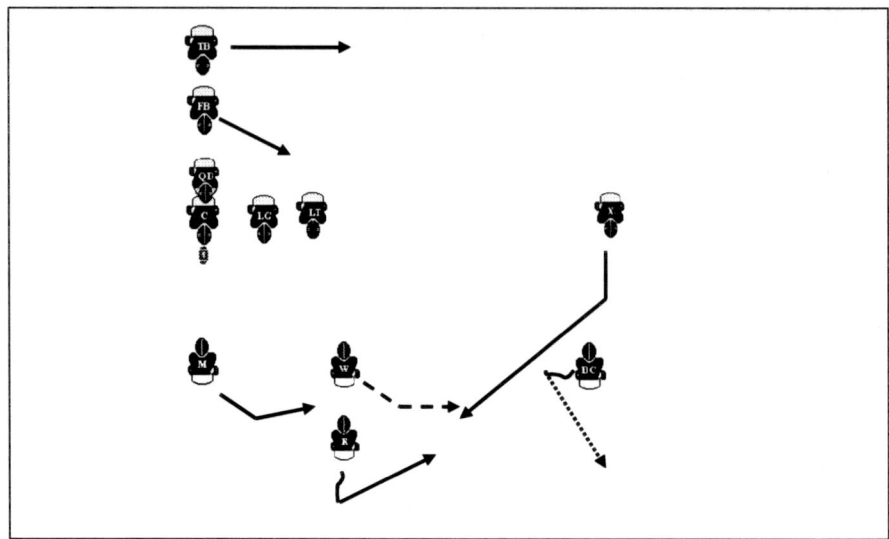

Figure 4-21. Cover 2 vs. weakside X slant

❏ Corner

Alignment: The corner stems to five yards deep and one yard inside of #1.

Keys: He keys the quarterback through the offensive tackle as he reroutes #1.

Responsibility: He shuffles inside for no more than three steps, then works for depth and width.

Coaching Points: He must shuffle inside on his five-yard highway. After three steps he must work for depth to the outside thinking that #1 may run a slant-corner.

❏ Will

Alignment: Will aligns in the defense that is called in the huddle.

Keys: He uses his normal linebacker keys.

Responsibility: When he reads pass, he drops three steps at a 45-degree angle and levels outside to the wall-curl-pull. He walls #1's slant route.

Coaching Point: He must take the slant route away by keeping his eyes on the quarterback as he feels for the slant route.

❑ Rover

Alignment: Rover aligns 10 yards deep, and then bails 12 to 14 yards on the hash. He slow shuffles two to three yards outside the hash.

Keys: He then keys the quarterback and the release of #1.

Responsibility: He comes off the hash and works over the top of #1 on the slant, thinking slant and go.

Coaching Points: He can come off the hash and over the top of #1 *only* if the quarterback's eyes are focused on the slant. He must always be concerned about the slant and go or wheel route by a back out of the backfield.

❑ Mike

Alignment: Mike aligns in the defense that is called in the huddle.

Keys. He uses his normal linebacker keys.

Responsibility: He opens and works to the outside staying on top of #3.

Coaching Point: Mike must stay on top of #3, but if #3's outside release continues to the outside, Will picks up #3 and Mike must play the slant by #1.

Cover 2 vs. Weakside Twins—X and Z Fades (Figure 4-22)

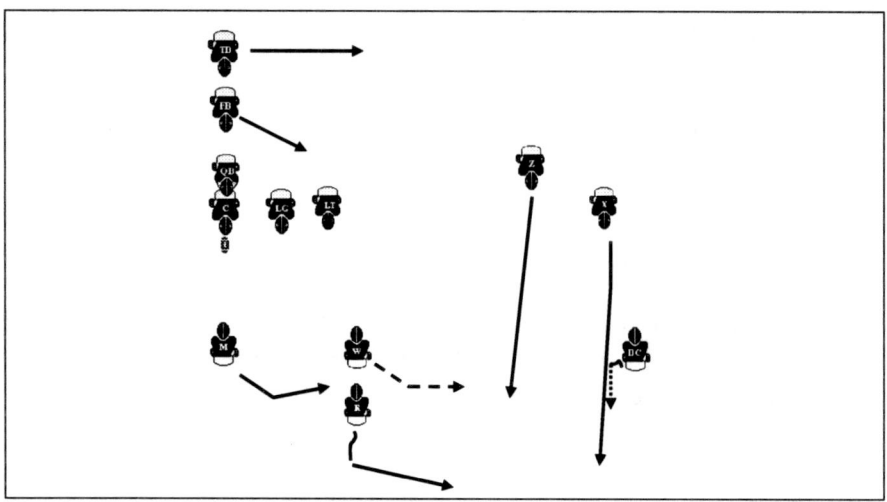

Figure 4-22. Cover 2 vs. weakside twins—X and Z fades

❑ Corner

Alignment: The corner stems to five yards deep and one yard outside of #1.

Keys: He keys the quarterback through #2.

Responsibility: He shuffles inside for no more than three steps to collision #1, and then he sinks with #1, as he reads #2.

Coaching Points: He will sink with #1 because there is no immediate threat to the flats. He must read #2 for any outside release.

❑ Will

Alignment: Will aligns in the defense called and makes a backer call; he widens about three steps to be able to wall #2.

Keys: He uses his normal linebacker keys.

Responsibility: Will drops three steps at a 45-degree angle and levels outside to the wall-curl-pull. He must collision #2 and settle in the curl.

Coaching Points: He cannot let #2 catch a straight up-the-field seam route. He can run with #2 on the vertical if Mike can handle the back out man-to-man.

❑ Rover

Alignment: Rover aligns 10 yards deep, and then bails 12 to 14 yards on the hash. He slow shuffles two to three yards outside the hash.

Keys: He keys the quarterback and the release of #2.

Responsibility: He comes off the hash and works over the top of #2 on the vertical.

Coaching Point: He must be able to play either vertical route by reading the quarterback.

❑ Mike

Alignment: Mike aligns in the defense that is called in the huddle. He gets a backer call by Will, so he slides three steps to the weakside.

Keys: He uses his normal linebacker keys.

Responsibility: He opens and works to the outside staying on top ot #3.

Coaching Points: If Will runs with #2 on the vertical, Mike plays #3 without any help.

Cover 2 vs. Weakside Twins—X Fade and Z Slant (Figure 4-23)

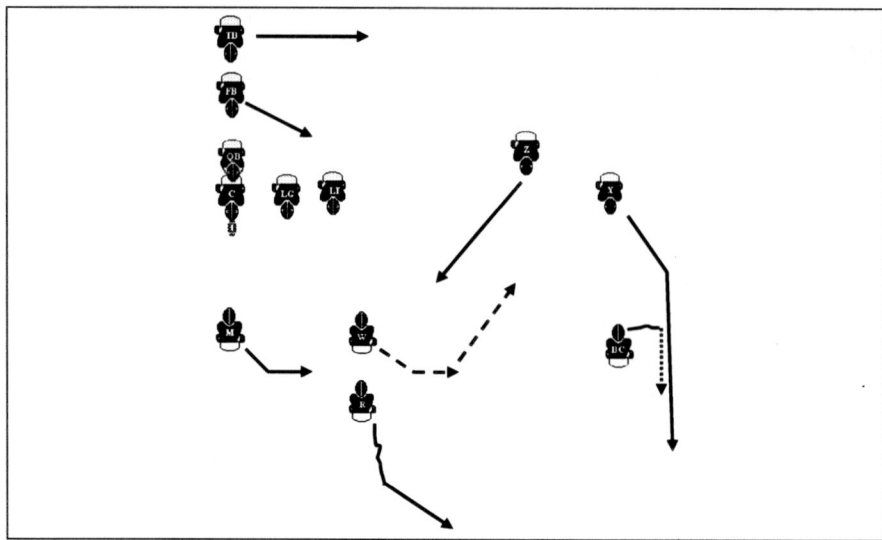

Figure 4-23. Cover 2 vs. weakside twins—X fade and Z slant

❏ Corner

Alignment: The corner stems to five yards deep and one yard outside of #1.

Keys: He keys the quarterback through #2.

Responsibility: He shuffles outside for no more than three steps to collision #1and then he sinks with #1 on the fade.

Coaching Points: The corner can sink with #1 because there is no immediate threat to the flats. He must see #2's route for a slant-corner.

❑ Will

Alignment: Will aligns in the defense called and makes a backer call. He widens about three steps to be able to wall #2.

Keys: He uses his normal linebacker keys.

Responsibility: Will drops three steps at a 45-degree angle and levels outside to the wall-curl-pull.

Coaching Points: He walls #2 and pulls to the back flaring, who now becomes #2. He makes a slant call to Mike, who then walls #2.

❑ Rover

Alignment: Rover aligns 10 yards deep, and then bails 12 to 14 yards on the hash. He slow shuffles two to three yards outside the hash.

Keys: He keys the quarterback and the release of #2 for his responsibilities.

Responsibility: He comes off the hash and works over the top of #1 and #2.

Coaching Points: He must look for the slant and go by #2.

❑ Mike

Alignment: Mike aligns in the defense that is called in the huddle. He gets a backer call by Will, so he slides three steps to the weakside.

Keys: He uses his normal linebacker keys.

Responsibility: He opens and works to the outside, staying on top of #3.

Coaching Points: As #3 widens outside, Mike walls #2's slant route. Mike and Will must communicate with each other on who plays the slant and who stays over the top of #3.

Cover 2 vs. Weakside Twins—X Fade and Z Out (Figure 4-24)

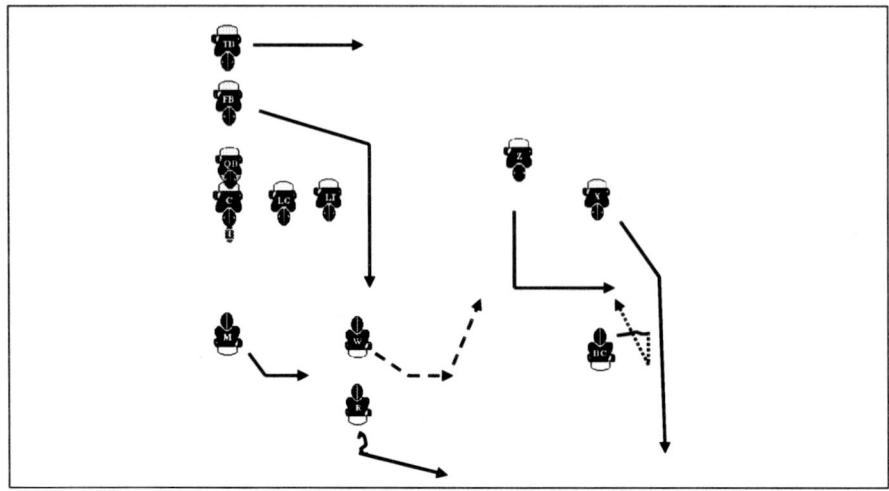

Figure 4-24. Cover 2 vs. weakside twins—X fade and Z out

❑ Corner

Alignment: The corner aligns five yards deep and one yard outside of #1.

Keys: He corner keys the quarterback through #2.

Responsibility: He shuffles outside for no more than three steps to collision #1. He then sinks with #1 into a position where he can break on #1 or #2 on the quarterback's throw.

Coaching Point: He can sink with #1 and rally back to #2 in the flats *only* when the ball is thrown to the flats.

❑ Will

Alignment: Will aligns in the defense called and makes a backer call. He widens about three steps to be able to wall #2.

Keys: He uses his normal linebacker keys.

Responsibility: Will drops three steps at a 45-degree angle and levels outside to the wall-curl-pull. He drops into the curl and breaks on the ball.

Coaching Point: He must read the quarterback's eyes to be able to break on the proper receiver.

❏ Rover

Alignment: Rover aligns 10 yards deep, and then bails 12 to 14 yards on the hash. He slow shuffles two to three yards outside the hash.

Keys: He keys the quarterback and the release of #2 for his responsibilities.

Responsibility: He comes off the hash and works over the top of #1.

Coaching Points: He must be aware of the vertical by #3. He must read the quarterback's eyes and break on the ball when it is thrown.

❏ Mike

Alignment: Mike aligns in the defense called in the huddle. He gets a backer call by Will, so he slides three steps to the weakside.

Keys: He uses his normal linebacker keys.

Responsibility: He opens and works to the outside, staying on top of #3.

Coaching Points: He must pick up #3 and run with him on the vertical. He must stay on top of #3 because Rover help may come late.

Cover 2 vs. Strongside Tight End (Y) Fade (Figure 4-25)

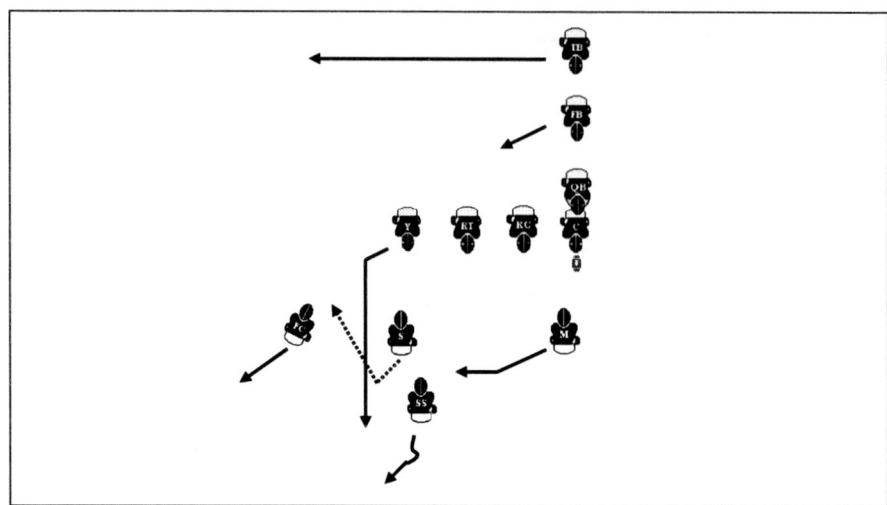

Figure 4-25. Cover 2 vs. strongside tight end (Y) fade

❑ Corner

Alignment: The corner aligns three yards by three yards off the tight end.

Keys: He turns his knees to the inside and keys the quarterback through the tight end for his read keys.

Responsibility: He drops at a 45- degree angle to the flats.

Coaching Point: He must think smash route by the tight end or wheel by the back.

❑ Sam

Alignment: Sam aligns in the defense that is called in the huddle.

Keys: He uses his normal linebacker keys.

Responsibility: He collisions the tight end and works to the pull, to cover the flaring back.

Coaching Points: He must attack the tight end and take away the quick hot route. He then pulls to the back.

❑ Strong safety

Alignment: The strong safety aligns eight yards deep over the top on the tight end.

Keys: He keys the quarterback and the tight end for a run/pass read.

Responsibility: He plays over the top of the tight end.

❑ Mike

Alignment: Mike aligns in the defense that is called in the huddle.

Keys: He uses his normal linebacker keys.

Responsibility: He and works to the strongside hook.

Coaching Points: As he opens to the strongside hook, he must read the route of the tight end. If the tight end comes inside, he walls him and runs with him.

Cover 2 vs. Strongside Pro Set—Z and Y Fades (Figure 4-26)

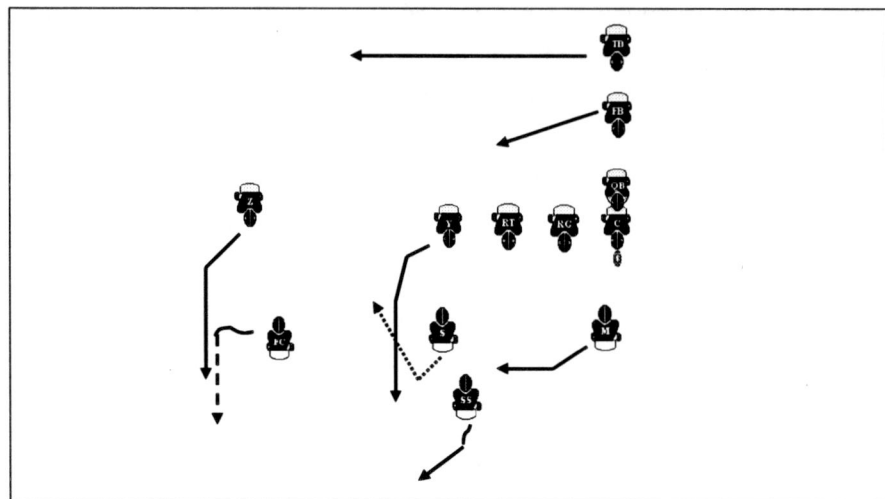

Figure 4-26. Cover 2 vs. strongside pro set—Z and Y fades

❑ Corner

Alignment: The corner aligns five yards deep and one yard inside of #1.

Keys: He keys the quarterback through the tight end for his read keys.

Responsibility: He shuffles outside no more than three steps to collision #1. As he drops, he reads the tight end on the vertical, so he "speed turns" and runs with #1 in a trail position.

Coaching Points: He can run with #1 because there is no immediate threat to the flats. He rallies back to the flats only when the ball is thrown.

❑ Sam

Alignment: Sam aligns in the defense that is called in the huddle.

Keys: He uses his normal linebacker keys.

Responsibility: He drops three steps at a 45-degree angle and levels outside to the wall-curl-pull. He then pulls on the back flaring.

Coaching Points: He must collision the tight end to defend against the hot route. He then pulls late on the halfback's flare route.

❑ Strong Safety

Alignment: The strong safety aligns 10 yards deep and bails 12 to 14 yards on the hash; his bail must not be more than three yards outside the hash.

Keys: He keys the quarterback to #2 to for a run/pass read.

Responsibility: He plays over the top of #2.

Coaching Points: He must take away #2's fade while reading the quarterback's eyes to know where the ball will be thrown. If the quarterback throws to #1, the safety must break to the ball.

❑ Mike

Alignment: Mike aligns in the defense that is called in the huddle.

Keys: He uses his normal linebacker keys.

Responsibility: He opens and works to get on top of #3.

Coaching Point: Because of the tight end's release, the tight end becomes #3, so the Mike runs with the tight end on the vertical.

Cover 2 vs. Strongside Pro Set—Z Fade and Y Out (Figure 4-27)

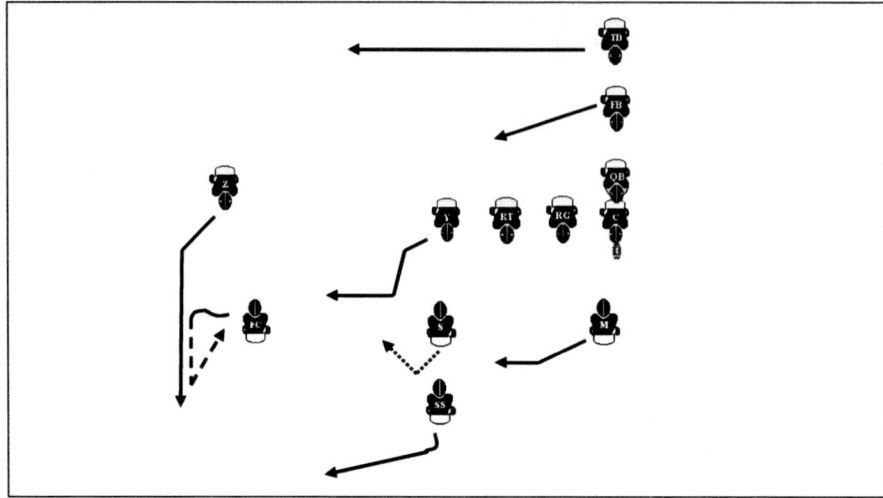

Figure 4-27. Cover 2 vs. strongside pro set—Z fade and Y out

❑ Corner

Alignment: The corner aligns five yards deep and one yard inside of #1.

Keys: He keys the quarterback through the tight end for his read keys.

Responsibility: He shuffles outside no more than three steps to collision #1. He can sink with #1.

Coaching Points: As he drops, he reads #2 outside, so he sinks with #1 and reads the quarterback. If the ball is thrown to #2, the corner rallies back to #2.

❑ Sam

Alignment: Sam aligns in the defense that is called in the huddle.

Keys: He uses his normal linebacker keys.

Responsibility: He drops three steps at a 45-degree angle and levels outside to the wall-curl-pull.

Coaching Point: He plays the pull on the back flaring or breaks on #2 in the flats.

❏ Strong Safety

Alignment: The strong safety aligns 10 yards deep and bails 12 to 14 yards on the hash; his bail must not be more than three yards outside the hash.

Keys: He keys the quarterback to #2 for a run/pass read.

Responsibility: He plays over the top of #1.

Coaching Point: Because #2 is flat to the outside, he plays the vertical by #1 if the quarterback is focusing in that direction.

❏ Mike

Alignment: Mike aligns in the defense that is called in the huddle.

Keys: He uses his normal linebacker keys.

Responsibility: He opens and works to get on top of #3.

Coaching Points: Because #2 and #3 are both outside, Mike settles in the strongside hook.

Cover 2 vs. Strongside Pro Set—Z Slant (Figure 4-28)

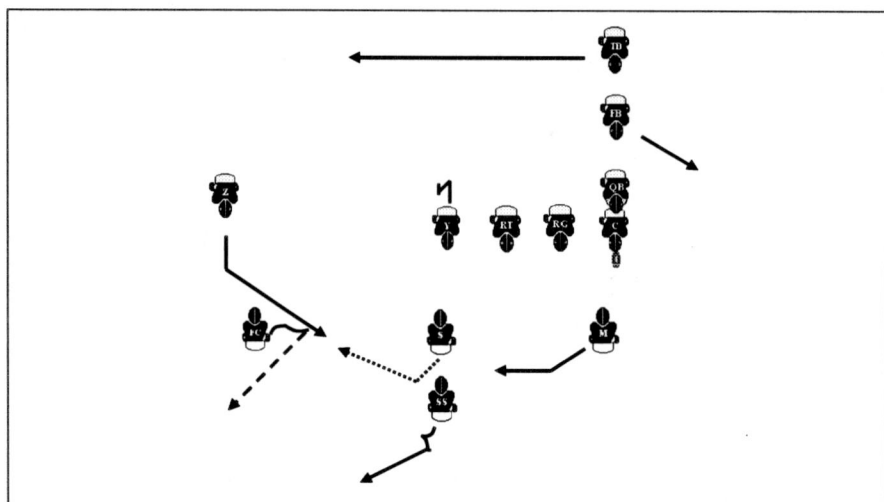

Figure 4-28. Cover 2 vs. strongside pro set—Z slant

❏ Corner

Alignment: The corner aligns five yards deep and one yard inside of #1.

Keys: He keys the quarterback through the tight end for his read keys.

Responsibility: He shuffles inside no more than three steps to collision #1.

Coaching Point: He gets depth and width, thinking smash route by the tight end or wheel route by the halfback.

❏ Sam

Alignment: Sam aligns in the defense that is called in the huddle.

Keys: He uses his normal linebacker keys.

Responsibility: He drops three steps at a 45-degree angle and levels outside to the wall-curl-pull. He walls #1 on the slant route.

Coaching Points: Sam must take away the slant route by looking at the quarterback as he feels for the slant route. He also breaks late on the back pull.

❏ Strong Safety

Alignment: The strong safety aligns 10 yards deep and bails 12 to 14 yards on the hash; his bail cannot be more than three yards outside the hash.

Keys: He keys the quarterback to #2 for a run/pass read.

Responsibility: He plays over the top of #1.

Coaching Points: He must read the quarterback's eyes as he plays over the top of the slant. He must think slant and go by #1.

❏ Mike

Alignment: Mike aligns in the defense that is called in the huddle.

Keys: He uses his normal linebacker keys.

Responsibility: He opens and works to get on top of #3.

Coaching Point: He walls #1 if Sam makes a slant call.

Cover 3

Cover 3 vs. a 21 Set (Figure 4-29)

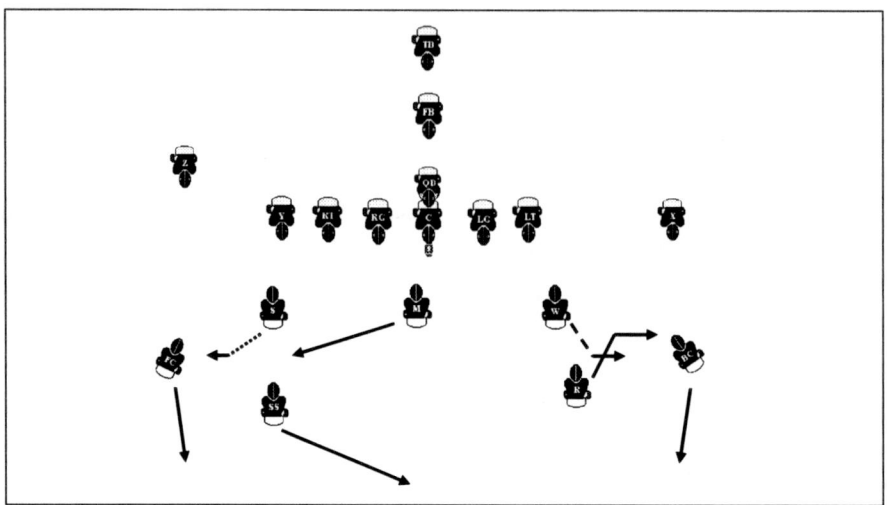

Figure 4-29. Cover 3 vs. a 21 set

Cover 3 is a three-deep with four underneath zone coverage, which is a pre-determined rotation to the weakside. The general concept in cover 3 is that the defenders will get in the middle of their zones and read the quarterback and receivers for routes, and then break on the ball. The corners play deep outside one-third. The strong safety plays the deep middle one-third, and Rover plays the weakside wall-curl-flats. Sam plays the strongside wall-curl-flats. Will plays the weakside hook/curl. Mike plays the strongside hook/curl.

Cover 3 Alignments, Stances, and Keys

❑ Field Corner

Alignment: The field corner aligns seven yards deep and one yard outside of a wideout. If no wideout is on his side, he aligns seven yards deep and four yards outside the tight end. From his cover 2 shell, on the snap of the ball, he backpedals into the middle of his outside one-third.

Stance: He aligns with the outside foot up and the inside foot back. He faces the quarterback at a 45-degree angle with his feet no more than armpits-width apart. His weight should be on the balls of his feet. He is bent at the waist and knees for explosion. His tail is down and his back is arched. His head is up with his chin slightly forward over his toes. His arms are outside his knees and relaxed and bent at the elbows. His eyes are looking to the inside for his read keys.

Keys: He keys the quarterback to #2 to #1.

Responsibilities: If pass occurs, he plays the deep outside one-third. He must keep everything in front of him by keeping a three-yard cushion on all receivers.
- Run to: He fits where he is needed. He has secondary contain. He cannot support the run until all threats of a pass are gone and the ball has crossed the line of scrimmage.
- Run away: He clears his outside one-third and takes a deep cut-off angle to the ball.
- Pass: He drops to the deep outside one-third on all passes. He must see the quarterback and read the routes of receivers.

❑ Boundary Corner

Alignment: The boundary corner aligns seven yards deep and one yard outside of a wideout. If no wideout is on his side, he aligns seven yards deep and four yards outside the tight end. From his cover 2 shell on the snap of the ball, he backpedals into the middle of his outside one-third.

Stance: He aligns with his outside foot up and his inside foot back. He faces the quarterback at a 45-degree angle with his feet no more than armpits-width apart. His weight should be on the balls of his feet. He is bent at the waist and knees for explosion. His tail is down and his back is arched. His head is up with his chin slightly forward over his toes. His arms are outside his knees and relaxed and bent at the elbows. His eyes are looking to the inside for his read keys.

Keys: He keys the quarterback to #2 to #1.

Responsibilities: If pass occurs, he plays the deep outside one-third. He must keep everything in front of him by keeping a three-yard cushion on all receivers.
- Run to: He fits where he is needed. He has secondary contain. He cannot support the run until all threats of a pass are gone and the ball has crossed the line of scrimmage.
- Run away: He clears his outside one-third and takes a deep cut-off angle to the ball.
- Pass: He drops to the deep outside one-third on all passes. He must see the quarterback and read the routes of receivers.

❑ Strong Safety

Alignment: The strong safety aligns in his cover 2 shell at 10 yards deep over a normal tight end alignment. He then stems to 12 yards deep in the middle one-third of the field.

Stance: He aligns in a square stance with his feet no more than armpits-width apart. His weight should be on the balls of his feet. He is bent at the waist and knees for explosion. His tail is down and his back is arched. His head is up with his chin slightly forward over his toes. His arms are outside his knees and relaxed and bent at the elbows. His eyes are looking at the quarterback for his read keys.

Keys: He keys the quarterback to #2 to #1 and is aware of high-hat by offensive linemen.

Responsibilities: The strong safety must think pass first and run second. On all runs, he fits where he is needed and becomes an inside-out alley player.
- Run strong: He reads to see if the quarterback is on the line or off the line of scrimmage. If the quarterback is on the line of scrimmage, the safety works flat, keeping an inside out position on the quarterback. He must be ready to fill inside-out on the ball. He must not overrun the ball.
- Run weak: He reads to see if the quarterback is on the line or off the line of scrimmage. If the quarterback is on the line of scrimmage, he works flat, keeping an inside-out position on the quarterback. He must be ready to fill inside-out on the ball. He must not overrun the ball.
- Pass: On all passes, he backpedals into the deep middle one-third. He must be deeper than all receivers. He must think post. He is responsible for the tight end hot, when veer passes occur.

❑ Rover

Alignment: Rover aligns in his cover 2 shell at 10 yards deep over a normal tight-end alignment. He then stems to four yards by four yards off a normal tight-end alignment. He aligns four yards deep and one yard inside of a slot. His width is dictated by the receiver's alignment and field position.

Stance: He aligns in a square stance with his feet no more than armpits-width apart. His weight should be on the balls of his feet. He is bent at the waist and knees for explosion. His tail is down and his back is arched. His head is up with his chin slightly forward over his toes. His arms are outside his knees and relaxed and bent at the elbows. His eyes are looking at the quarterback for his read keys.

Keys: He keys the quarterback to #2 and the offensive linemen for high-hat.

Responsibilities: He must think run first and pass second.
- Run to: He has outside containment.
- Run away: He turns his knees to the inside and drops on a five-yard fence playing reverses and counters. When all threats are clear, he drives through the deep middle one-third to the ball.
- Pass: On all passes, he drops to the weakside wall-curl-flats.

❏ Sam

Alignment: Sam aligns in the front that is called in the huddle.

Stance: He aligns in his normal linebacker stance.

Keys: He uses his normal linebacker keys.

Responsibilities: On all passes, he opens to the outside at a 45-degree angle and drops to the strongside wall-curl-flats.

❏ Mike

Alignment: Mike aligns in the front that is called in the huddle.

Stance: He aligns in his normal linebacker stance.

Keys: He uses his normal linebacker keys.

Responsibilities: On all passes, he drops to the strongside hook/curl.

❏ Will

Alignment: Will aligns in the front that is called in the huddle.

Stance: He aligns in his normal linebacker stance.

Keys: He uses his normal linebacker keys.

Responsibilities: On all passes, he opens to the outside at a 45-degree angle and drops to the weakside hook/curl.

Cover 3 vs. a 12 Set (Figures 4-30 and 4-31)

The field corner aligns seven yards deep and four yards outside of the tight end. The boundary corner aligns seven yards deep and one yard outside of #1. The strong safety aligns 12 yards deep in the middle of the field. Rover aligns four yards deep and one yard inside of #2. Sam, Mike, and Will align in the defense that is called.

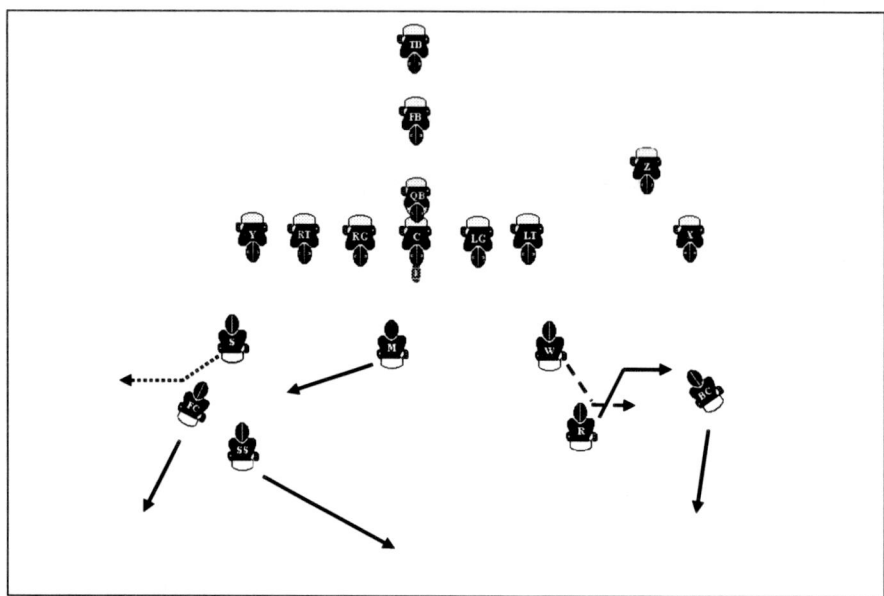

Figure 4-30. Cover 3 vs. a 12 set

Position	Pass responsibility
Sam	Drops to the strongside flats.
Mike	Drops to the strongside hook.
Will	Drops to the weakside hook/curl.
Strong safety	Drops to the deep middle one-third.
Rover	Drops to the weakside wall-curl-flats.
Field corner	Drops to the deep outside one-third.
Boundary corner	Drops to the deep outside one-third.

Figure 4-31. Position and pass responsibility for cover 3 vs. a 12 set

Cover 3 vs. a 13 Set (Figures 4-32 and 4-33)

The field corner aligns seven yards deep and four yards outside of the tight end. The boundary corner aligns seven yards deep and one yard outside of #1. The strong safety aligns 12 yards deep in the middle of the field. Rover aligns four yards deep and one yard inside of #2. Sam, Mike, and Will align in the defense that is called.

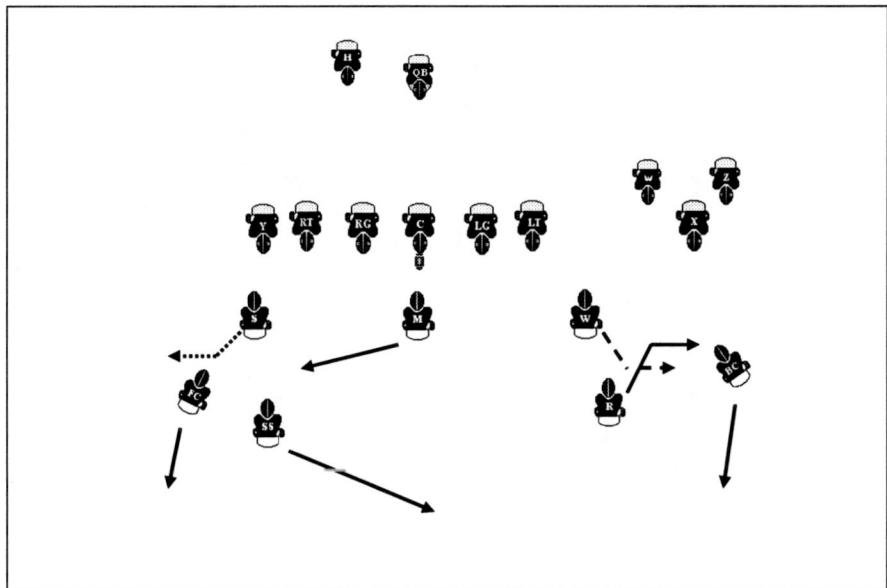

Figure 4-32. Cover 3 vs. a 13 set

Position	Pass responsibility
Sam	Drops to the strongside flats.
Mike	Drops to the strongside hook.
Will	Drops to the weakside hook/curl.
Strong safety	Drops to the deep middle one-third.
Rover	Drops to the weakside wall-curl-flats.
Field corner	Drops to the deep outside one-third.
Boundary corner	Drops to the deep outside one-third.

Figure 4-33. Position and pass responsibility for cover 3 vs. a 13 set

Cover 3 vs. a 14 Set (Figures 4-34 and 4-35)

The field corner aligns seven yards deep and four yards outside of the tight end. The boundary corner aligns seven yards deep and one yard outside of #1. The strong safety aligns 12 yards deep in the middle of the field. Rover aligns four yards deep and one yard inside of #2. Sam, Mike, and Will align in the defense that is called.

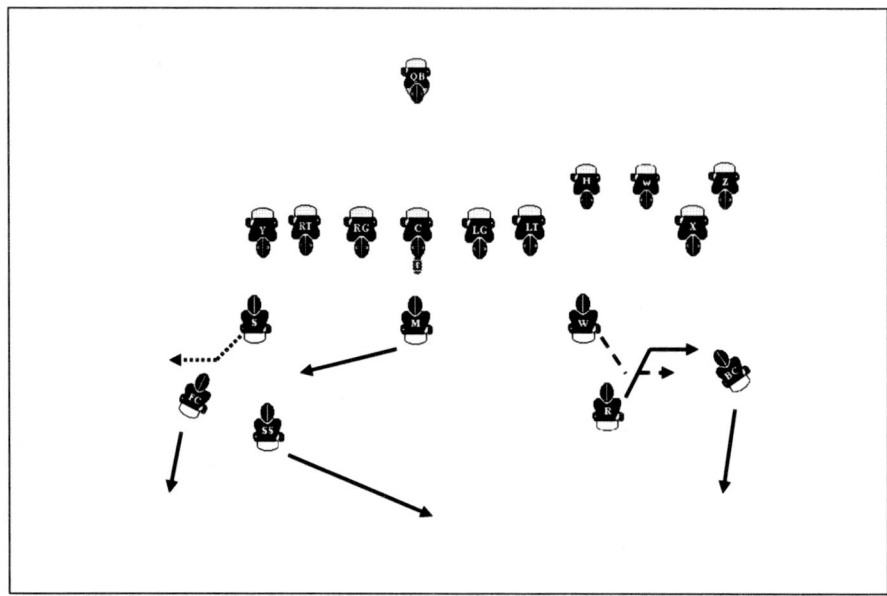

Figure 4-34. Cover 3 vs. a 14 set

Position	Pass responsibility
Sam	Drops to the strongside flats.
Mike	Drops to the strongside hook.
Will	Drops to the weakside hook/curl.
Strong safety	Drops to the deep middle one-third.
Rover	Drops to the weakside wall-curl-flats.
Field corner	Drops to the deep outside one-third.
Boundary corner	Drops to the deep outside one-third.

Figure 4-35. Position and pass responsibility for cover 3 vs. a 14 set

Cover 3 vs. a 22 Set (Figures 4-36 and 4-37)

The corners align seven yards deep and one yard outside of #1. The strong safety aligns 12 yards deep in the middle of the field. Rover aligns four yards deep and one yard inside of #2. Sam, Mike, and Will align in the defense that is called.

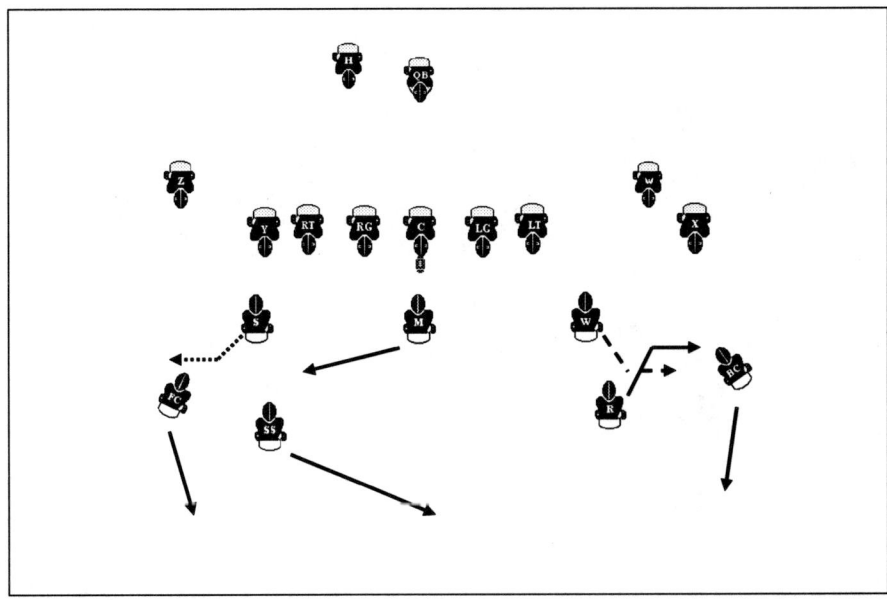

Figure 4-36. Cover 3 vs. a 22 set

Position	Pass responsibility
Sam	Drops to the strongside wall-curl-flats.
Mike	Drops to the strongside hook/curl.
Will	Drops to the weakside hook/curl.
Strong safety	Drops to the deep middle one-third.
Rover	Drops to the weakside wall-curl-flats.
Field corner	Drops to the deep outside one-third.
Boundary corner	Drops to the deep outside one-third.

Figure 4-37. Position and pass responsibility for cover 3 vs. a 22 set

Cover 3 vs. a 23 Set (Figures 4-38 and 4-39)

The corners align seven yards deep and one yard outside of #1.The strong safety aligns 12 yards deep in the middle of the field. Rover aligns four yards deep and one yard inside of #2. Sam , Mike, and Will align in the defense that is called.

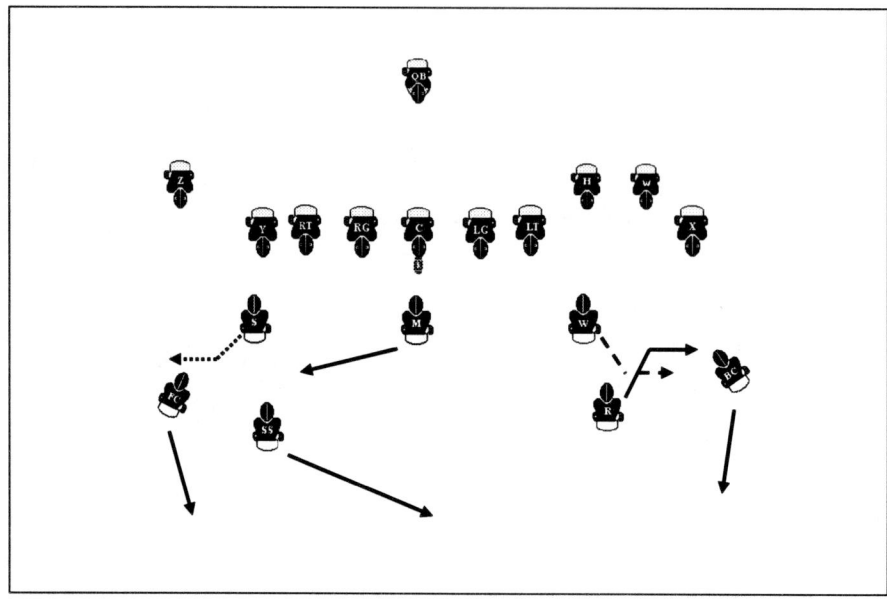

Figure 4-38. Cover 3 vs. a 23 set

Position	Pass responsibility
Sam	Drops to the strongside wall-curl-flats.
Mike	Drops to the strongside hook/curl.
Will	Drops to the weakside hook/curl.
Strong safety	Drops to the deep middle one-third.
Rover	Drops to the weakside wall-curl-flats.
Field corner	Drops to the deep outside one-third.
Boundary corner	Drops to the deep outside one-third.

Figure 4-39. Position and pass responsibility for cover 3 vs. a 23 set

Cover 3 vs. a 31 Set (Figures 4-40 and 4-41)

The corners align seven yards deep and one yard outside of #1. The strong safety aligns 12 yards deep in the middle of the field. Rover aligns four yards deep and one yard inside of #2. Sam, Mike, and Will align in the defense that is called.

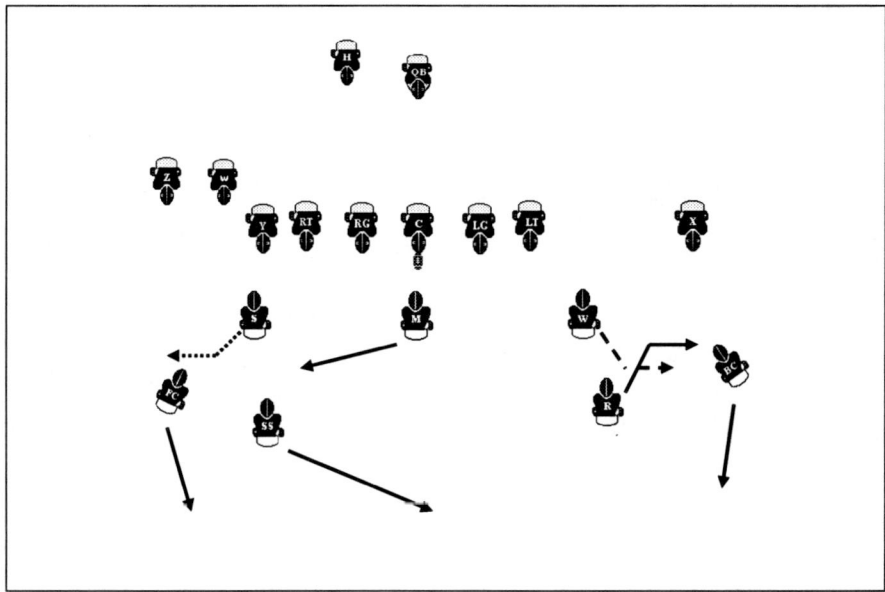

Figure 4-40. Cover 3 vs. a 31 set

Position	Pass responsibility
Sam	Drops to the strongside wall-curl-flats.
Mike	Drops to the strongside hook/curl.
Will	Drops to the weakside hook/curl.
Strong safety	Drops to the deep middle one-third.
Rover	Drops to the weakside wall-curl-flats.
Field corner	Drops to the deep outside one-third.
Boundary corner	Drops to the deep outside one-third.

Figure 4-41. Position and pass responsibility for cover 3 vs. a 31 set

Cover 3 vs. a 32 Set (Figures 4-42 and 4-43)

The corners align seven yards deep and one yard outside of #1. The strong safety aligns 12 yards deep in the middle of the field. Rover aligns four yards deep and one yard inside of #2. Sam, Mike, and Will align in the defense that is called.

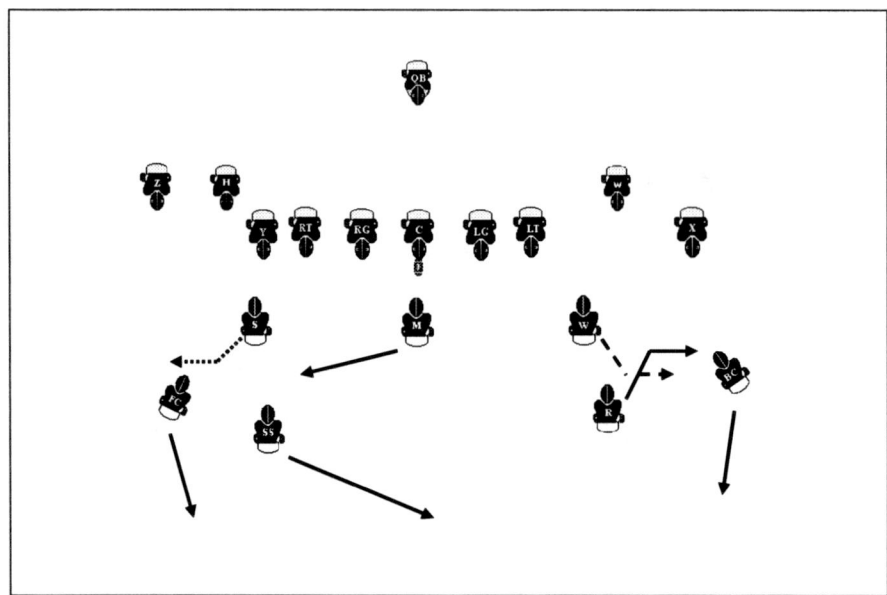

Figure 4-42. Cover 3 vs. a 32 set

Position	Pass responsibility
Sam	Drops to the strongside wall-curl-flats.
Mike	Drops to the strongside hook/curl.
Will	Drops to the weakside hook/curl.
Strong safety	Drops to the deep middle one-third.
Rover	Drops to the weakside wall-curl-flats.
Field corner	Drops to the deep outside one-third.
Boundary corner	Drops to the deep outside one-third.

Figure 4-43. Position and pass responsibility for cover 3 vs. a 32 set

Cover 3 vs. a 41 Set (Figures 4-44 and 4-45)

The corners align seven yards deep and one yard outside of #1. The strong safety aligns 12 yards deep in the middle of the field. Rover aligns four yards deep and four yards outside the tackle. Sam, Mike, and Will align in the defense that is called.

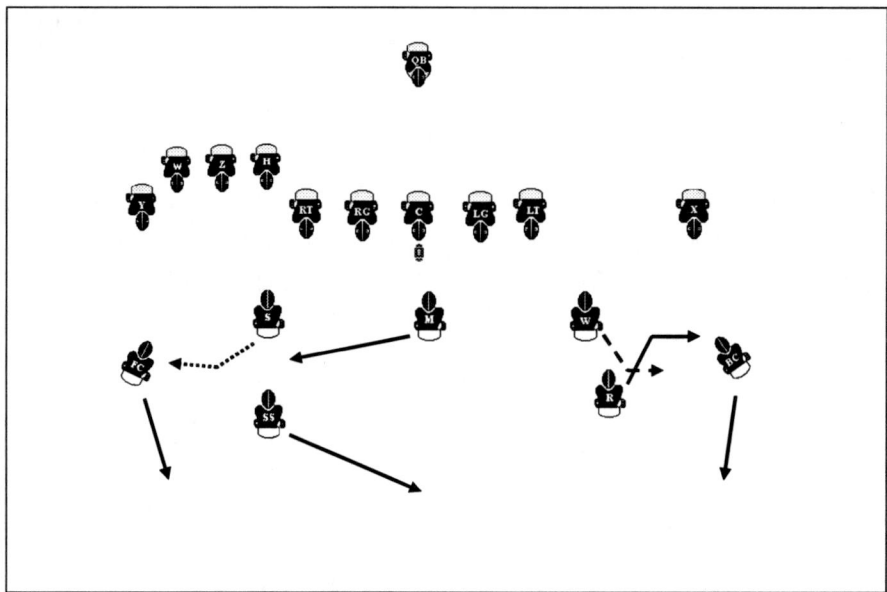

Figure 4-44. Cover 3 vs. a 41 set

Position	Pass responsibility
Sam	Drops to the strongside wall-curl-flats.
Mike	Drops to the strongside hook/curl.
Will	Drops to the weakside hook/curl.
Strong safety	Drops to the deep middle one-third.
Rover	Drops to the weakside wall-curl-flats.
Field corner	Drops to the deep outside one-third.
Boundary corner	Drops to the deep outside one-third.

Figure 4-45. Position and pass responsibility for cover 3 vs. a 41 set

Cover 3 Rhino

Cover 3 Rhino is a three-deep five underneath zone coverage. It is basically cover 3 with a pre-determined weakside roll and is used mainly with the Arizona package. In Cover 3 Rhino, Rover spins down into the low hole and Geronimo plays the weakside wall-curl-flats. The corners play the deep outside one-thirds. The strong safety plays the deep middle one-third. Sam plays the strongside wall-curl-flats. Mike has the strongside hook/curl. Will has the weakside hook/curl.

Cover 3 Rhino vs. a 21 Set (Figures 4-46 and 4-47)

The corners align seven yards deep and one yard outside of #1. The strong safety aligns 12 yards deep in the middle of the field. Rover aligns in the low hole at eight yards deep. Sam, Mike, and Will align in the defense that is called. Geronimo aligns four yards deep and four yards outside of the tackle.

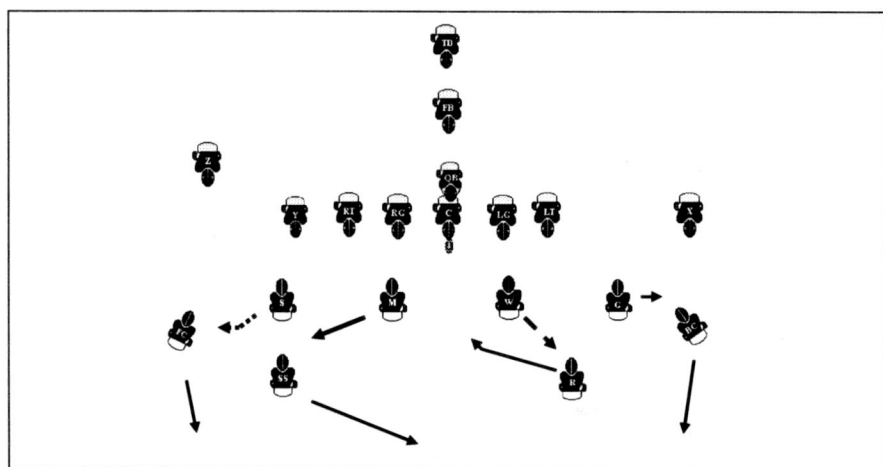

Figure 4-46. Cover 3 Rhino vs. a 21 set

Position	Pass responsibility
Sam	Drops to the strongside wall-curl-flats.
Mike	Drops to the strongside hook/curl.
Will	Drops to the weakside hook/curl.
Strong safety	Drops to the deep middle one-third.
Rover	Drops into the low hole.
Field corner	Drops to the deep outside one-third.
Boundary corner	Drops to the deep outside one-third.
Geronimo	Drops to the weakside wall-curl-flats.

Figure 4-47. Position and pass responsibility for cover 3 Rhino vs. a 21 set

Cover 3 Rhino vs. a 22 Set (Figures 4-48 and 4-49)

Cover 3 Rhino vs. a 22 set is a three-deep five underneath zone coverage. The corners align seven yards deep and 1 yard outside of #1. The strong safety aligns 12 yards deep in the middle of the field. Rover aligns in the low hole at eight yards deep. Mike and Will align in the defense that is called. Sam aligns four yards deep and one yard inside of #2. Geronimo aligns four yards deep and one yard inside of #2.

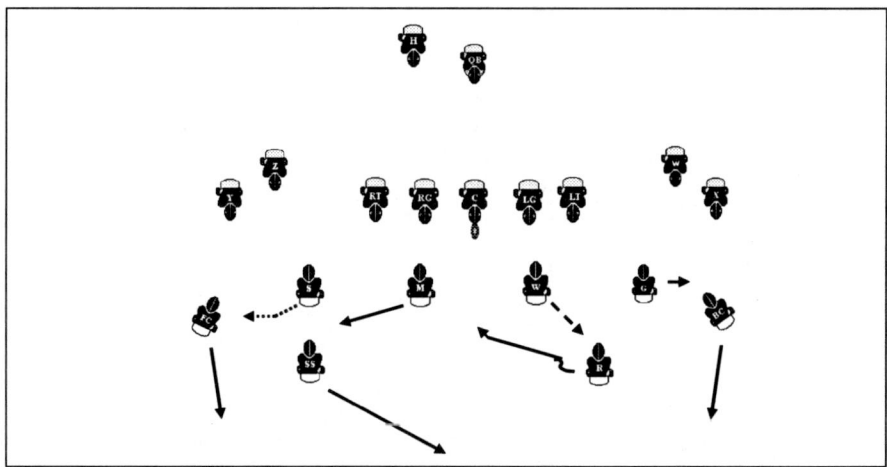

Figure 4-48. Cover 3 Rhino vs. a 22 set

Position	Pass responsibility
Sam	Drops to the strongside wall-curl-flats.
Mike	Drops to the strongside hook/curl.
Will	Drops to the weakside hook/curl.
Strong safety	Drops to the deep middle one-third.
Rover	Drops into the low hole.
Field corner	Drops to the deep outside one-third.
Boundary corner	Drops to the deep outside one-third.
Geronimo	Drops to the weakside wall-curl-flats.

Figure 4-49. Position and pass responsibility for cover 3 Rhino vs. a 22 set

Cover 6

Cover 6 vs. a 21 Set (Figure 4-50)

This coverage is a pre-determined roll to the strongside. The corners play deep outside one-thirds. Rover plays deep middle one-third, and the strong safety plays the strongside wall-curl-flats. Sam plays the strongside hook/curl. Will plays the weakside wall-curl-flats. Mike plays the weakside hook/curl. Basically, cover 6 is the opposite of cover 3.

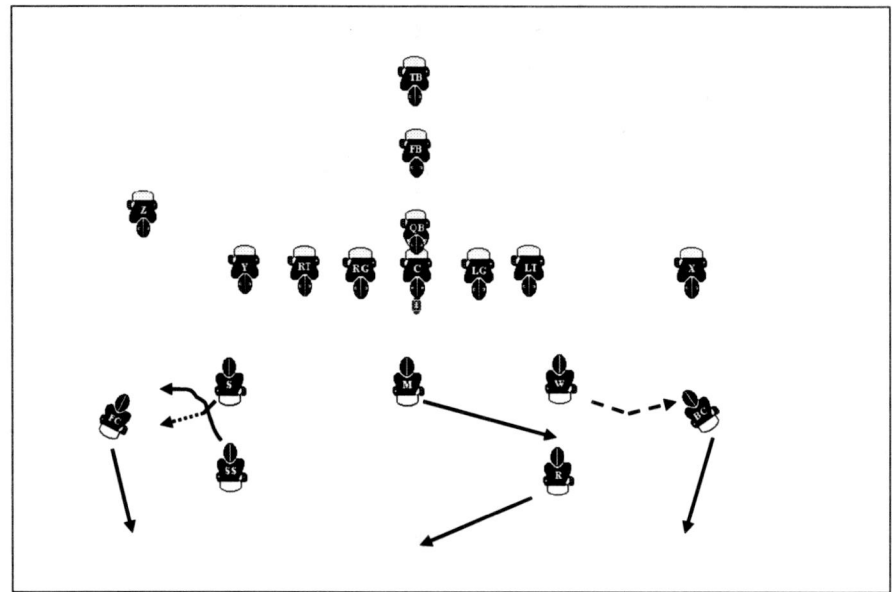

Figure 4-50. Cover 6 vs. a 21 set

Cover 6 Alignments, Stances, and Keys

❑ Field Corner

Alignment: The field corner aligns seven yards deep and one yard outside of a wideout. If no wideout is on his side, he aligns seven yards deep and four yards outside the tight end. From his cover 2 shell, on the snap of the ball, he backpedals into the middle of his outside one-third.

Stance: He aligns with his outside foot up and his inside foot back. He faces the quarterback at a 45-degree angle with his feet no more than armpits-width apart. His weight should be on the balls of his feet. He is bent at the waist and knees for explosion. His tail is down and his back is arched. His head is up with his chin slightly forward over his toes. His arms are outside his knees and relaxed and bent at the elbows. His eyes are looking to the inside for his read keys.

Keys: He keys the quarterback to #2 to #1.

Responsibilities: If pass occurs, he plays the deep outside one-third. He must keep everything in front of him by keeping a three-yard cushion on all receivers.
- Run to: He fits where he is needed. He has secondary contain. He cannot support the run until all threats of a pass are gone and the ball has crossed the line of scrimmage.
- Run away: He clears his outside one-third and takes a deep cutoff angle to the ball.
- Pass: He drops to the deep outside one-third on all passes. He must see the quarterback and read the routes of receivers.

❑ Boundary Corner

Alignment: The field corner aligns seven yards deep and one yard outside of a wideout. If no wideout is on his side, he aligns seven yards deep and four yards outside the tight end. From his cover 2 shell, on the snap of the ball, he backpedals into the middle of his outside one-third.

Stance: He aligns with his outside foot up and his inside foot back. He faces the quarterback at a 45-degree angle with his feet no more than armpits-width apart. His weight should be on the balls of his feet. He is bent at the waist and knees for explosion. His tail is down and his back is arched. His head is up with his chin slightly forward over his toes. His arms are outside his knees and relaxed and bent at the elbows. His eyes are looking to the inside for his read keys.

Keys: He keys the quarterback to #2 to #1.

Responsibilities: If pass occurs, he plays the deep outside one-third. He must keep everything in front of him by keeping a three-yard cushion on all receivers.
- Run to: He fits where he is needed. He has secondary contain. He cannot support the run until all threats of a pass are gone and the ball has crossed the line of scrimmage.
- Run away: He clears his outside one-third and takes a deep cutoff angle to the ball.
- Pass: He drops to the deep outside one-third on all passes. He must see the quarterback and read the routes of receivers.

❑ Strong Safety

Alignment: The strong safety aligns in his cover 2 shell at 10 yards deep over a normal tight end alignment. He then stems to four yards by four yards off a normal tight end alignment. He aligns four yards deep and one yard inside of a slot. The strong safety's width is dictated by the receiver's alignment and field position.

Stance: He aligns in a square stance with his feet no more than armpits-width apart. His weight should be on the balls of his feet. He is bent at the waist and knees for explosion. His tail is down and his back is arched. his head is up with his chin slightly forward over his toes. His arms are outside his knees and relaxed and bent at the elbows. His eyes are looking at the quarterback for his read keys.

Keys: He keys the quarterback to #2 and the offensive linemen for high-hat.

Responsibilities: He must think run first and pass second.
- Run to: He has outside containment.
- Run away: He turns his knees to the inside and drops on a five-yard fence, playing reverses and counters. When all threats are clear, he drives through the deep middle one-third to the ball.
- Pass: On all passes, he drops to the weakside wall-curl-flats.

❑ Rover

Alignment: Rover aligns in his cover 2 shell at 10 yards deep over a normal tight end alignment. He then stems to 12 yards deep in the middle one-third of the field.

Stance: He aligns in a square stance with his feet no more than armpits-width apart. His weight should be on the balls of his feet. He is bent at the waist and knees for explosion. His tail is down and his back is arched. His head is up with his chin slightly forward over his toes. His arms are outside his knees and relaxed and bent at the elbows. His eyes are looking at the quarterback for his read keys.

Keys: He keys the quarterback to #2 to #1 and is aware of high-hat by offensive linemen.

Responsibilities: He must think pass first and run second. On all runs, he fits where he is needed and becomes an inside-out alley player.

- Run strong: He reads to see if the quarterback is on or off the line of scrimmage. If the quarterback is on the line of scrimmage, Rover works flat, keeping an inside-out position on the quarterback. He must be ready to fill inside-out on the ball. He must not over run the ball.
- Run weak: He reads to see if the quarterback is on or off the line of scrimmage. If the quarterback is on the line of scrimmage, he works flat, keeping an inside-out position on the quarterback. He must be ready to fill inside-out on the ball. He must not over run the ball.
- Pass: On all passes, he backpedals into the deep middle one-third. He must be deeper than all receivers. He must think post. He is responsible for the tight end hot, when veer passes occur.

❏ Sam

Alignment: Sam aligns in the front that is called in the huddle.

Stance: He aligns in a normal linebacker stance.

Keys: He uses his normal linebacker keys.

Responsibilities: On all passes, he drops to the strongside hook/curl.

❏ Mike

Alignment: Mike aligns in the front that is called in the huddle.

Stance: He aligns in his normal linebacker stance.

Keys: He uses his normal linebacker keys.

Responsibilities: On all passes, he drops to the weakside hook/curl.

❏ Will

Alignment: Will aligns in the front that is called in the huddle.

Stance: He aligns in his normal linebacker stance.

Keys: He uses his normal linebacker keys.

Responsibilities: On all passes, he drops to the weakside wall-curl-flats.

Cover 6 Snake

Cover 6 Snake vs. a 21 Set (Figures 4-51 and 4-52)

Cover 6 snake is used with the Arizona package. It is the same coverage as cover 6, except the strong safety spins down into the low hole, which is a pre-determined strongside roll. The corners play the deep outside one-thirds. Rover plays the deep middle one-third. Sam has the strongside wall-curl-flats. Mike has the strongside hook/curl. Will has the weakside hook/curl. Geronimo has the weakside wall-curl-flats.

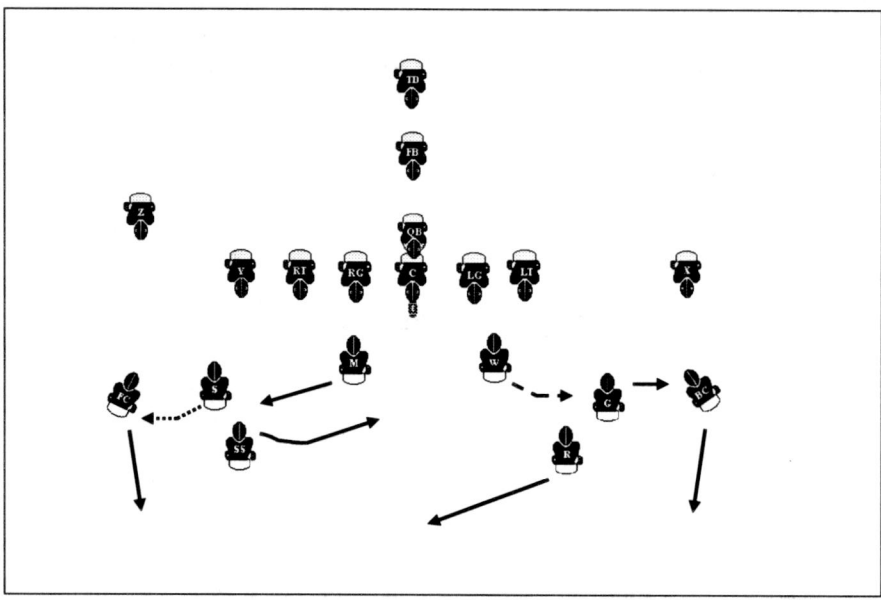

Figure 4-51. Cover 6 snake vs. a 21 set

Position	Pass responsibility
Sam	Drops to the strongside wall-curl-flats.
Mike	Drops to the strongside hook/curl.
Will	Drops to the weakside hook/curl.
Strong safety	Drops into the low hole.
Rover	Drops to the deep middle one-third.
Field corner	Drops to the deep outside one-third.
Boundary corner	Drops to the deep outside one-third.
Geronimo	Drops to the weakside wall-curl-flats.

Figure 4-52. Position and pass responsibilities from cover 6 snake vs. a 21 set

5

Man/Zone Combination Coverages

Man/zone coverages are pass coverages that include both man and zone techniques. These coverages include Toro, cover 4, and cover 5.

Toro

Toro vs. a 21 Set (Figures 5-1 through 5-4)

Toro coverage involves man-free techniques. Mike, Will, Rover, and the strong safety read backfield flow in order to determine their responsibilities. Toro vs. a 21 set is a combination man-to-man and zone coverage. The strong safety and Rover read fullback flow. If the fullback flow goes to the strongside, the strong safety plays him man-to-man and Rover drops free into the deep middle one-third. If the fullback goes to the weakside, Rover plays him man-to-man and the strong safety drops free into the deep middle one-third. Mike and Will use their normal back reads, but on all passes, they must react to the flow of the tailback. If the tailback goes to the strongside, Mike plays him man-to-man and Will drops to the low hole. If the tailback goes to the weakside, Will plays him man-to-man and Mike drops to the low hole. Sam plays #2 strong man-to-man. The corners play the #1s man-to-man.

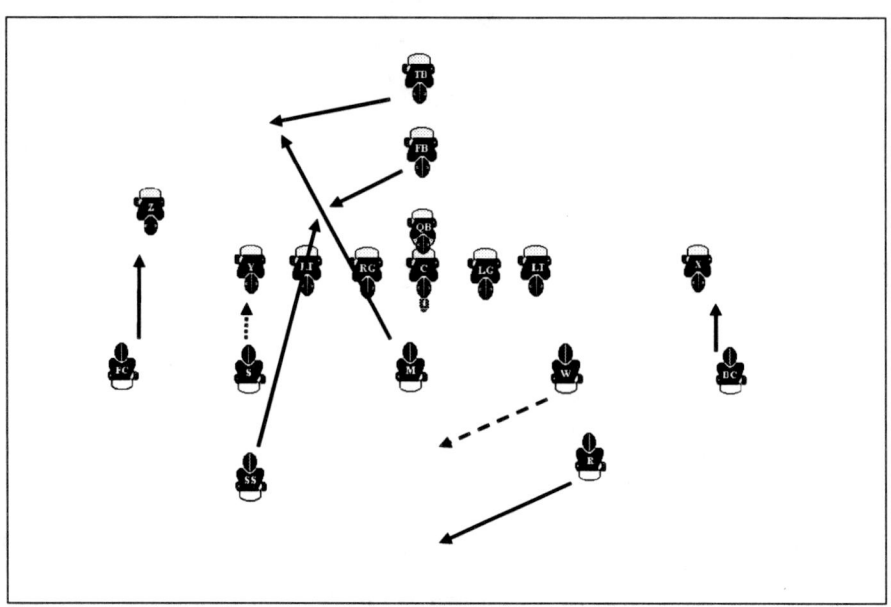

Figure 5-1. Toro vs. a 21 set with strongside flow

Position	Pass responsibility
Sam	Plays the tight end man-to-man.
Mike	Uses his normal key reads but plays the tailback man-to-man on all passes.
Will	Uses his normal key reads but drops to the low hole on all passes.
Strong safety	Plays the fullback man-to-man.
Rover	Drops to the deep middle one-third and plays man-free.
Field corner	Plays #1 man-to-man.
Boundary corner	Plays #1 man-to-man.

Figure 5-2. Position and pass responsibility from Toro vs. a 21 set with strongside flow

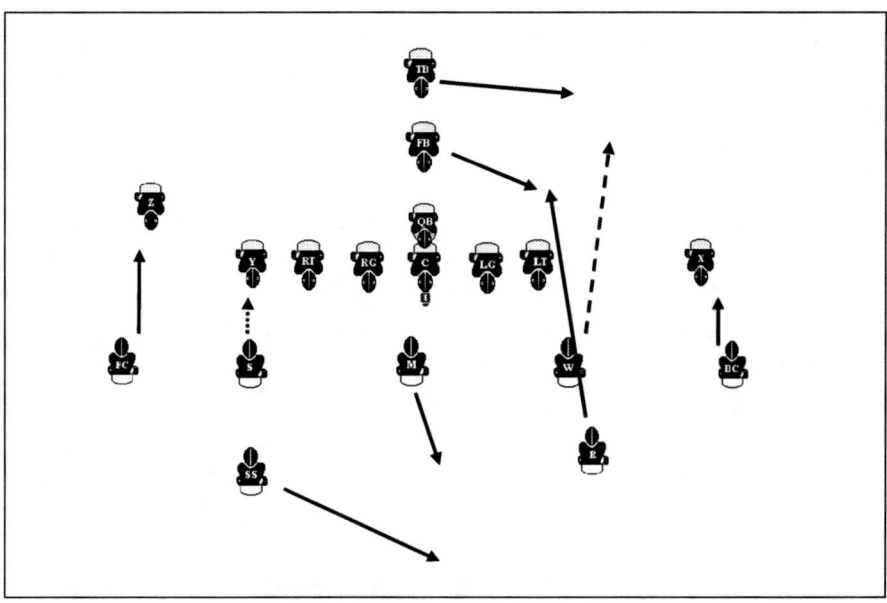

Figure 5-3. Toro vs. a 21 set with weakside flow

Position	Pass responsibility
Sam	Plays the tight end man-to-man.
Mike	Uses his normal key reads but drops to the low hole on all passes.
Will	Uses his normal key reads but plays the tailback man-to-man on all passes.
Strong safety	Drops to the deep middle one-third and plays man-free.
Rover	Plays the fullback man-to-man.
Field corner	Plays #1 man-to-man.
Boundary corner	Plays #1 man-to-man.

Figure 5-4. Position and pass responsibility from Toro vs. a 21 set with weakside flow

Toro Alignments, Stances, and Keys

❏ Field Corner

Alignment: The field corner aligns in his cover 2 shell, seven yards deep and one yard outside of #1. Just prior to the snap of the ball, he stems to man-to-man coverage on #1. Because he has middle field help, he must have an outside alignment on #1. He can choose either man-cloud or man-sky alignment. If he chooses man cloud, he aligns in an Opie alignment, which is an on the line of scrimmage alignment with his inside foot on the outside foot of #1. If he uses man sky, he aligns seven yards deep and one yard outside of #1.

Stance: From an Opie alignment, he aligns in a square stance with his toes parallel to the line of scrimmage and pointing straight ahead. His feet are no wider than armpits-width apart with his weight on the balls of his feet. He is bent at the waist and knees for explosion. His arms are outside his knees and are relaxed and bent at the elbows. His hands are at shoulder-level with his fingers spread and his thumbs inside. His tail is down with his back arched. He has a slight forward lean at the waist. His head is up with his chin slightly over his toes. If he aligns in man sky, he tilts at a 45-degree angle facing the quarterback. His inside foot is back and his outside foot is forward.

Keys: From an Opie alignment, he reads the outside hip of #1. From a sky alignment, he reads the quarterback's drop.
- Three-step drop: He attacks #1's route immediately, thinking short routes and fade.
- Five-step drop: He backpedals keeping over-the-top coverage on #1, thinking medium-to-deep routes.
- Seven-step drop: He backpedals, keeping over-the-top coverage on #1, thinking deep routes.

Responsibilities: He plays #1 man-to-man. He must not get beat deep. He supports the run late, only after the ball has crossed the line of scrimmage.

❏ Boundary Corner

Alignment: The boundary corner aligns in his cover 2 shell, seven yards deep and one yard outside of #1. Just prior to the snap of the ball, he stems to man-to-man coverage on #1. Because he has middle field help, he must have an outside alignment on #1. He can choose either man cloud or man sky alignment. If he chooses man cloud, he aligns in an Opie alignment, which is an on the line of scrimmage alignment with his inside foot on the outside foot of #1. If he uses man sky, he aligns seven yards deep and one yard outside of #1.

Stance: From an Opie alignment, he aligns in a square stance with his toes parallel to the line of scrimmage and pointing straight ahead. His feet are no wider than armpits-width apart with his weight on the balls of his feet. He is bent at the waist and knees for explosion. His arms are outside his knees and are relaxed and bent at the elbows. His hands are at shoulder-level with his fingers spread and his thumbs inside. His tail is down with his back arched. His has a slight forward lean at the waist. His head is up with his chin slightly over his toes. If he aligns in man sky, he tilts at a 45-degree angle facing the quarterback. His inside foot is back and his outside foot is forward.

Keys: From an Opie alignment, he reads the outside hip of #1. From a sky alignment, he reads the quarterback's drop.
- Three-step drop: He attacks #1's route immediately, thinking short routes and fade.
- Five-step drop: He backpedals, keeping over-the-top coverage on #1, thinking medium-to-deep routes.
- Seven-step drop: He backpedals, keeping over-the-top coverage on #1, thinking deep routes.

Responsibilities: He plays #1 man-to-man. He must not get beat deep. He supports the run late, only after the ball has crossed the line of scrimmage.

❏ Strong Safety

Alignment: The strong safety aligns in a cover 2 shell at 10 yards deep over the tight end area.

Stance: He aligns with his toes parallel to the line of scrimmage. His outside foot is staggered back in a toe-to-heel relationship with his inside foot. His feet are no more than armpits-width apart. His weight should be on the balls of his feet. He is bent at the waist and knees for explosion. His tail is down and his back is arched. His head is up with his chin slightly forward over his toes. His arms are outside his knees and relaxed and bent at the elbows. His eyes are looking to the fullback for his read keys.

Keys: He keys the fullback.

Responsibilities: If the fullback comes to the strongside, the strong safety plays him man-to-man. If the fullback goes to the weakside, the strong safety drops free into the middle one-third. If the play is a run to the strongside, the linebacker on the strongside wrong-shoulders all inside plays and spills the ball outside to the strong safety. The strong safety plays the spill from the outside in. If the play is run to the weakside, the safety from the deep middle one-third fits where needed from the middle of the field.

❏ Rover

Alignment: Rover aligns in a cover 2 shell at 10 yards deep over the tight end area.

Stance: He aligns with his toes parallel to the line of scrimmage. His outside foot is staggered back in a toe-to-heel relationship with his inside foot. His feet are no more than armpits–width apart. His weight should be on the balls of his feet. He is bent at the waist and knees for explosion. His tail is down and his back is arched. His head is up with his chin slightly forward over his toes. His arms are outside his knees and relaxed and bent at the elbows. His eyes are looking to the fullback for his read keys.

Keys: He keys the fullback.

Responsibilities: If the fullback comes to the weakside, Rover plays him man-to-man. If the fullback goes to the strongside, Rover drops free into the middle one-third. If the play is a run to the weakside, the linebacker on the weakside wrong shoulders all inside plays and spills the ball outside to Rover. Rover plays the spill from the outside in. If the play is run to the strongside, Rover from the deep middle one-third fits where he is needed from the middle of the field.

❏ Sam

Alignment: Sam uses his normal linebacker stance, unless he is aligned on a wideout, then he aligns in an Opie or sky position.

Stance: From an Opie alignment, he aligns in a square stance with his toes parallel to the line of scrimmage and pointing straight ahead. His feet are no wider than armpits-width apart with his weight on the balls of his feet. He is bent at the waist and knees for explosion. His arms are outside his knees and are relaxed and bent at the elbows. His hands are at shoulder-level with his fingers spread and his thumbs inside. His tail is down with his back arched. His has a slight forward lean at the waist. His head is up with his chin slightly over his toes. If he aligns in man sky, he tilts at a 45-degree angle facing the quarterback. His inside foot is back and his outside foot is forward.

Keys: From an Opie alignment, he reads the outside hip of #2. From a sky alignment, he reads the quarterback's drop.
  • Three-step drop: He attacks #2's route immediately, thinking short routes and fade.

- Five-step drop: He backpedals, keeping over-the-top coverage on #2, thinking medium-to-deep routes.
- Seven-step drop: He backpedals, keeping over-the-top coverage on #2, thinking deep routes.

Responsibilities: He has #2 strong or the second back out to the strongside man-to-man. If no #2 is present, he drops to the strongside hook/curl.

❏ Mike

Alignment: Mike aligns in the front that is called in the huddle.

Stance: He uses his normal linebacker stance.

Keys: He uses his normal linebacker keys, except on all passes, he must key the tailback.

Responsibilities: He keys the fullback, but plays the tailback man-to-man if he releases on the strongside. If the tailback goes to the weakside, Mike drops to the low hole.

❏ Will

Alignment: Will aligns in the front called in the huddle. Offensive formations will exist that require Will to align on wideouts.

Stance: He uses his normal linebacker stance. If he aligns on a wideout, he uses his Opie or man sky alignments.

Keys: He uses his normal linebacker keys, except on all passes, he must key the tailback.

Responsibilities: He uses his normal linebacker keys, but on all passes, he keys the tailback. If the tailback goes to the strongside, he drops to the low hole. If the tailback comes to the weakside, he plays him man-to-man. If Will aligns on a wideout, he uses his Opie or man sky techniques.

Toro vs. a 12 Set (Figures 5-5 through 5-8)

The field corner supers over and aligns in a Marvin alignment on #2. The boundary aligns in an Opie alignment on #1. The linebackers align in their normal alignments. The strong safety and Rover align in their Cover 2 shell. Toro vs. a 12 set with strongside flow is shown in Figures 5-5 and 5-6. Toro vs. a 12 set with weakside flow is shown in Figures 5-7 and 5-8.

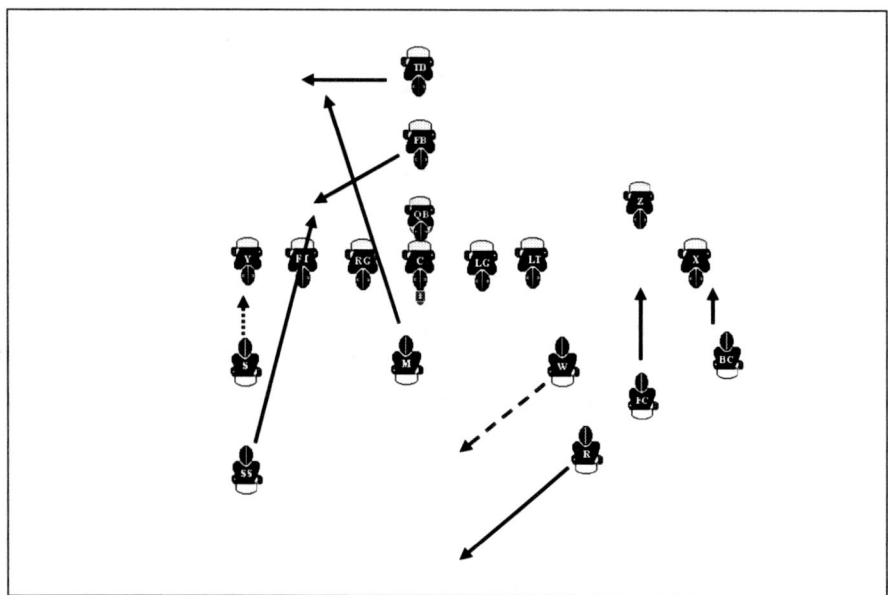

Figure 5-5. Toro vs. a 12 set with strongside flow

Position	Pass responsibility
Sam	Plays the tight end man-to-man because of the super call.
Mike	Uses his normal key reads but plays the tailback man-to-man on all passes.
Will	Uses his normal key reads but drops to the low hole on all passes.
Strong safety	Plays the fullback man-to-man.
Rover	Drops to the middle one-third and plays man-free.
Field corner	Supers over to the weakside and plays #2 man-to-man.
Boundary corner	Plays #1 man-to-man.

Figure 5-6. Position and pass responsibility for Toro vs. a 12 set with strongside flow

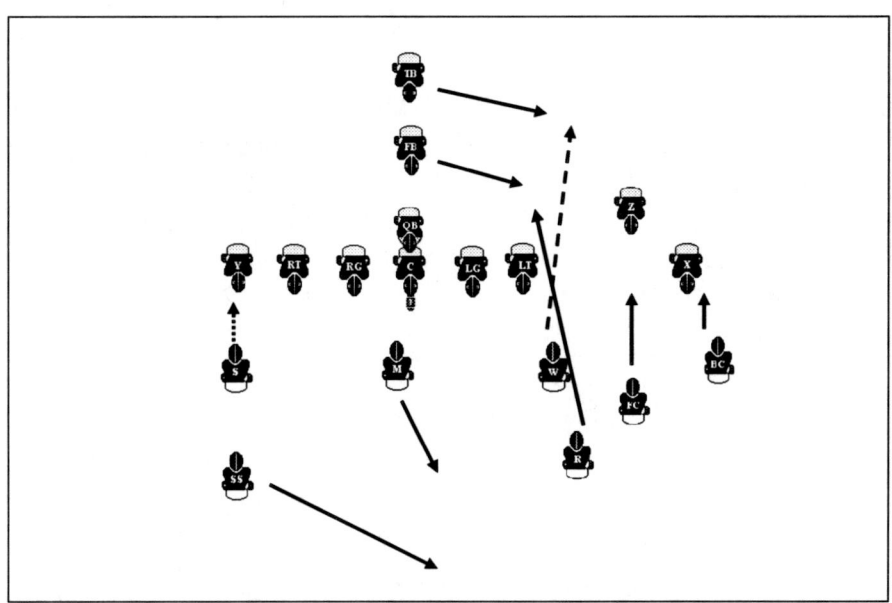

Figure 5-7. Toro vs. a 12 set with weakside flow

Position	Pass responsibility
Sam	Plays the tight end man-to-man because of the super call.
Mike	Uses his normal key reads but drops to the low hole on all passes.
Will	Uses his normal key reads but plays the tailback man-to-man on all passes.
Strong safety	Drops to the middle one-third and plays man-free.
Rover	Plays the fullback man-to-man.
Field corner	Supers over to the weakside and plays #2 man-to-man.
Boundary corner	Plays #1 man-to-man.

Figure 5-8. Position and pass responsibility for Toro vs. a 12 set with weakside flow

Toro vs. a 13 Set (Figures 5-9 through 5-12)

The field corner supers over and aligns in a Marvin alignment on #2. The boundary corner aligns in an Opie alignment on #1. The linebackers align in their normal alignments. The strong safety aligns free in the middle one-third. Rover aligns in a sky alignment on #3. Think of this formation as if the fullback had released to the weakside. Toro vs. a 13 set with strongside flow is as shown in Figures 5-9 and 5-10. Toro vs. a 13 set with weakside flow is shown in Figures 5-11 and 5-12.

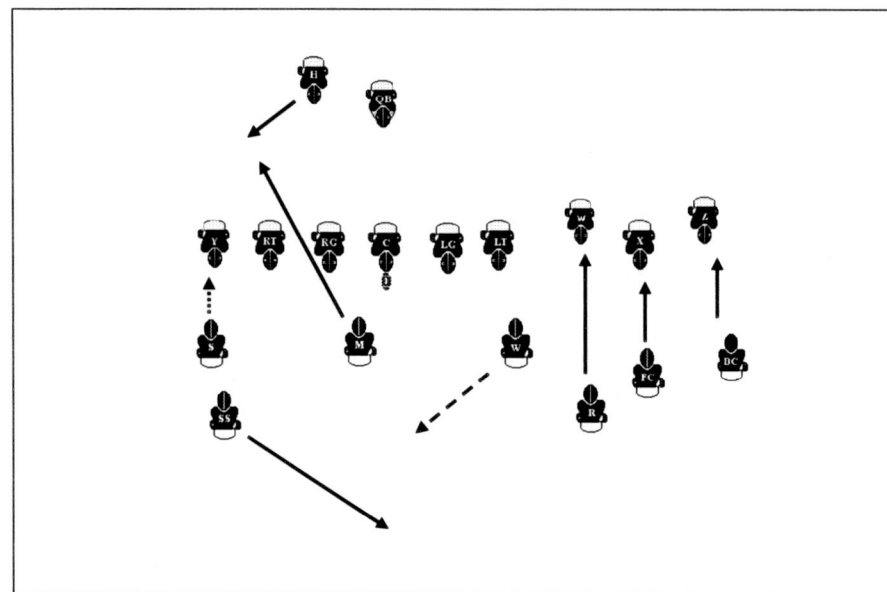

Figure 5-9. Toro vs. a 13 set with strongside flow

Position	Pass responsibility
Sam	Plays the tight end man-to-man because of the super call.
Mike	Uses his normal key reads but plays the H back man-to-man on all passes.
Will	Uses his normal key reads but drops to the low hole on all passes.
Strong safety	Drops to the middle one-third and plays man-free.
Rover	Plays #3 man-to-man.
Field corner	Supers over to the weakside and plays #2 man-to-man.
Boundary corner	Plays #1 man-to-man.

Figure 5-10. Position and pass responsibility for Toro vs. a 13 set with strongside flow

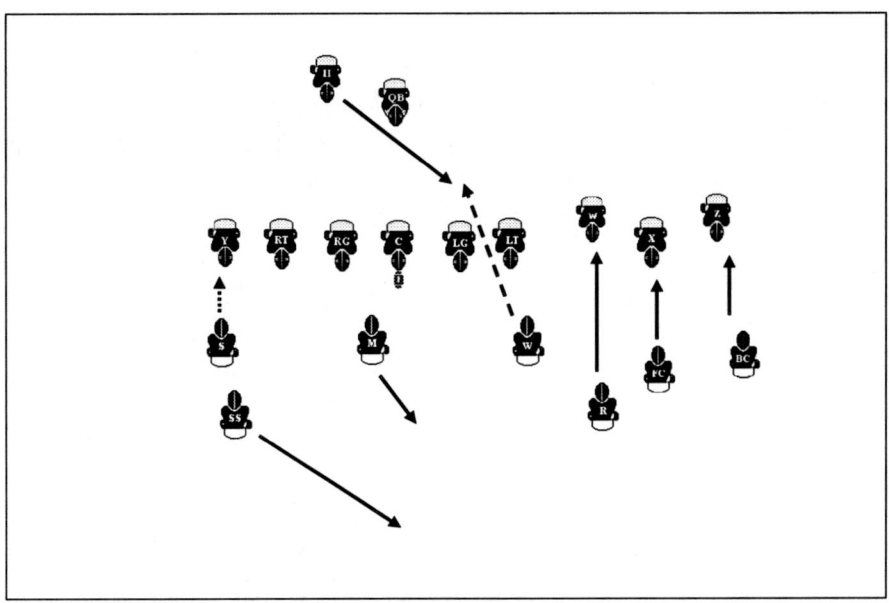

Figure 5-11. Toro vs. a 13 set with weakside flow

Position	Pass responsibility
Sam	Plays the tight end man-to-man because of the super call.
Mike	Uses his normal key reads but drops to the low hole on all passes.
Will	Uses his normal key reads but plays the H back man-to-man on all passes.
Strong safety	Drops to the middle one-third and plays man-free.
Rover	Plays #3 man-to-man.
Field corner	Supers over and plays #2 man-to-man.
Boundary corner	Plays #1 man-to-man.

Figure 5-12. Position and pass responsibility for Toro vs. a 13 set with weakside flow

Toro vs. a 14 Set (Figures 5-13 and 5-14)

The field corner supers over and aligns in a Marvin alignment on #2. The boundary corner aligns in a sky alignment on #1. Mike and Sam align in their normal alignments. Will aligns in a sky alignment on #4. The strong safety aligns free in the middle one-third. Rover aligns in a sky alignment on #3. Think of this formation as if both backs had released to the weakside.

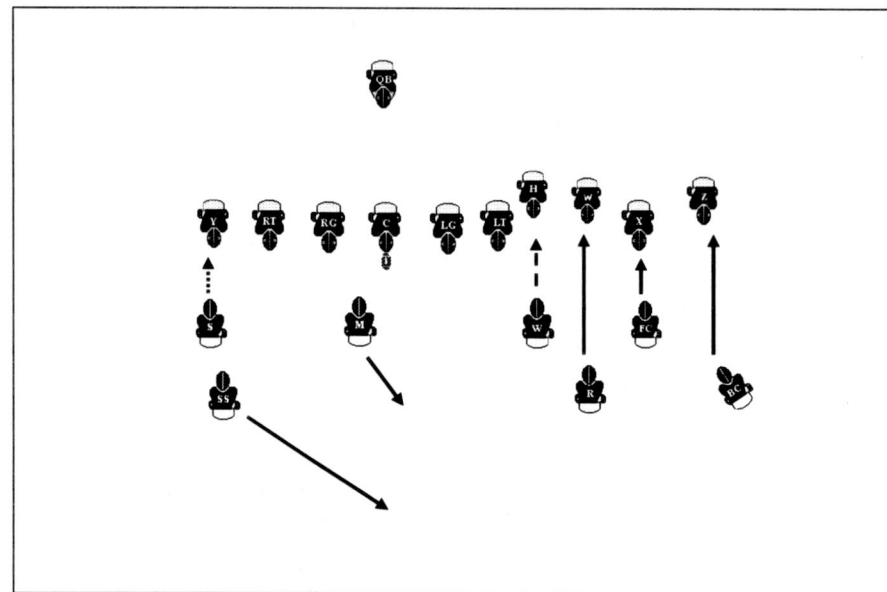

Figure 5-13. Toro vs. a 14 set

Position	Pass responsibility
Sam	Plays the tight end man-to-man because of the super call.
Mike	Drops to the low hole and mirrors the quarterback.
Will	Plays #4 man-to-man.
Strong safety	Drops to the middle one-third and plays man-free.
Rover	Plays #3 man-to-man.
Field corner	Supers over and plays #2 man-to-man.
Boundary corner	Plays #1 man-to-man.

Figure 5-14. Position and pass responsibility for Toro vs. a 14 set

Toro vs. a 22 Set (Figures 5-15 through 5-18)

The corners align in an Opie alignment on the #1s. Mike and Will align in their normal alignment. Sam uses a sky alignment on #2. The strong safety aligns free in the middle one-third. Rover aligns in a sky alignment on #2. Think of this formation as if the fullback had released to the weakside. Toro vs. as 22 set with strongside flow is shown in Figures 5-15 and 5-16. Toro vs. 22 set with weakside flow is shown in Figures 5-17 and 5-18.

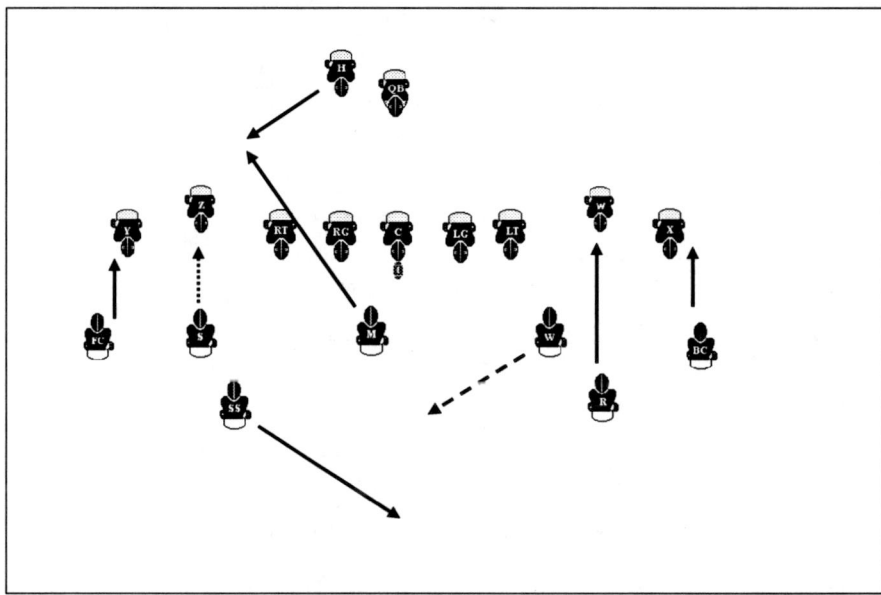

Figure 5-15. Toro vs. a 22 set with strongside flow

Position	Pass responsibility
Sam	Plays #2 man-to-man.
Mike	Uses his normal key reads but drops to the low hole on all passes.
Will	Uses his normal key reads but plays the H back man-to-man on all passes.
Strong safety	Drops to the middle one-third and plays man-free.
Rover	Plays #2 man-to-man.
Field corner	Plays #1 man-to-man.
Boundary corner	Plays #1 man-to-man.

Figure 5-16. Position and pass responsibility for Toro vs. a 22 set with strongside flow

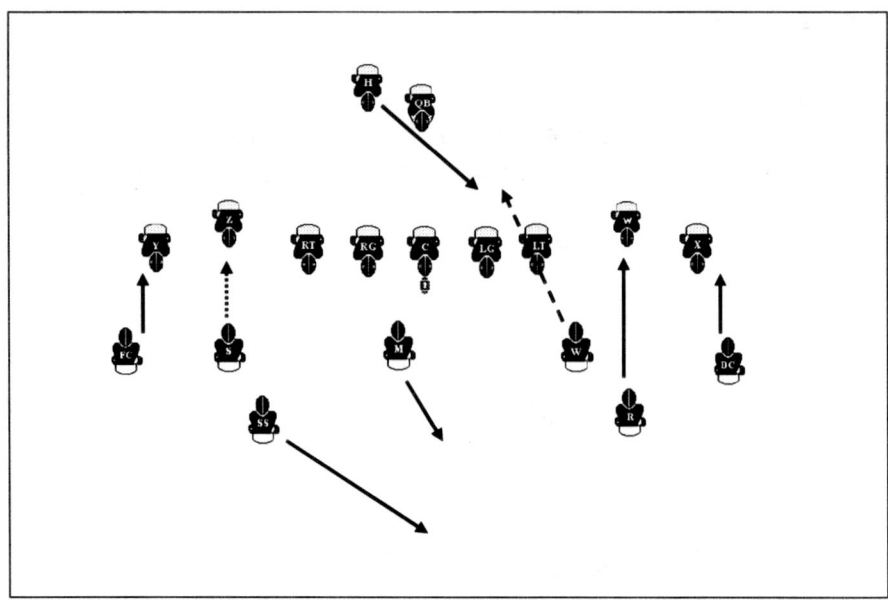

Figure 5-17. Toro vs. a 22 set with weakside flow

Position	Pass responsibility
Sam	Plays #2 man-to-man.
Mike	Uses his normal key reads but plays the H back man-to-man on all passes.
Will	Uses his normal key reads but drops to the low hole on all passes.
Strong safety	Drops to the middle one-third and plays man-free.
Rover	Plays #2 man-to-man.
Field corner	Plays #1 man-to-man.
Boundary corner	Plays #1 man-to-man.

Figure 5-18. Position and pass responsibility for Toro vs. a 22 set with weakside flow

Toro vs. a 23 Set (Figures 5-19 and 5-20)

The corners align in an Opie alignment on the #1s. Mike aligns in his normal alignment. Will aligns a sky alignment on #3. Sam uses his normal alignment. The strong safety aligns free in the middle one-third. Rover aligns in a sky alignment on #2. Think of this formation as if both backs had released to the weakside.

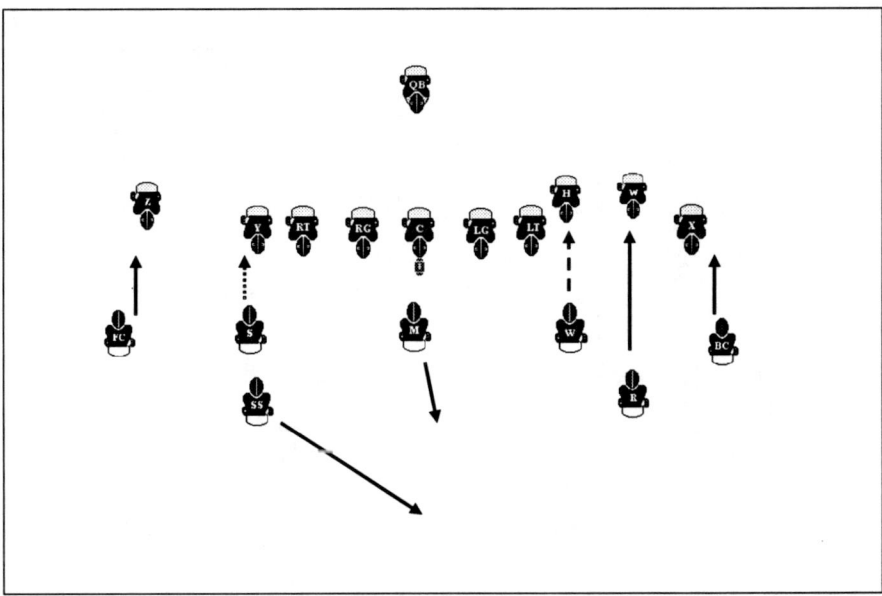

Figure 5-19. Toro vs. a 23 set

Position	Pass responsibility
Sam	Plays the tight end man-to-man.
Mike	Uses his normal key reads but drops to the low hole on all passes.
Will	Plays #3 man-to-man.
Strong safety	Drops to the middle one-third and plays man-free.
Rover	Plays #2 man-to-man.
Field corner	Plays #1 man-to-man.
Boundary corner	Plays #1 man-to-man.

Figure 5-20. Position and pass responsibility for Toro vs. a 23 set

Toro vs. a 31 Set (Figures 5-21 through 5-24)

The corners align in an Opie alignment on the #1s. Mike, Will, and Sam align in their normal alignments. The strong safety aligns in a sky alignment on #2. Rover aligns free in the middle one-third. Think of this formation as if the fullback had released to the strongside. Toro vs. as 31 set with strongside flow is shown in Figures 5-21 and 5-22. Toro vs. a 31 set with weakside flow is shown in Figures 5-23 and 5-24.

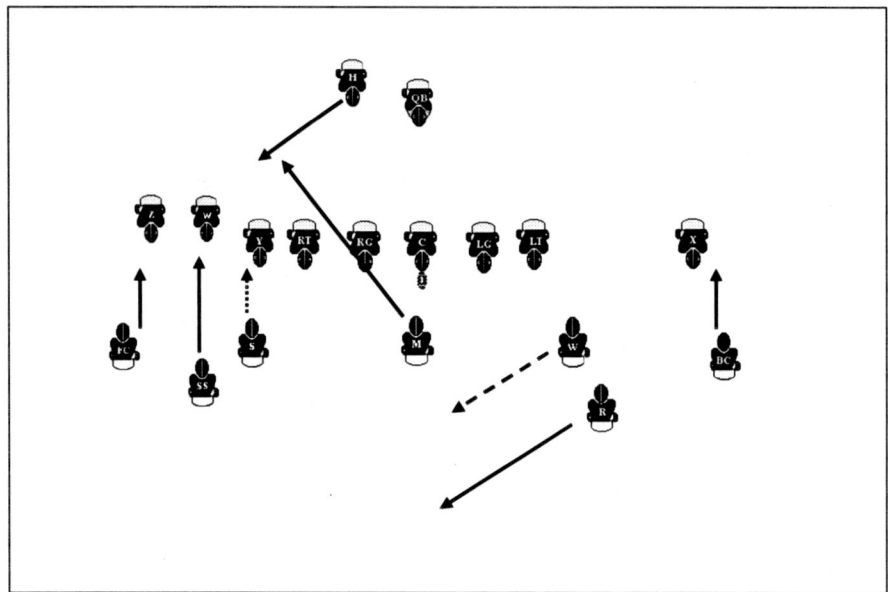

Figure 5-21. Toro vs. a 31 set with strongside flow

Position	Pass responsibility
Sam	Plays the tight end man-to-man.
Mike	Uses his normal key reads but plays the H back man-to-man on all passes.
Will	Uses his normal key reads but drops to the low hole on all passes.
Strong safety	Plays #2 man-to-man.
Rover	Drops to the middle one-third and plays man-free.
Field corner	Plays #1 man-to-man.
Boundary corner	Plays #1 man-to-man.

Figure 5-22. Position and pass responsibility for Toro vs. a 31 set with strongside flow

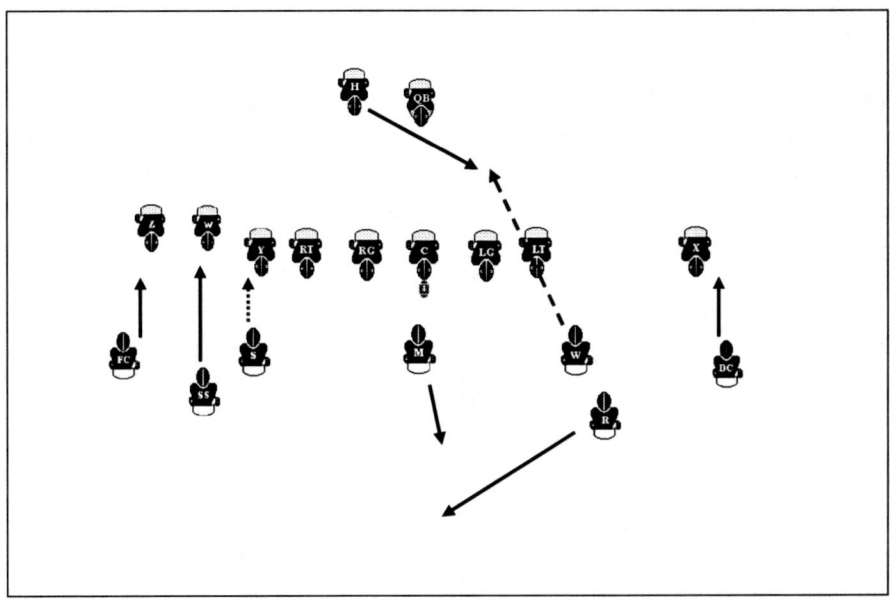

Figure 5-23. Toro vs. a 31 set with weakside flow

Position	Pass responsibility
Sam	Plays the tight end man-to-man.
Mike	Uses his normal key reads but drops to the low hole on all passes.
Will	Uses his normal key reads but plays the H back man-to-man on all passes.
Strong safety	Plays #2 man-to-man.
Rover	Drops to the middle one-third and plays man-free.
Field corner	Plays #1 man-to-man.
Boundary corner	Plays #1 man-to-man.

Figure 5-24. Position and pass responsibility for Toro vs. a 31 set with weakside flow

Toro vs. a 32 Set (Figures 5-25 and 5-26)

The corners align in an Opie alignment on the #1s. Mike and Sam aligns in their normal alignments. Will aligns in a sky alignment over #2. The strong safety aligns in a sky alignment on #2. Rover aligns free in the middle one-third. Think of this formation as if the fullback had released to the strongside and the tailback had released to the weakside.

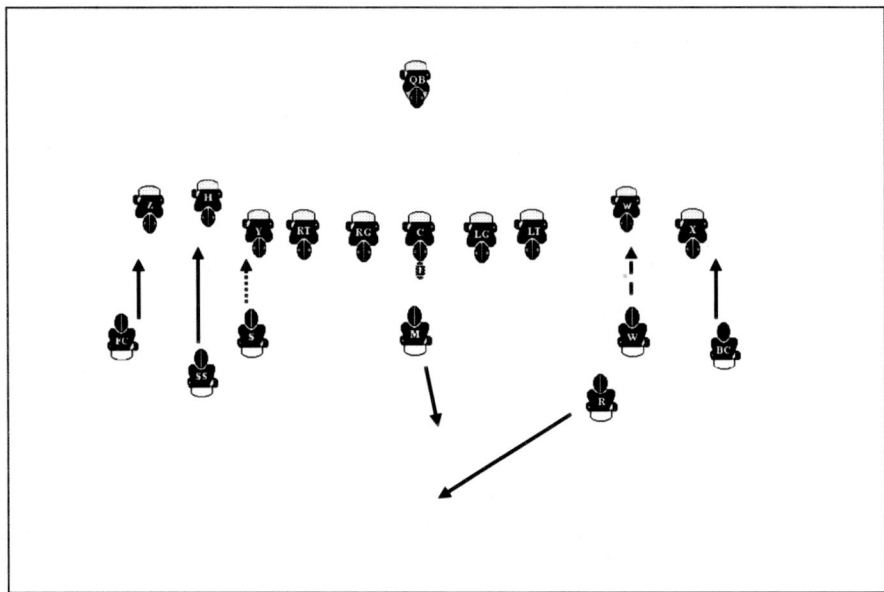

Figure 5-25. Toro vs. a 32 set

Position	Pass responsibility
Sam	Plays the tight end man-to-man.
Mike	Uses his normal key reads but drops to the low hole on all passes.
Will	Plays #2 man-to-man.
Strong safety	Plays #2 man-to-man.
Rover	Drops to the middle one-third and plays man-free.
Field corner	Plays #1 man-to-man.
Boundary corner	Plays #1 man-to-man.

Figure 5-26. Position and pass responsibility for Toro vs. a 32 set

Toro vs. a 41 Set (Figures 5-27 and 5-28)

The field corner aligns in a sky alignment on #1. The boundary corner aligns in an Opie alignment on #1. Mike and Sam align in their normal alignments. Will aligns in a sky alignment over #3 strong. The strong safety aligns in a Marvin alignment on #2. Rover aligns free in the middle one-third. Think of this formation as if both backs had released to the strongside.

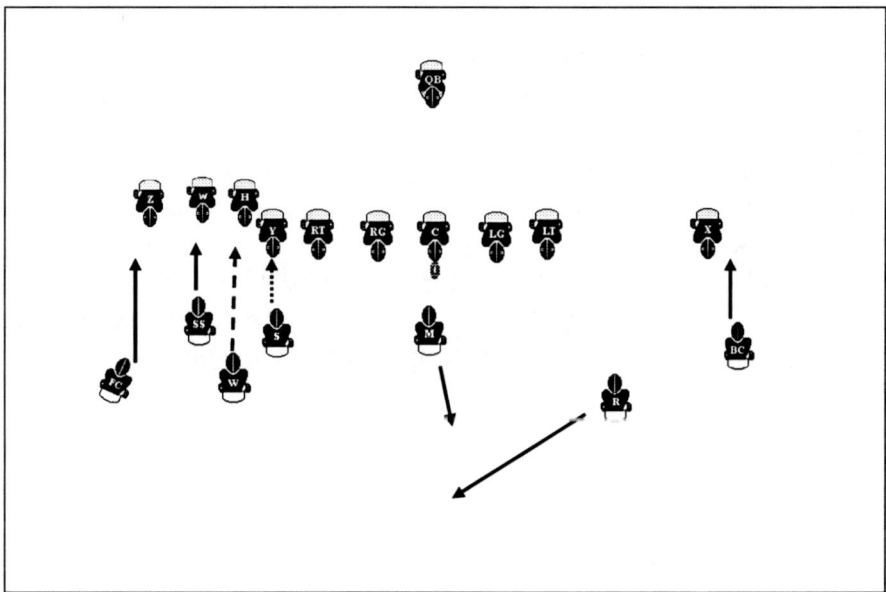

Figure 5-27. Toro vs. a 41 set

Position	Pass responsibility
Sam	Plays the tight end man-to-man.
Mike	Uses his normal key reads but drops to the low hole on all passes.
Will	Moves to the strongside and plays #3 man-to-man.
Strong safety	Plays #2 man-to-man.
Rover	Drops to the middle one-third and plays man-free.
Field corner	Plays #1 man-to-man.
Boundary corner	Plays #1 man-to-man.

Figure 5-28. Position and pass responsibility for Toro vs. a 41 set

Cover 4

Cover 4 is basically cover 2, except instead of playing two-deep with five underneath zone, the underneath coverage plays man-to-man. This coverage can be used with regular personnel, but it is best played from the Arizona package. The secondary can stem and prowl to this coverage.

Cover 4 vs. a 21 Set (Figure 5-29)

The corners play the #1s man-to-man. Sam and Geronimo play the #2s man-to-man. Mike plays the first back out to the strongside man-to-man, or he drops to the low hole. Will has the second back out to the weakside man-to-man, or he drops to the high hole. The strong safety and Rover bail to the hashes and play deep halves; they cannot pattern read receivers as they do in cover 2. They must read the quarterback's eyes as they weave in their backpedal. The man-to-man coverage techniques played from cover 4 are Ike. Opie is sometimes called to help on outside routes. In addition, sometimes Sky is called and the defender plays over the top of the receivers, even though he has two-deep safety help behind the underneath coverage.

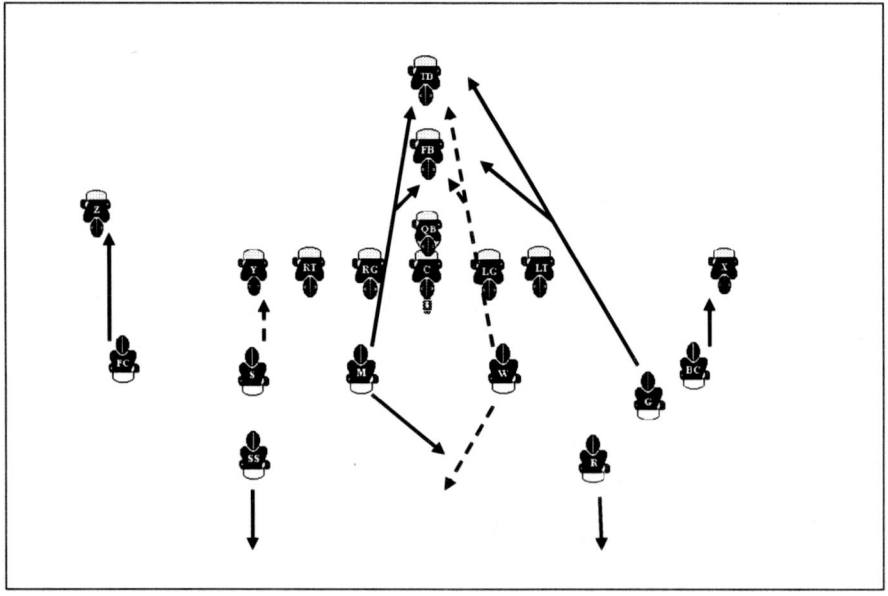

Figure 5-29. Cover 4 vs. a 21 set

Cover 4 Alignments, Stances, and Keys

❏ Field Corner

Alignment: The field corner aligns in his cover 2 shell, seven yards deep and one yard outside of #1. Just prior to the snap of the ball, he stems to man-to-man coverage on #1. The corner can use an Ike alignment on #1, which is an on the line of scrimmage alignment with his outside foot on the inside foot of #1.

Stance: From an Ike alignment, he aligns in a square stance with his toes parallel to the line of scrimmage and pointing straight ahead. His feet are no wider than armpits-width apart with his weight on the balls of his feet. He is bent at the waist and knees for explosion. His arms are outside his knees and are relaxed and bent at the elbows. His hands are at shoulder-level with his fingers spread and his thumbs inside. His tail is down with his back arched. He has a slight forward lean at the waist. His head is up with his chin slightly over his toes.

Keys: From an Ike alignment, he reads the inside hip of #1.

Responsibilities: The defender plays #1 man-to-man. He must stay between the quarterback and the receiver. He supports the run late, only after the safety makes a run call.

❏ Boundary Corner

Alignment: The boundary corner aligns in his cover 2 shell, seven yards deep and one yard outside of #1. Just prior to the snap of the ball, he stems to man-to-man coverage on #1. The corner can use an Ike alignment on #1, which is an on the line of scrimmage alignment with his outside foot on the inside foot of #1.

Stance: From an Ike alignment, he aligns in a square stance with his toes parallel to the line of scrimmage and pointing straight ahead. His feet are no wider than armpits-width apart with his weight on the balls of his feet. He is bent at the waist and knees for explosion. His arms are outside his knees and are relaxed and bent at the elbows. His hands are at shoulder-level with his fingers spread and his thumbs inside. His tail is down with his back arched. He has a slight forward lean at the waist. His head is up with his chin slightly over his toes.

Keys: From an Ike alignment, he reads the inside hip of #1.

Responsibilities: He plays #1 man-to-man. He must stay between the quarterback and the receiver. He supports the run late, only after the safety makes a run call.

❑ Strong Safety

Alignment: The strong safety aligns in a cover 2 shell at 10 yards deep over the tight end area. Just prior to the snap, he bails 12 to 14 yards deep on the strong hash. If he only has a tight end on his side, he aligns at eight yards deep.

Stance: He aligns with his toes parallel to the line of scrimmage. His outside foot is staggered back in a toe-to-heel relationship with his inside foot. His feet are no more than armpits-width apart. His weight should be on the balls of his feet. He is bent at the waist and knees for explosion. His tail is down with his back arched. His head is up with his chin slightly forward over his toes. His arms are outside his knees and relaxed and bent at the elbows. His eyes are looking to the quarterback for his read keys.

Keys: He keys the quarterback.

Responsibilities: He thinks pass first and run second. He bails to the hash and reads the quarterback. He weaves in his backpedal in the direction that the quarterback's eyes are looking.

- Flow toward: He drops to the deep strongside half until no threat of a pass occurs, and then he fits where he is needed.
- Flow away: He drops to the deep strongside half, and then takes a flat pursuit angle looking for cutbacks. He fits where he is needed, playing the ball from the inside-out.
- Pass: He must read the quarterback's drop and eyes. He then weaves in the direction that the quarterback is looking. A three-step drop makes him think slant or fade. A five-step drop makes him think medium-to-deep routes. A seven-step-drop makes him think deep routes. He must keep everything in front of him and cannot let anything get even or behind him.
- Because all underneath coverage is playing man-to-man, he must give a "run!" or "pass!" call to the underneath coverage.

❑ Rover

Alignment: Rover aligns in a cover 2 shell at 10 yards deep over the tight end area. Just prior to the snap, he bails 12 to 14 yards deep on the weak hash. If he only has a tight end on his side, he aligns at eight yards deep.

Stance: He aligns with his toes parallel to the line of scrimmage. His outside foot is staggered back in a toe-to-heel relationship with his inside foot. His feet are no more than armpits-width apart. His weight should be on the balls of his feet. He is bent at the waist and knees for explosion. His tail is down with his back arched. His head is up with his chin slightly forward over his toes. His arms are outside his knees and relaxed and bent at the elbows. His eyes are looking to the quarterback for his read keys.

Keys: He keys the quarterback.

Responsibilities: He thinks pass first and run second. He bails to the hash and reads the quarterback. He weaves in his backpedal in the direction that the quarterback's eyes are looking.
- Flow toward: He drops to the deep weakside deep half until no threat of a pass occurs, and then he fits where he is needed.
- Flow away: He drops to the deep weakside half, and then takes a flat pursuit angle looking for cutbacks. He fits where he is needed, playing the ball from the inside-out.
- Pass: He must read the quarterback's drop and eyes. He then weaves in the direction that the quarterback is looking. A three-step drop makes him think slant or fade. A five-step drop makes him think medium-to-deep routes. A seven-step-drop makes him think deep routes. In addition, the release of #2 helps him to get a jump on the ball. If #2 is inside or vertical, he sinks over the top of #2. If #2 is flat, he widens and sinks over the top of #1. If no #2 is on his side, the strong safety reads the quarterback's drops and eyes for his reaction.
- Because all underneath coverage is playing man-to-man, Rover must give a "run!" or "pass!" call to the underneath coverage.

❑ Sam

Alignment: Sam aligns in the front that is called in the huddle.

Stance: He uses his normal linebacker stance.

Keys: He uses his normal linebacker keys.

Responsibilities: He plays #2 strong man-to-man. He has cover 2 help behind him, so he can play the receiver in an Ike alignment, and he can use a trail technique. He has no run responsibilities until he hears a run call from the safety.

❑ Mike

Alignment: Mike aligns in the front that is called in the huddle.

Stance: He uses his normal linebacker stance.

Keys: He uses his normal linebacker keys.

Responsibilities: He plays the first back out strong man-to-man, or he drops to the low hole.

❑ Will

Alignment: Will aligns in the front that is called in the huddle.

Stance: He uses his normal linebacker stance.

Keys: He uses his normal linebacker keys.

Responsibilities: He plays #3 weak man-to-man on all passes. He has cover 2 help behind him, so he plays the receiver in an Ike alignment, and he can use a trail technique. He has no run responsibilities until he hears a run call from Rover. If no #3 is present, he drops to the high hole.

❏ Geronimo

Alignment: Geronimo aligns in the front that is called.

Stance: He uses his normal stance, unless he is aligned on a wideout, and then he aligns in an Ike position.

Keys: From man cloud, he uses an Ike alignment and reads the inside hip of #2.

Responsibilities: He plays #2 man-to-man. He has cover 2 help behind him, so he can play the receiver in an Ike alignment, and he can use a trail technique. He has no run responsibilities until he hears a run call from Rover.

Cover 4 vs. a 12 Set (Figures 5-30 and 5-31)

The field corner plays #1 man-to-man from an Opie alignment. The boundary corner plays #1 man-to-man in an Ike alignment. Sam and Geronimo play #2s man-to-man from a sky alignment. Mike and Will play their normal linebacker alignments. The strong safety and Rover align 12 to 14 yards deep on the hashes.

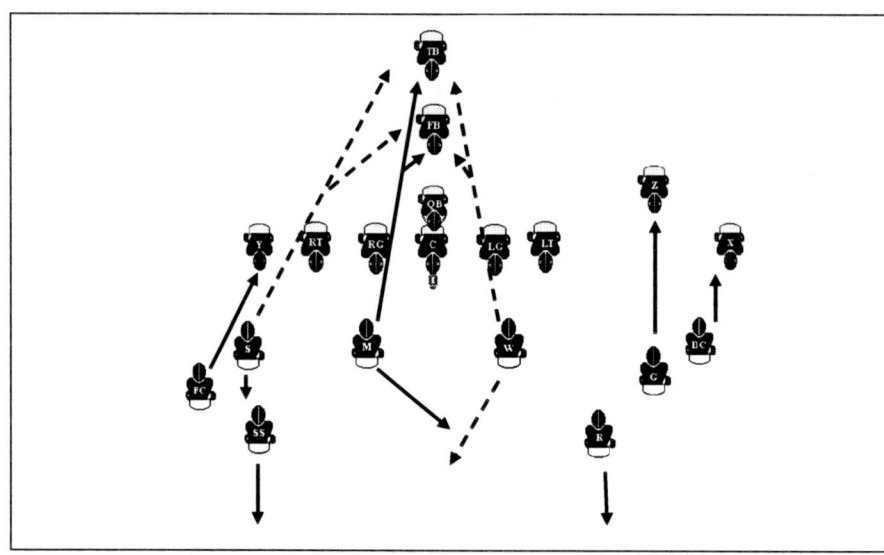

Figure 5-30. Cover 4 vs. a 12 set

Position	Pass responsibility
Sam	Plays the first back out strong man-to-man or drops to the strongside hook/curl.
Mike	Plays the second back out either side man-to-man or drops to the low hole and mirrors the quarterback.
Will	Plays the first back out to the weakside man-to-man or drops to the high hole.
Strong safety	Drops to the hash and plays the deep strongside half.
Rover	Drops to the hash and plays the deep weakside half.
Field corner	Plays the tight end man-to-man.
Boundary corner	Plays #1 man-to-man.
Geronimo	Plays #2 weak man-to-man.

Figure 5-31. Position and responsibility for cover 4 vs. a 12 set

Cover 4 vs. a 13 Set (Figures 5-32 and 5-33)

The field corner supers over and plays #2 man-to-man from a Marvin alignment. The boundary corner plays #1 man-to-man from an Ike alignment. Geronimo plays #3 man-to-man from a sky alignment. Sam, Mike, and Will play their normal linebacker alignments. The strong safety and Rover align 12 to 14 yards deep on the hashes.

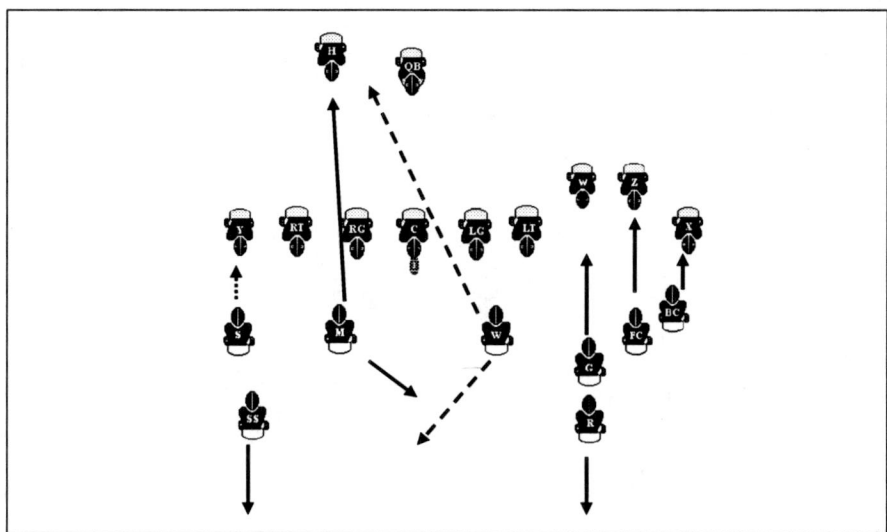

Figure 5-32. Cover 4 vs. a 13 set

Position	Pass responsibility
Sam	Plays the tight end man-to-man because of the super call.
Mike	Plays the first back out to the strongside man-to-man or drops to the low hole.
Will	Plays the first back out to the weakside man-to-man or drops to the high hole.
Strong safety	Drops to the hash and plays the deep strongside half.
Rover	Drops to the hash and plays the deep weakside half.
Field corner	"Supers" over to the weakside and plays #2 man-to-man.
Boundary corner	Plays #1 man-to-man.
Geronimo	Plays #3 man-to-man on the weakside.

Figure 5-33. Position and responsibility for cover 4 vs. a 13 set

Cover 4 vs. a 14 Set (Figures 5-34 and 5-35)

The field corner supers over and plays #2 man-to-man from a Marvin alignment. The boundary corner plays #1 man-to-man from an Ike alignment. Geronimo plays #3 man-to-man from a sky alignment. Sam and Mike play their normal linebacker alignments. Will plays #4 man-to-man from a sky alignment. The strong safety and Rover align 12 to 14 yards deep on the hashes.

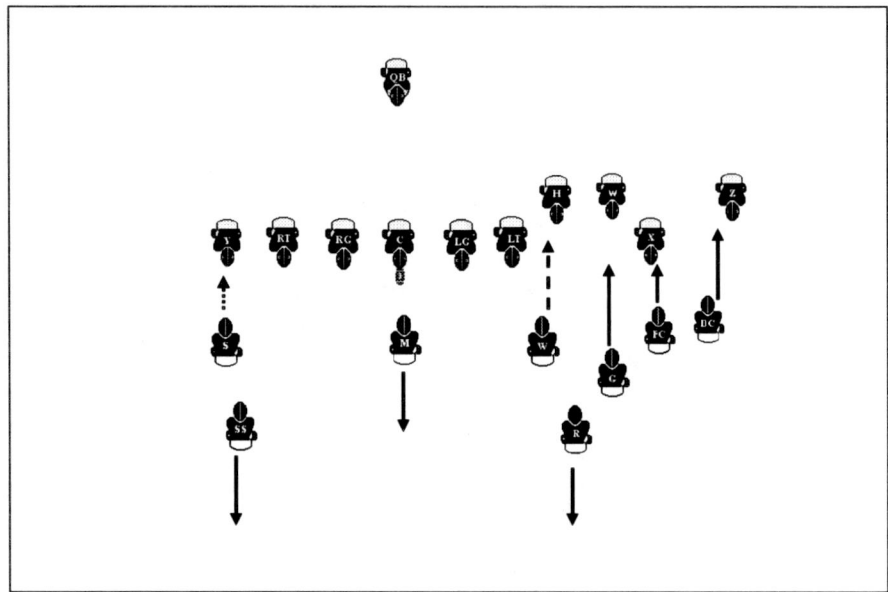

Figure 5-34. Cover 4 vs. a 14 set

Position	Pass responsibility
Sam	Plays the tight end man-to-man because of the super call.
Mike	Drops to the low hole and mirrors the quarterback.
Will	Plays #4 man-to-man.
Strong safety	Drops to the hash and plays the deep strongside half.
Rover	Drops to the hash and plays the deep weakside half.
Field corner	"Supers" over to the weakside and plays #2 man-to-man.
Boundary corner	Plays #1 man-to-man.
Geronimo	Plays #3 man-to-man on the weakside.

Figure 5-35. Position and responsibility for cover 4 vs. a 14 set

Cover 4 vs. a 22 Set (Figures 5-36 and 5-37)

The corners play #1s man-to-man from an Ike alignment. Sam and Geronimo play #2s man-to-man from a Marvin alignment. Mike and Will play their normal linebacker alignments. The strong safety and Rover align 12 to 14 yards deep on the hashes.

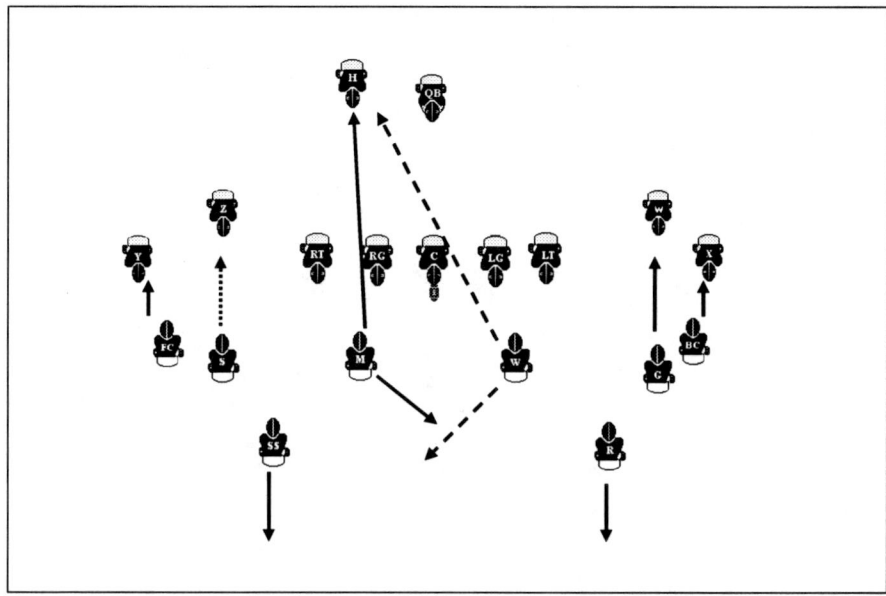

Figure 5-36. Cover 4 vs. a 22 set

Position	Pass responsibility
Sam	Plays #2 man-to-man.
Mike	Plays the first back out to the strongside man-to-man or drops to the low hole and mirrors the quarterback.
Will	Plays the first back out to the weakside man-to-man or drops to the high hole.
Strong safety	Drops to the hash and plays the deep strongside half.
Rover	Drops to the hash and plays the deep weakside half.
Field corner	Plays #1 man-to-man.
Boundary corner	Plays #1 man-to-man.
Geronimo	Plays #2 man-to-man on the weakside.

Figure 5-37. Position and responsibility for cover 4 vs. a 22 set

Cover 4 vs. a 23 Set (Figures 5-38 and 5-39)

The corners play #1s man-to-man from an Ike alignment. Sam plays #2 from his normal linebacker alignment. Geronimo plays the #2 man-to-man from a Marvin alignment. Mike aligns in his normal linebacker alignment. Will plays #3 man-to-man from a sky alignment. The strong safety and Rover align 12 to 14 yards deep on the hashes.

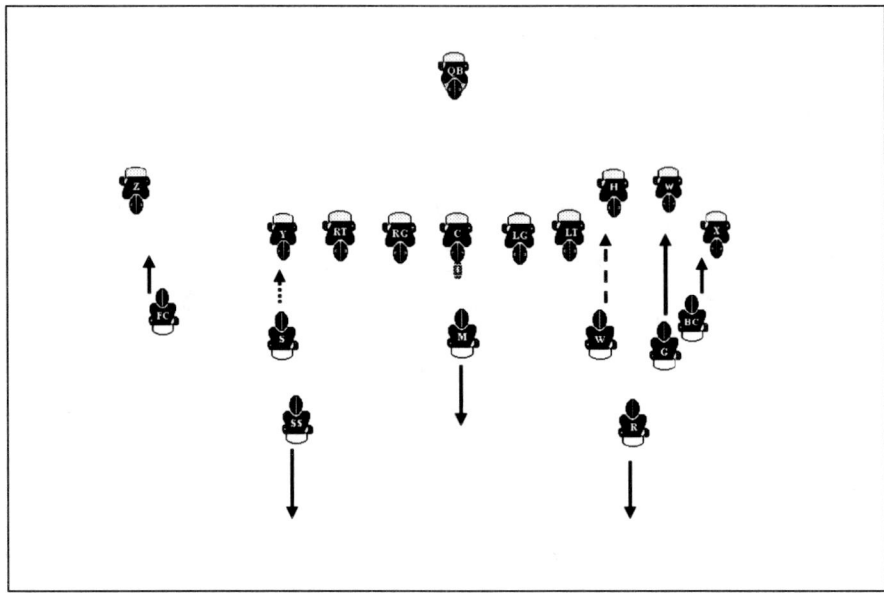

Figure 5-38. Cover 4 vs. a 23 set

Position	Pass responsibility
Sam	Plays the tight end man-to-man.
Mike	Drops to the low hole and mirrors the quarterback.
Will	Plays #3 man-to-man.
Strong safety	Drops to the hash and plays the deep strongside half.
Rover	Drops to the hash and plays the deep weakside half.
Field corner	Plays #1 man-to-man.
Boundary corner	Plays #1 man-to-man.
Geronimo	Plays #2 man-to-man on the weakside.

Figure 5-39. Position and responsibility for cover 4 vs. a 23 set

Cover 4 vs. a 31 Set (Figures 5-40 and 5-41)

The corners play #1s man-to-man from an Ike alignment. Sam plays #3 man-to-man from his normal linebacker alignment. Geronimo plays #2 strong man-to-man from a Marvin alignment. Mike and Will align their normal linebacker alignments. The strong safety and Rover align 12 to 14 yards deep on the hashes.

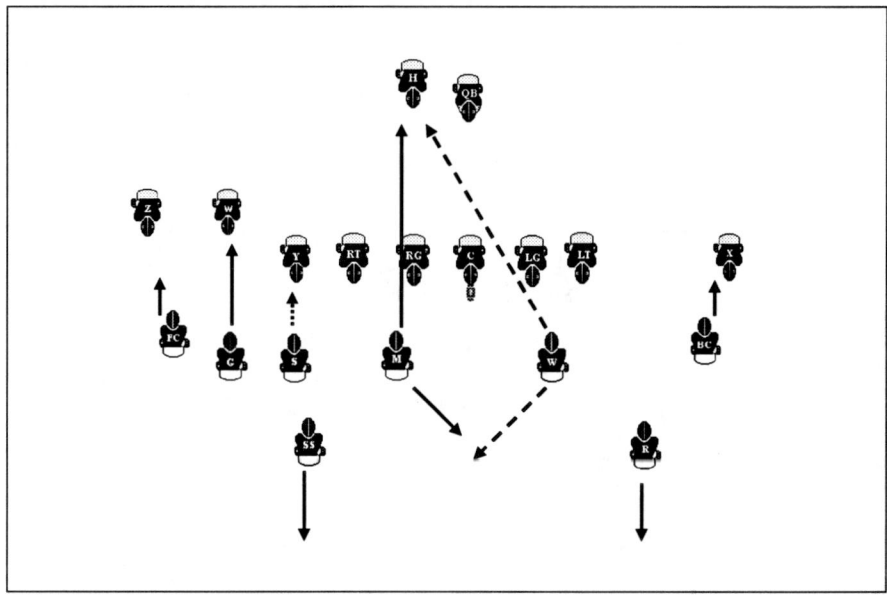

Figure 5-40. Cover 4 vs. a 31 set

Position	Pass responsibility
Sam	Plays the tight end man-to-man.
Mike	Plays the first back out on the strongside man-to-man or drops to the low hole.
Will	Plays the first back out on the weakside man-to-man or drops to the high hole.
Strong safety	Drops to the hash and plays the deep strongside half.
Rover	Drops to the hash and plays the deep weakside half.
Field corner	Plays #1 man-to-man.
Boundary corner	Plays #1 man-to-man.
Geronimo	Plays #2 man-to-man on the strongside.

Figure 5-41. Position and responsibility for cover 4 vs. a 31 set

Cover 4 vs. a 32 Set (Figures 5-42 and 5-43)

The corners play #1s man-to-man from an Ike alignment. Sam plays the tight end man-to-man from his normal linebacker alignment. Geronimo plays #2 strong man-to-man from a Marvin alignment. Mike aligns in his normal linebacker alignment. Will plays #2 man-to-man from a Marvin alignment. The strong safety and Rover align 12 to 14 yards deep on the hashes.

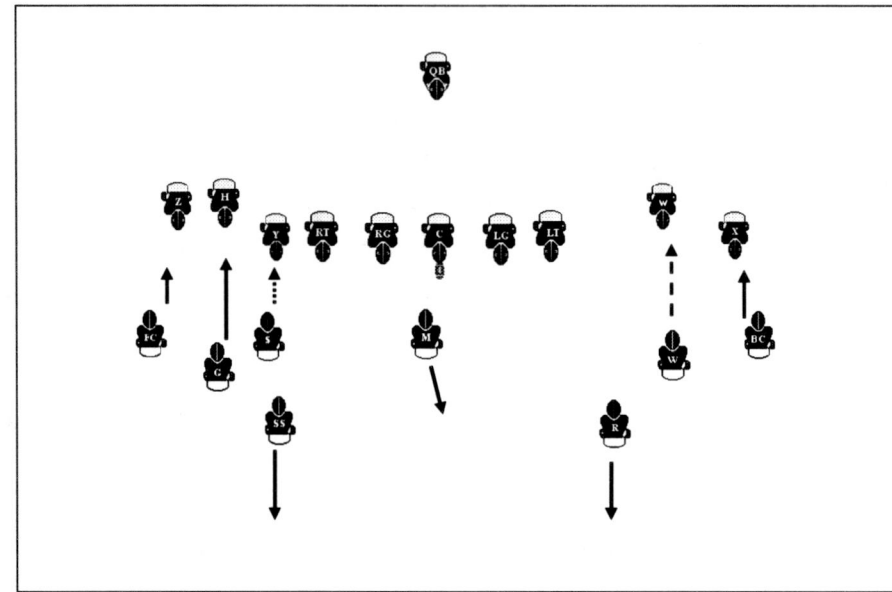

Figure 5-42. Cover 4 vs. a 32 set

Position	Pass responsibility
Sam	Plays the tight end man-to-man.
Mike	Drops to the low hole and mirrors the quarterback.
Will	Plays #2 man-to-man on the weakside.
Strong safety	Drops to the hash and plays the deep strongside half.
Rover	Drops to the hash and plays the deep weakside half.
Field corner	Plays #1 man-to-man.
Boundary corner	Plays #1 man-to-man.
Geronimo	Plays #2 man-to-man on the strongside.

Figure 5-43. Position and responsibility for cover 4 vs. a 32 set

Cover 4 vs. a 41 Set (Figures 5-44 and 5-45)

The corners play #1s from an Ike alignment. Sam plays the tight end man-to-man from his normal linebacker alignment. Geronimo plays #2 strong man-to-man from a Marvin alignment. Mike aligns in his normal linebacker alignment. Will plays #3 strong man-to-man from a sky alignment. The strong safety and Rover align 12 to 14 yards deep on the hashes.

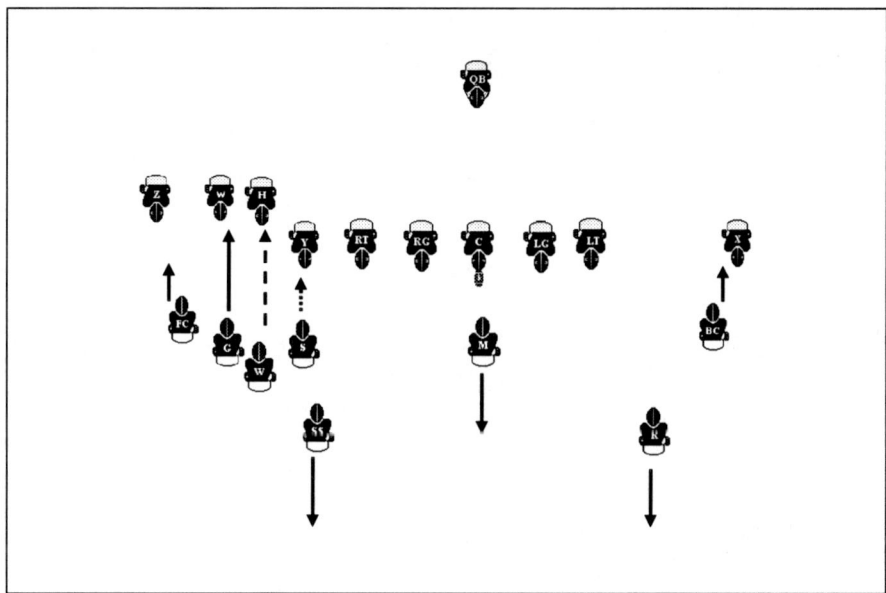

Figure 5-44. Cover 4 vs. a 41 set

Position	Pass responsibility
Sam	Plays the tight end man-to-man.
Mike	Drops to the low hole and mirrors the quarterback.
Will	Plays #3 man-to-man on the strongside.
Strong safety	Drops to the hash and plays the deep strongside half.
Rover	Drops to the hash and plays the deep weakside half.
Field corner	Plays #1 man-to-man.
Boundary corner	Plays #1 man-to-man.
Geronimo	Plays #2 man-to-man on the strongside.

Figure 5-45. Position and responsibility for cover 4 vs. a 41 set

Cover 5

Cover 5 vs. a 21 Set (Figure 5-46)

Cover 5 can be run from any defense, but is best from the Arizona package, which is a quarter-read type coverage. To the strongside, the defenders read the release of the tight end with Sam and the strong safety reacting accordingly. To the weakside, Rover and the corner play bracket coverage. Geronimo plays wall-curl-pull. Mike plays the first back out strong, or he drops to the low hole. Will has the first back out to the weakside, or he drops to the high hole.

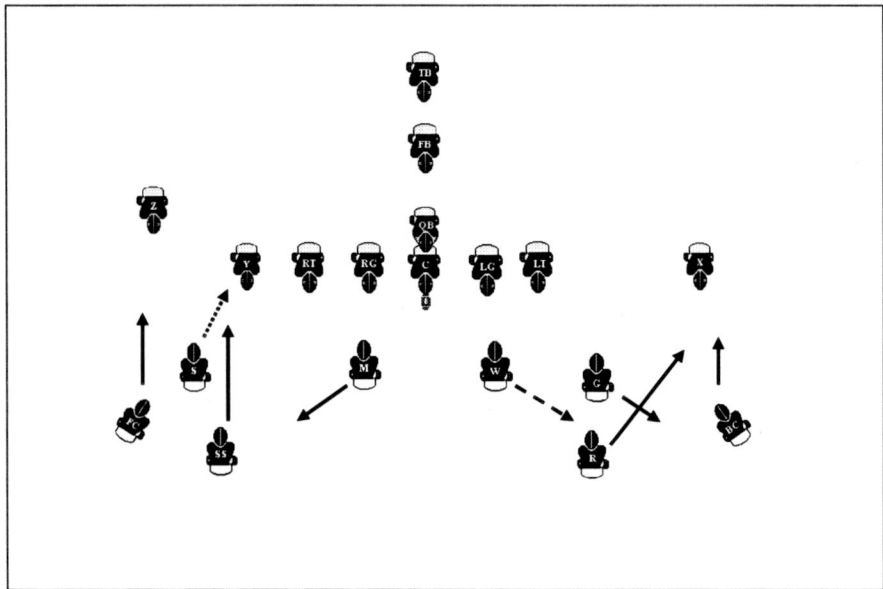

Figure 5-46. Cover 5 vs. a 21 set

Cover 5 Alignments, Stances, and Keys

❑ Field Corner

Alignment: The field corner aligns seven yards deep and one yard outside of #1. He aligns in a sky alignment.

Stance: His arms are relaxed and bent at the elbows. His tail is down with his knees bent and his back arched. His head is up with his chin slightly over his toes. From a sky alignment, he tilts at a 45-degree angle facing the quarterback. His inside foot is back and his outside foot is forward.

Keys: From man sky, he reads the quarterback for either a pass or run key.
- Three-step drop: The corner immediately attacks #1's route, thinking short routes and fade.
- Five-step drop: The corner backpedals, keeping over-the-top coverage on #1, thinking medium-to-deep routes.
- Seven-step drop: The corner backpedals, keeping over-the-top coverage on #1, thinking deep routes.

Responsibilities: The corner has #1 man-to-man. He must not get beat deep. He supports the run late, *only* after ball has crossed the line of scrimmage.

❑ Boundary Corner

Alignment: The boundary corner aligns seven yards deep and one yard outside of #1. He aligns in a sky alignment.

Stance: His arms are relaxed and bent at the elbows. His tail is down with his knees bent and his back arched. His head is up with his chin slightly over his toes. From a sky alignment, he tilts at a 45-degree angle facing the quarterback. His inside foot is back and his outside foot is forward.

Keys: From man sky, he reads the quarterback for either a pass or run key.
- Three-step drop: The corner immediately attacks #1's route, thinking short routes and fade.
- Five-step drop: The corner backpedals, keeping over-the-top coverage on #1, thinking medium-to-deep routes.
- Seven-step drop: The corner backpedals, keeping over-the-top coverage on #1, thinking deep routes.

Responsibilities: The corner has #1 man-to-man. He must not get beat deep. He supports the run late, only after ball has crossed the line of scrimmage.

❑ Strong Safety

Alignment: The strong safety aligns 10 yards deep over a normal tight end alignment. He then stems to seven yards by two yards off the tight end.

Stance: He aligns in a square stand facing the tight end. His arms are relaxed and bent at the elbows. His tail is down with his knees bent and his back arched. His head is up with his chin slightly over his toes.

Keys: He keys the quarterback through the tight end. He must have slow feet and bounce in place until the play is diagnosed, instead of backpedaling. The tight end and the quarterback give the strong safety his run or pass key read.

Responsibilities: He has #2 man-to-man over the top. He must think pass first and run second.
- Flow to: With the tight end blocking, he supports outside of Sam and fits where he is needed. With the tight end releasing, he plays the tight end man-to-man for the "hot" route, and then he plays the quarterback on the option.
- Flow away: With the tight end blocking, he plays the cutback from the edge to the B gap. With the tight end releasing, he plays the tight end man-to-man over-the-top into the middle one-third.
- Pass: If the tight end is vertical, the strong safety plays the tight end man-to-man over the top. If the tight end releases inside, the strong safety rotates to the middle one-third, keeping over-the-top on the tight end. If the tight end releases to the flats, the strong safety will focus on #1's route. He will bracket #1 by playing the post-to-curl. The strong safety is under all routes by #1, and the corner is over the top of all routes by #1.

❑ Rover

Alignment: Rover aligns 10 yards deep over a normal tight end alignment, and then he stems to seven yards by two yards off the tight end.

Stance: He aligns in a square stand facing the tight end. The defender's arms are relaxed and bent at the elbows. His tail is down with his knees bent and his back arched. His head is up with his chin slightly over his toes.

Keys: He reads the quarterback to the uncovered offensive linemen. He bounces in place until the play is diagnosed, instead of backpedaling.

Responsibilities: He must think run first and pass second.
- Flow to: He plays contain pitch.
- Flow away: He plays the cutback from the edge to the B gap.
- Pass: He brackets #1 from the post-to-curl. He is under all routes by #1, and the corner plays over the top of #1. If #2 releases on a vertical, Rover plays him man-to-man and #2 is the back out of the backfield.

❑ Sam

Alignment: He aligns in the front that is called in the huddle. If he aligns in a Raven alignment, he plays four yards deep and one yard inside of #2.

Stance: He uses his normal linebacker stance.

Keys: He keys the tight end to the quarterback. He keys #2 if he is playing a Raven alignment.

Responsibilities: He reacts to the block or release of the tight end.
- Flow to: He plays contain on all running plays.
- Flow away: He turns his knees inside and drops on a five-yard fence, looking for reverses, cutbacks, and drag routes.
- Pass: If the tight end is vertical, Sam drops to the curl and brackets underneath #1 and the corner has #1 over the top. If the tight end releases inside, Sam drops to the curl and brackets underneath #1 and the corner has #1 over the top. If the tight end releases to the flats, Sam plays the tight end man-to-man, thinking wheel route.

❑ Mike

Alignment: Mike aligns in the front that is called in the huddle.

Stance: He uses his normal linebacker stance.

Keys: He uses his normal linebacker keys.

Responsibilities: He stays over the top of #3 on all passes.

❑ Will

Alignment: Will aligns in the front that is called in the huddle. If he aligns in a Raven alignment, he plays four yards deep and one yard inside of #2.

Stance: He uses his normal linebacker stance.

Keys: He uses his normal linebacker keys. If he is playing a Raven alignment, he keys #2.

Responsibilities: If pass occurs, he must stay on the top of the first back out to the weakside.

❑ Geronimo

Alignment: Geronimo aligns in the front that is called in the huddle. If he aligns in a Raven alignment, he plays four yards deep and one yard inside of #2.

Stance: He aligns in a square stance. The defender's arms are relaxed and bent at the elbows. His tail is down with his knees bent and his back arched. His head is up with his chin slightly over his toes.

Keys: He uses his normal keys.

Responsibilities: He plays the run first and the pass second.
- Flow to: He keeps outside contain on all runs.
- Flow away: He turns his knees to the inside and drops on a five-yard fence, looking for reverses, cutback, and drags.
- Pass: He plays the weakside wall-curl-pull.

Raven Coverage

Raven is used against strong or weak twin sets. It is a progression read coverage using the following rules.

❑ Corner

The corner uses his normal alignment and keys #2 using the following reads:
- If #2 releases inside or up the field, he plays #1 man-to-man from a sky alignment.
- If #2 releases outside, he plays #2 man-to-man, thinking wheel route by #2.

❑ Strong Safety or Rover

The strong safety or Rover aligns 10 yards deep directly over #2. They key #2 using the following rules:
- If #2 releases inside or upfield, he plays him man-to-man.
- If #2 releases outside, he plays #1 man-to-man over the top.

❑ Sam, Will, Geronimo, Tonto, or the Super Corner

Sam, Will, Geronimo, or the super corner alignments from a Raven call are four yards deep and one yard inside of #2. They use the following reads:

- If #2 releases inside or upfield, the defender jams him and plays the wall-curl-pull. He must not let the receiver catch a quick seam route.
- If #2 releases outside, the defender plays wall-curl-pull. If #2 goes outside, the defender must always think #1 is coming inside.
- The #2 receiver must be rerouted but cannot be chased.

Cover 5 vs. a 12 Set (Figures 5-47 and 5-48)

The field corner aligns three yards by three yards off the tight end. The boundary corner aligns seven yards deep and one yard outside of #1. All linebackers align in their normal linebacker alignments. The strong safety aligns seven yards deep and two yards outside of the tight end. Rover aligns 10 yards deep over #2. Geronimo aligns four yards deep and one yard inside of #2.

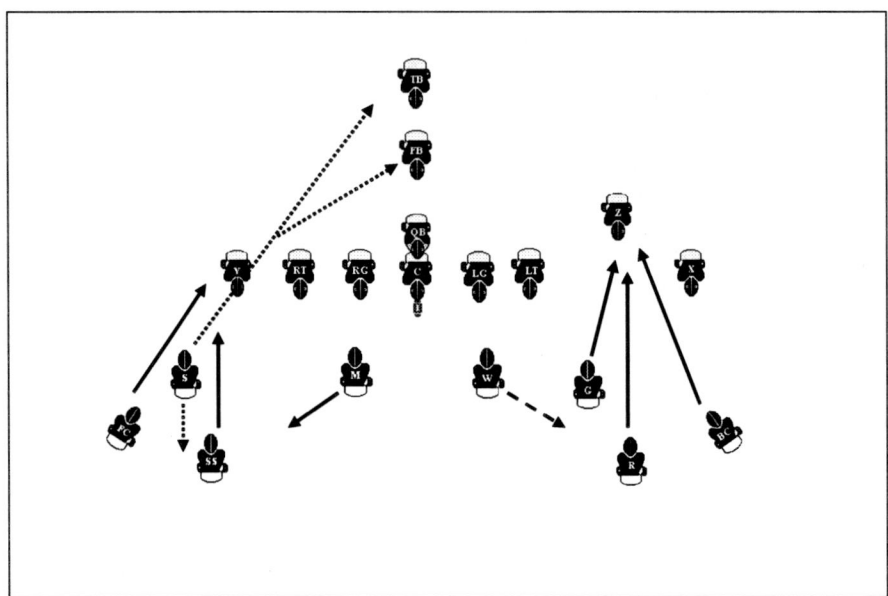

Figure 5-47. Cover 5 vs. a 12 set

Position	Pass responsibility
Sam	Plays the first back out to the strongside man-to-man or drops to the strongside hook/curl.
Mike	Plays man-to-man on the second back out to the strongside or weakside or drops to the low hole.
Will	Plays man-to-man on the first back out to the weak or drops to the high hole.
Strong safety	Reads the tight end for his responsibilities.
Rover	Reads #2 for his responsibilities.
Field corner	Reads the tight end for his responsibilities.
Boundary corner	Reads #2 for his responsibilities.
Geronimo	Reads #2 for his responsibilities.

Figure 5-48. Position and pass responsibility for cover 5 vs. a 12 set

Cover 5 vs. a 13 Set (Figures 5-49 and 5-50)

The field corner supers over and aligns four yards deep and one yard inside of #2. The boundary corner aligns seven yards deep and one yard outside of #1. All linebackers use their normal linebacker alignments. The strong safety aligns seven yards deep and two yards outside the tight end. Rover aligns 10 yards deep over #2. Geronimo plays a sky alignment on #3.

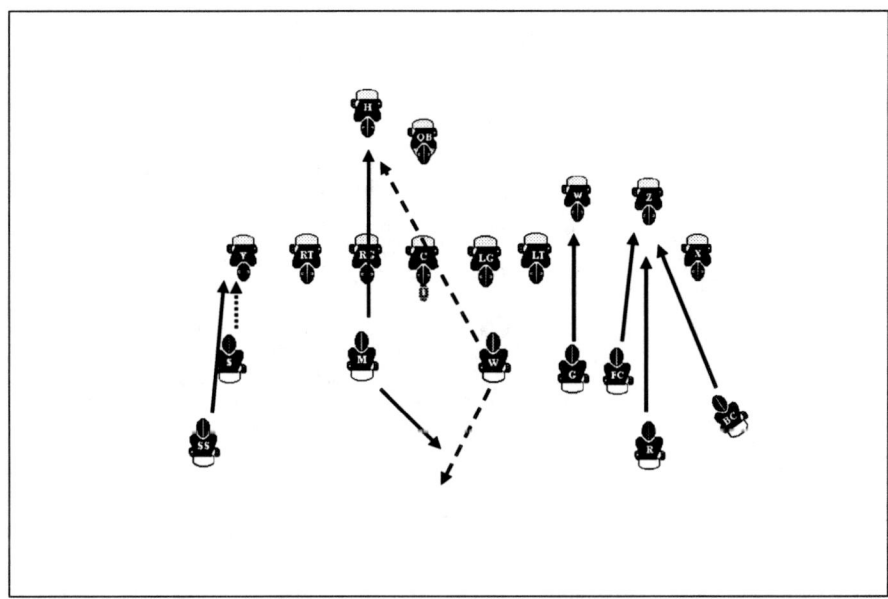

Figure 5-49. Cover 5 vs. a 13 set

Position	Pass responsibility
Sam	Reads the tight end for his responsibilities.
Mike	Plays man-to-man on the first back out to the strongside or drops to the low hole.
Will	Plays man-to-man on the first back out to the weakside or drops to the high hole.
Strong safety	Reads the tight end for his responsibilities.
Rover	Reads #2 for his responsibilities.
Field corner	Reads #2 for his responsibilities.
Boundary corner	Reads #2 for his responsibilities.
Geronimo	Plays #3 man-to-man on the weakside.

Figure 5-50. Position and pass responsibility for cover 5 vs. a 13 set

Cover 5 vs. a 14 Set (Figures 5-51 and 5-52)

Cover 5 vs. a 14 set is a progression read coverage. The field corner supers over and aligns four yards deep and one yard inside of #2. Sam aligns in his normal linebacker alignment. Mike aligns over the center. Will aligns in a sky position over #4. The strong safety aligns seven yards deep and two yards outside the tight end. Rover aligns 10 yards deep over #2. Geronimo plays a sky alignment on #3.

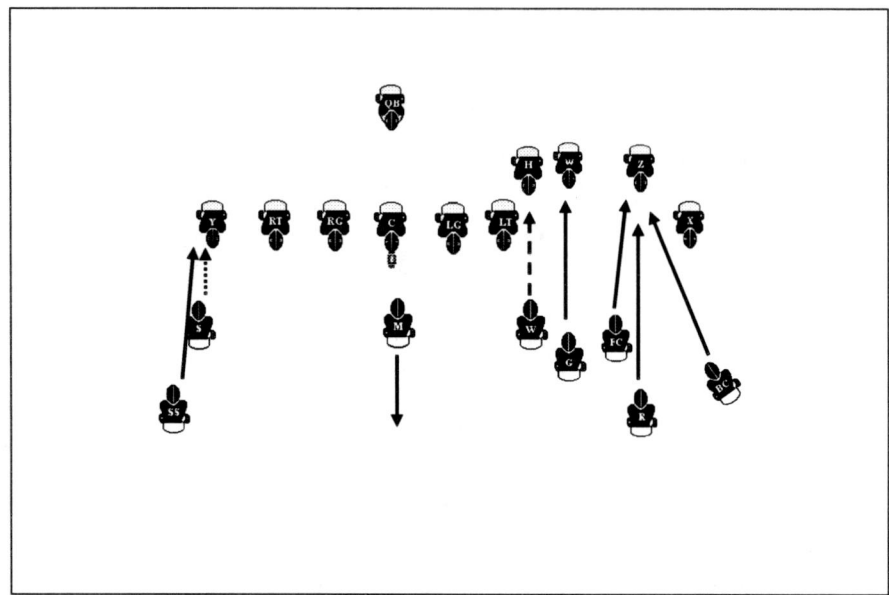

Figure 5-51. Cover 5 vs. a 14 set

Position	Pass responsibility
Sam	Reads the tight end for his responsibilities.
Mike	Drops to the low hole and mirrors the quarterback.
Will	Plays #4 man-to-man on the weakside.
Strong safety	Reads the tight end for his responsibilities.
Rover	Reads #2 for his responsibilities.
Field corner	Reads #2 for his responsibilities.
Boundary corner	Reads #2 for his responsibilities.
Geronimo	Plays #3 man-to-man on the weakside.

Figure 5-52. Position and pass responsibility for cover 5 vs. a 14 set

Cover 5 vs. a 22 Set (Figures 5-53 and 5-54)

Cover 5 vs. a 22 set is a progression read coverage. The corners align seven yards deep and one yard outside of #1. The linebackers align in their normal linebacker alignments. The strong safety aligns seven yards deep and two yards outside the tight end. Rover aligns 10 yards deep over #2. Geronimo aligns four yards deep and one yard inside of #2.

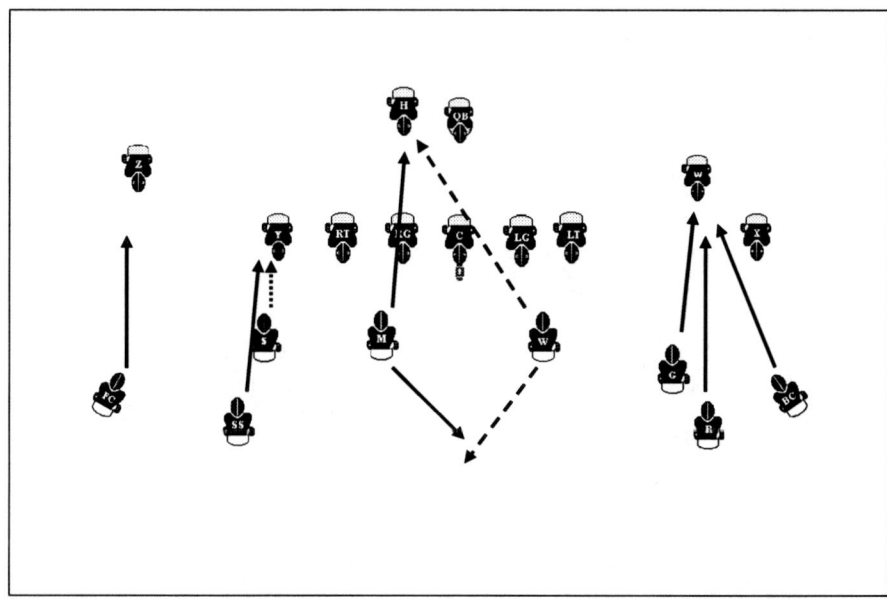

Figure 5-53. Cover 5 vs. a 22 set

Position	Pass responsibility
Sam	Reads the tight end for his responsibilities.
Mike	Plays the first back out to the strongside man-to-man or drops to the low hole.
Will	Plays man-to-man on the first back out to the weakside or drops to the high hole.
Strong safety	Reads the tight end for his responsibilities.
Rover	Reads #2 for his responsibilities.
Field corner	Plays man-to-man on #1.
Boundary corner	Reads #2 for his responsibilities.
Geronimo	Reads #2 for his responsibilities.

Figure 5-54. Position and pass responsibility for cover 5 vs. a 22 set

Cover 5 vs. a 23 Set (Figures 5-55 and 5-56)

Cover 5 vs. a 23 set is a progression read coverage. The corners align seven yards deep and one yard outside of #1. Sam aligns in his normal linebacker alignment. Mike aligns over the center. Will aligns four yards deep and one yard inside of #2. The strong safety aligns seven yards deep and two yards outside the tight end. Rover aligns 10 yards deep over #2. Geronimo aligns over #3 in a sky alignment.

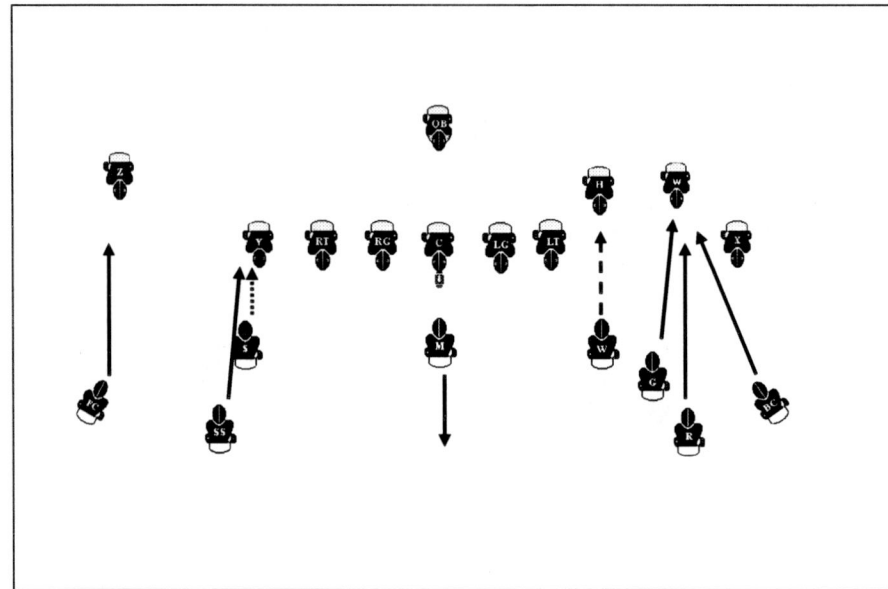

Figure 5-55. Cover 5 vs. a 23 set

Position	Pass responsibility
Sam	Reads the tight end for his responsibilities.
Mike	Drops to the low hole and mirrors the quarterback.
Will	Reads #2 for his responsibilities.
Strong safety	Reads the tight end for his responsibilities.
Rover	Reads #2 for his responsibilities.
Field corner	Plays #1 man-to-man.
Boundary corner	Reads #2 for his responsibilities.
Geronimo	Plays #3 man-to-man on the weakside.

Figure 5-56. Position and pass responsibility for cover 5 vs. a 23 set

Cover 5 vs. a 31 Set (Figures 5-57 and 5-58)

Cover 5 vs. a 31 set is a progression read coverage. The corners align seven yards deep and one yard outside of #1. The linebackers align in their normal linebacker alignments. The strong safety aligns 10 yards deep over #2. Rover aligns seven yards deep and two yards outside the tackle. Geronimo aligns four yards deep and one yard inside of #2.

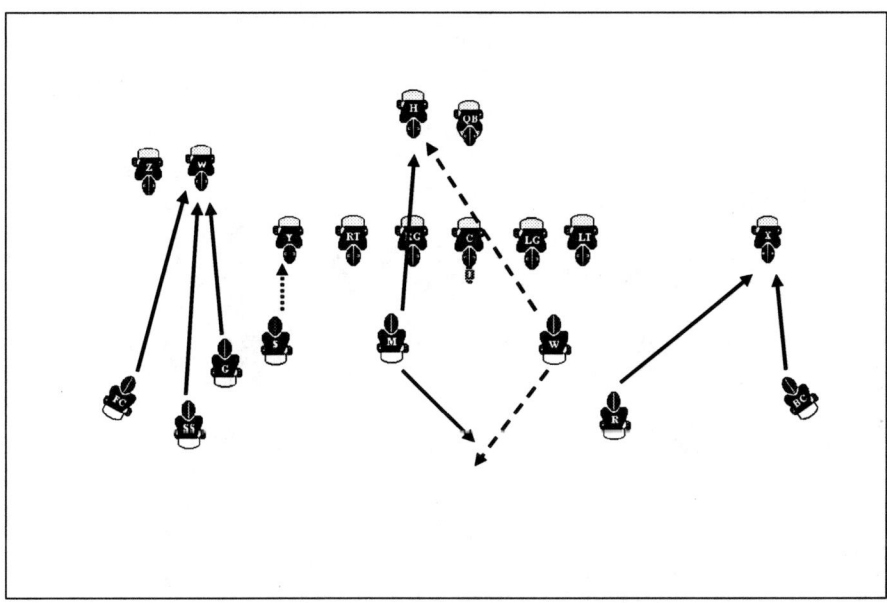

Figure 5-57. Cover 5 vs. a 31 set

Position	Pass responsibility
Sam	Plays the tight end man-to-man.
Mike	Plays the first back out strong man-to-man or drops to the low hole.
Will	Plays the first back out weak man-to-man or drops to the high hole.
Strong safety	Reads #2 for his responsibilities.
Rover	Reads #1 for his responsibilities.
Field corner	Reads #2 for his responsibilities.
Boundary corner	Plays #1 man-to-man.
Geronimo	Reads #2 strong for his responsibilities.

Figure 5-58. Position and pass responsibility for cover 5 vs. a 31 set

Cover 5 vs. a 32 Set (Figures 5-59 and 5-60)

Cover 5 vs. a 32 set is a progression read coverage. The corners align seven yards deep and one yard outside of #1. Sam aligns in his normal linebacker alignment. Mike aligns over the center. Will aligns four yards deep and one yard inside of #2. The strong safety aligns 10 yards deep over #2. Rover aligns 10 yards deep over #2. Geronimo aligns four yards deep and one yard inside of #2.

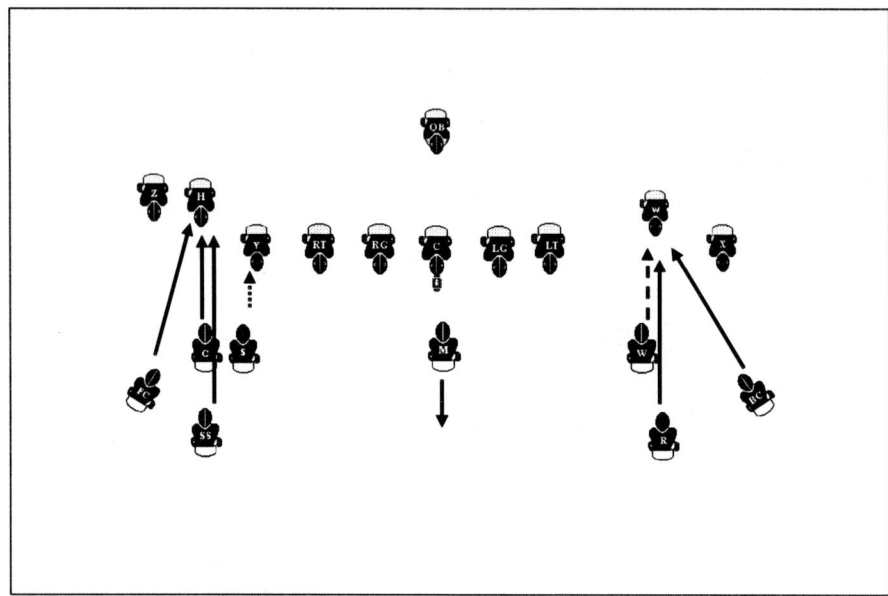

Figure 5-59. Cover 5 vs. a 32 set

Position	Pass responsibility
Sam	Plays the tight end man-to-man.
Mike	Drops to the low hole and mirrors the quarterback.
Will	Reads #2 weak for his responsibilities.
Strong safety	Reads #2 for his responsibilities.
Rover	Reads #2 for his responsibilities.
Field corner	Reads #2 for his responsibilities.
Boundary corner	Reads #2 for his responsibilities.
Geronimo	Reads #2 strong for his responsibilities.

Figure 5-60. Position and pass responsibility for cover 5 vs. a 32 set

Cover 5 vs. a 41 Set (Figures 5-61 and 5-62)

Cover 5 vs. a 41 set is a progression read coverage. The corners align seven yards deep and one yard outside of #1. Sam aligns in his normal linebacker alignment. Mike aligns over the center. Will aligns four yards deep and one yard inside of #2 on the strongside. The strong safety aligns 10 yards deep over #2. Rover aligns seven yards deep and two yards off the tackle. Geronimo aligns in a sky alignment over #3.

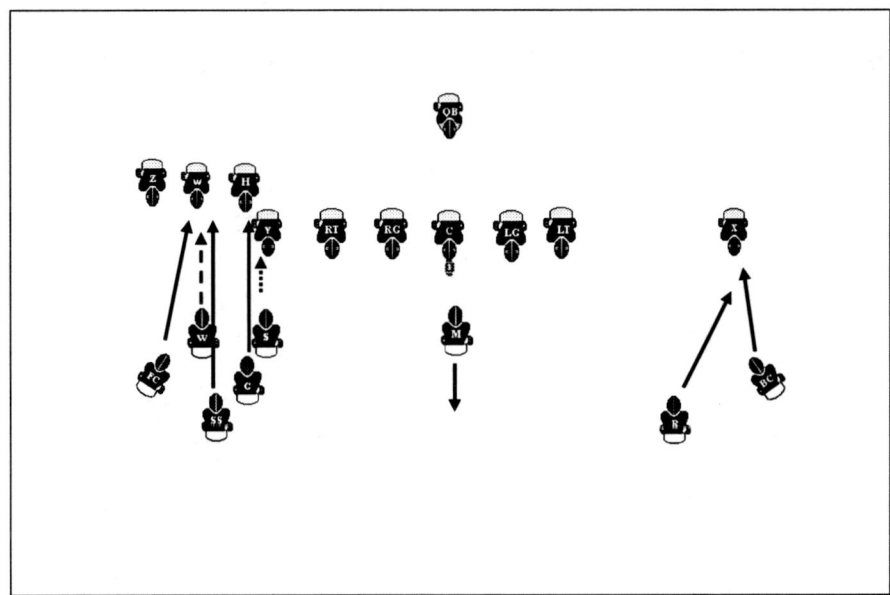

Figure 5-61. Cover 5 vs. a 41 set

Position	Pass responsibility
Sam	Plays the tight end man-to-man.
Mike	Drops to the low hole and mirrors the quarterback.
Will	Reads #2 strong for his responsibilities.
Strong safety	Reads #2 for his responsibilities.
Rover	Reads #1 for his responsibilities.
Field corner	Reads #2 for his responsibilities.
Boundary corner	Plays #1 man-to-man.
Geronimo	Plays #3 man-to-man on the strongside.

Figure 5-62. Position and responsibility for cover 5 vs. a 41 set

Zippo

Zippo vs. a 22 Set (Figures 5-63 through 5-66)

Zippo coverage is a combination of Toro and Cover 3. Zippo is used only with the Arizona package. The back read is the halfback. The corners play the deep outside one-thirds. Sam and Geronimo play the wall-curl-flats. Mike and Will use their Toro rules. The strong safety and Rover use their Toro rules, but the middle of the field dropper now plays zone instead of man free. Zippo vs. a 22 set with strongside flow is shown in Figures 5-63 and 5-64. Zippo vs. a 22 set with weakside flow is shown in Figures 5-65 and 5-66.

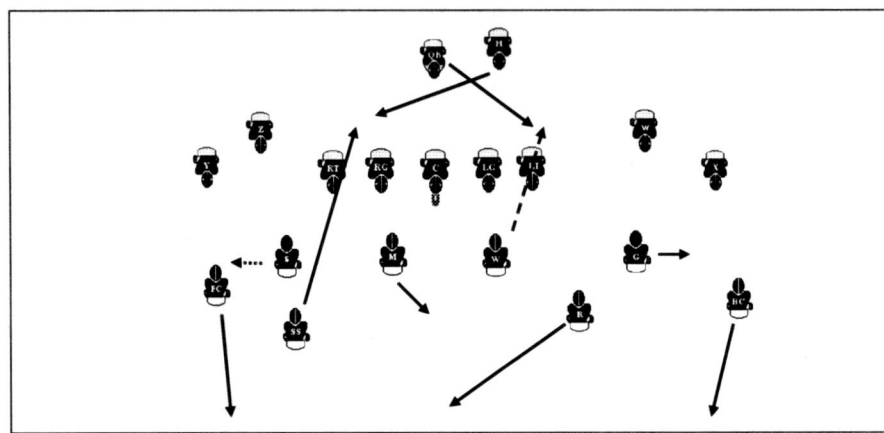

Figure 5-63. Zippo vs. a 22 set with strongside flow

Position	Pass responsibility
Sam	Plays the strongside wall-curl-flats.
Mike	Keys the H back coming to him, so he spills the halfback outside on all runs. He drops to the low hole on all passes.
Will	Keys the H back going away from him, so he plays the quarterback man-to-man.
Strong safety	Keys the H back coming to his side, so he plays the halfback man-to-man on all passes. He plays the spill from Mike on all runs.
Rover	Keys the H back going away from him, so he drops to the deep middle one-third and plays his cover 6 rules.
Field corner	Plays the deep strong outside one-third.
Boundary corner	Plays the deep weak outside one-third.
Geronimo	Plays the weakside wall-curl-flats.

Figure 5-64. Position and responsibility for Zippo vs. a 22 set with strongside flow

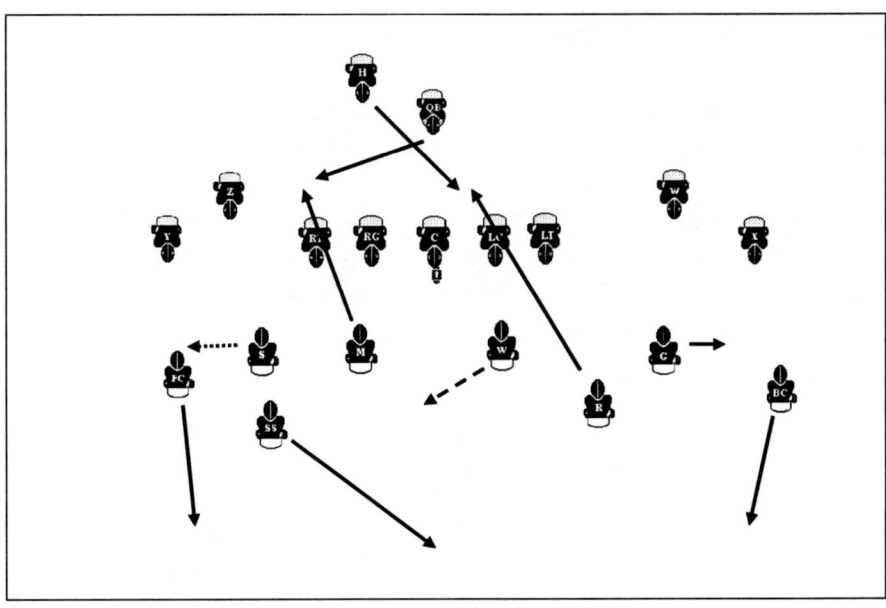

Figure 5-65. Zippo vs. a 22 set with weakside flow

Position	Pass responsibility
Sam	Plays the strongside wall-curl-flats.
Mike	Keys the H back going away from him, so he plays the quarterback man-to-man.
Will	Keys the H back going away from him, so he drops to the deep middle one-third and plays his cover 3 rules.
Strong safety	Keys the H back coming to his side, so he plays the halfback man-to-man. Will spills all weakside runs outside to Rover.
Rover	Keys the H back coming to him, so he plays the H back man-to-man.
Field corner	Plays the deep strong outside one-third.
Boundary corner	Plays the deep strong outside one-third.
Geronimo	Plays the weakside wall-curl-flats.

Figure 5-66. Position and responsibility for Zippo vs. a 22 set with weakside flow

Zippo Quarterback vs. a 22 Set (Figures 5-67 through 5-70)

Zippo Quarterback coverage is the same as Zippo, but the back read becomes the quarterback, instead of the halfback back. The corners play the deep outside one-thirds. Sam and Geronimo play the wall-curl-flats. Mike and Will use their Toro rules, but they key the quarterback instead of the halfback. The strong safety and Rover use their Toro rules, but they key the quarterback instead of the halfback. Zippo vs. a 22 set with strongside flow is shown in Figures 5-67 and 5-68. Zippo quarterback vs. a 22 set with weakside flow is shown in Figures 5-69 and 5-70.

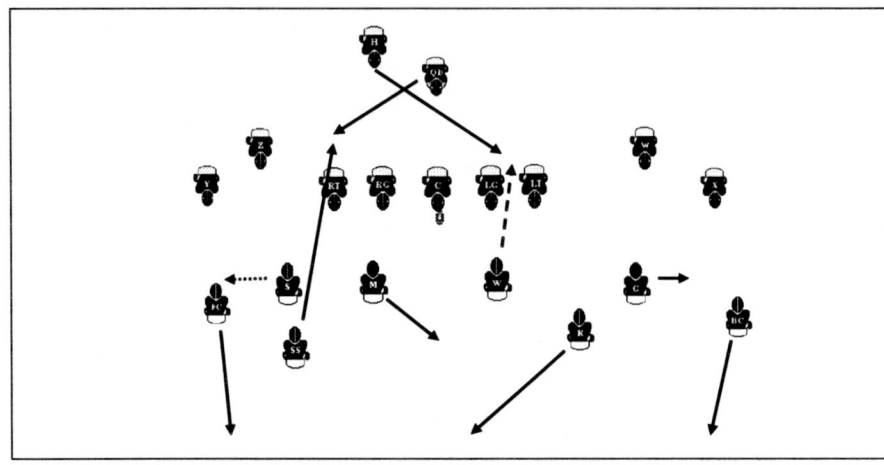

Figure 5-67. Zippo quarterback vs. a 22 set with strongside flow

Position	Pass responsibility
Sam	Plays the strongside wall-curl-flats.
Mike	Keys the quarterback. He reads the quarterback coming to him, so he spills him outside on all runs and drops to the low hole on all passes.
Will	Keys the quarterback going away from him, so he plays the H back man-to-man on all passes. He holds the backside on all runs.
Strong safety	Keys the quarterback coming to him, so he plays the quarterback man-to-man.
Rover	Keys the quarterback going away, so he drops to the deep middle one-third and plays his cover 6 rules.
Field corner	Plays the deep strong outside one-third.
Boundary corner	Plays the deep weak outside one-third.
Geronimo	Plays the weakside wall-curl-flats.

Figure 5-68. Position and responsibility for Zippo quarterback vs. a 22 set with strongside flow

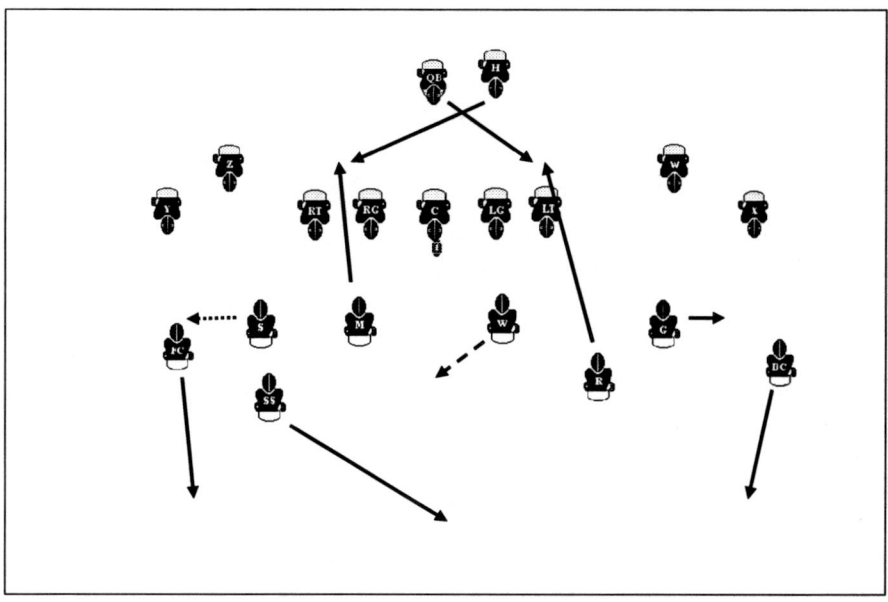

Figure 5-69. Zippo quarterback vs. a 22 set with weakside flow

Position	Pass responsibility
Sam	Plays the strongside wall-curl-flats.
Mike	Keys the quarterback going away from him, so he plays the H back man-to-man on all passes. He holds the backside on all runs.
Will	Keys the quarterback coming to him, so he spills the quarterback outside on all runs and drops to the low hole on passes.
Strong safety	Keys the quarterback going away from him, so he drops to the deep middle one-third and plays his cover 3 rules.
Rover	Keys the quarterback coming to him, so he plays the quarterback man-to-man on all passes.
Field corner	Plays the deep strong outside one-third.
Boundary corner	Plays the deep weak outside one-third.
Geronimo	Plays the weakside wall-curl-flats.

Figure 5-70. Position and responsibility for Zippo quarterback vs. a 22 set with weakside flow

Special Coverages

Cherokee Coverages

When a special scheme is created within the defensive scheme, a purpose must exist for its use. One such special scheme is Cherokee. The purpose of Cherokee is to disguise fronts and coverages and help defend against the evolution of the spread offense. Cherokee is run from a Crazy Horse front and incorporates several pass coverages. The general concept is to align Geronimo in the high hole at a depth of eight yards. Geronimo can use prowling and movement to align in the desired location inside the box, which helps the defense to defend various offensive plays. Cherokee allows not only Geronimo, but also Sam, Will, Rover, and the strong safety to help in the box. Cherokee uses prowling and movement in order to blitz, confuse quarterback reads, and to get advantageous alignments against both the run and the pass. This chapter looks at Cherokee and its various coverages vs. a 22 set.

Cherokee Cover 2 (Figures 6-1 and 6-2)

Cherokee cover 2 is a Crazy Horse alignment with cover 2 coverage. The purpose of this coverage is to play cover 2 with the addition of coverage in the high hole, which gives the defense better coverage against crossing routes and screens. Everyone is playing cover 2 except Geronimo who squats in the high hole. Linebackers align in a Crazy Horse front with Sam and Will widening to the outside enough to execute their cover 2 responsibilities. The secondary aligns in a cover 2 shell.

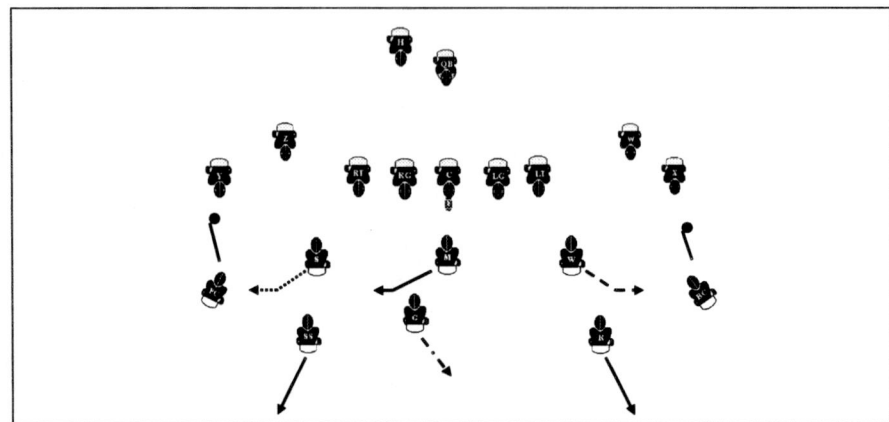

Figure 6-1. Cherokee cover 2 vs. a 22 set

Position	Pass responsibility
Sam	Uses his cover 2 rules and plays the strongside wall-curl-pull.
Mike	Uses his cover 2 rules and plays over the top of #3.
Will	Uses his cover 2 rules and plays the weakside wall-curl-pull.
Strong safety	Uses his cover 2 rules and plays the deep strongside half.
Rover	Uses his cover 2 rules and plays the deep weakside half.
Field corner	Uses his cover 2 rules, reroutes #1, and plays the flats.
Boundary corner	Uses his cover 2 rules, reroutes #1, and plays the flats.
Geronimo	Plays the high hole and attacks all inside crossing routes and screens.

Figure 6-2. Position and pass responsibility for Cherokee cover 2 vs. a 22 set

Cherokee Cover 2 Scooter (Figures 6-3 and 6-4)

Cherokee cover 2 scooter is a Crazy Horse alignment with cover 2 coverage. The purpose of this coverage is to let the strong safety and Rover come off their hashes and cheat on deep outside routes. Everyone is playing cover 2, except Geronimo who drops to the deep middle one-third from the high hole.

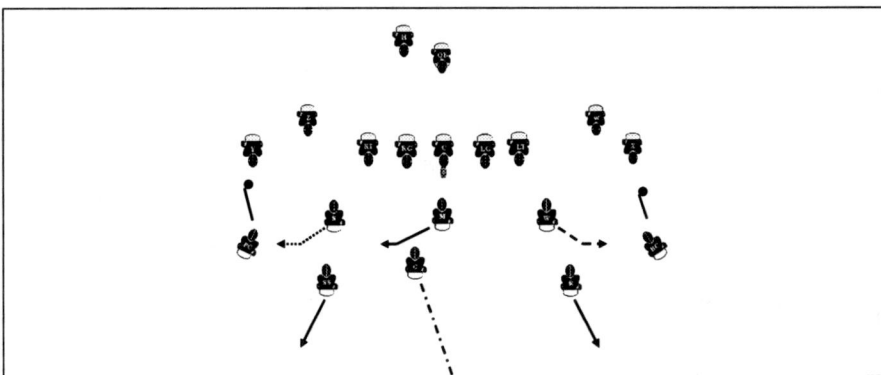

Figure 6-3. Cherokee cover 2 scooter vs. a 22 set

Position	Pass responsibility
Sam	Uses his cover 2 rules and plays the strongside wall-curl-pull.
Mike	Uses his cover 2 rules and plays over the top of #3.
Will	Uses his cover 2 rules and plays the weakside wall-curl-pull.
Strong safety	Uses his cover 2 rules and plays the deep strongside half. Because of the inside play of Geronimo, he can cheat off the hash to the outside and be more alert to deep outside routes.
Rover	Uses his cover 2 rules and plays the deep weakside half. Because of the inside play of Geronimo, he can cheat off the hash to the outside and be more alert to deep outside routes.
Field corner	Uses his cover 2 rules, reroutes #1, and plays the flats.
Boundary corner	Uses his cover 2 rules, reroutes #1, and plays the flats.
Geronimo	Drops to the deep middle one-third. He has deep outside help from the strong safety and Rover, allowing him to concentrate on deep middle routes.

Figure 6-4. Position and pass responsibility for Cherokee cover 2 scooter vs. a 22 set

Cherokee Cover 2 Sink (Figures 6-5 and 6-6)

Cherokee Cover 2 sink is a Crazy Horse front with cover 2 coverage. The purpose of this coverage is to give the secondary better coverage on deep-to-medium routes. Everyone is playing cover 2, except the corners, strong safety, and Rover sink into quarter coverage and divide the medium-to-deep zones into four zones instead of two zones. Geronimo squats in the high hole.

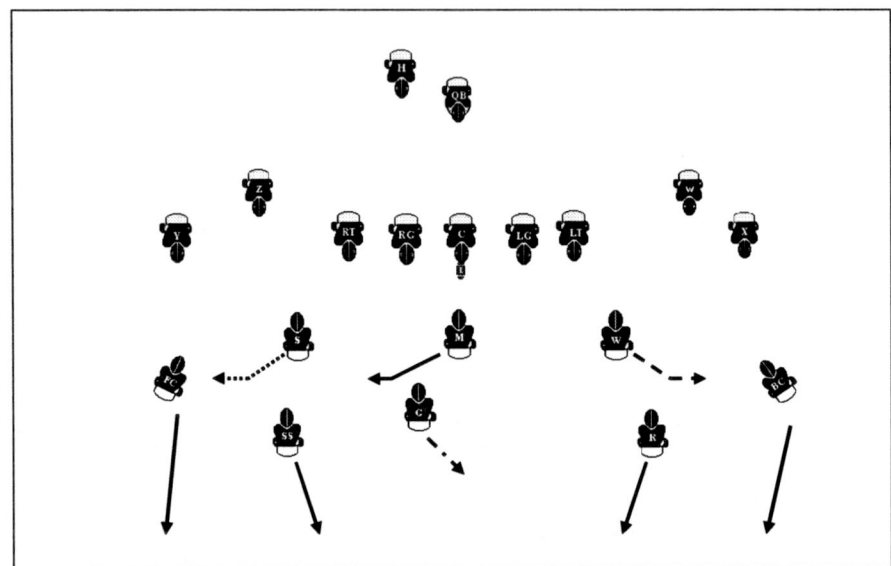

Figure 6-5. Cherokee cover 2 sink vs. a 22 set

Position	Pass responsibility
Sam	Uses his cover 2 rules and plays the strongside wall-curl-flats.
Mike	Uses his cover 2 rules and plays over the top of #3.
Will	Uses his cover 2 rules and plays the weakside wall-curl-flats.
Strong safety	Plays the strong inside one-quarter.
Rover	Plays the weak inside one-quarter.
Field corner	Plays the strong outside one-quarter.
Boundary corner	Plays the weak outside one-quarter.
Geronimo	Plays the high hole and attacks all inside crossing routes and screens.

Figure 6-6. Position and pass responsibility for Cherokee cover 2 sink vs. a 22 set

Cherokee Cover 2 Strike (Figures 6-7 and 6-8)

Cherokee Cover 2 strike is a Crazy Horse front with cover 2 coverage. The purpose of this coverage is to give coverage help on any strongside vertical route. Everyone is playing cover 2 except the strong safety plays over the top of any strongside vertical. He reads #2 to #1. If both #1 and #2 are on verticals, he plays over the top of #2. Geronimo bails to the deep strongside half.

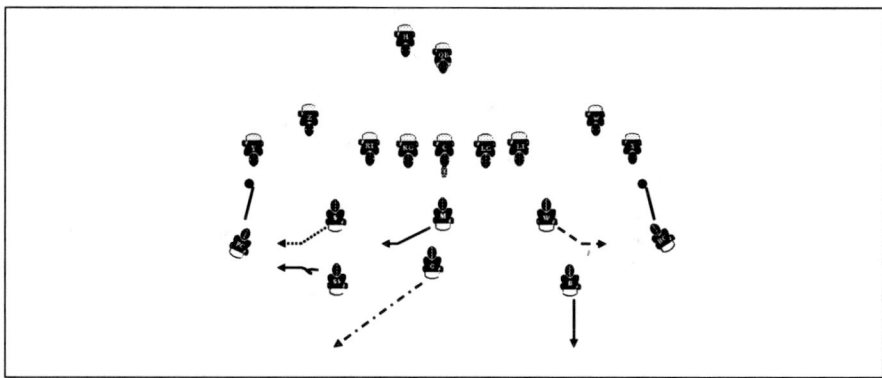

Figure 6-7. Cherokee cover 2 strike vs. a 22 set

Position	Pass responsibility
Sam	Uses his cover 2 rules and plays the strongside wall-curl-pull.
Mike	Uses his cover 2 rules and plays over the top of #3.
Will	Uses his cover 2 rules and plays the weakside wall-curl-pull.
Strong safety	Plays over the top of any strongside vertical or first inside route. He has Geronimo help behind him, so he can play very aggressively on all verticals and inside routes.
Rover	Uses his cover 2 rules and plays the deep weakside half.
Field corner	Reads #2. If #2 is inside or vertical, he sinks with #1. If #2 is outside, he attacks him immediately.
Boundary corner	Uses his cover 2 rules, re-routes #1, and plays the flats.
Geronimo	Drops to the deep strongside half. He has vertical help by the strong safety and corner, which allows him to concentrate on the quarterback in order to get a jump on the ball.

Figure 6-8. Position and pass responsibility for Cherokee cover 2 strike vs. a 22 set

Cherokee Cover 2 Whip (Figures 6-9 and 6-10)

Cherokee Cover 2 whip is a Crazy Horse front with cover 2 coverage. The purpose of this coverage is to give help on weakside vertical routes. Everyone is playing cover 2 except Rover plays over the top of any weakside vertical. He reads #2 to #1. If both #1 and #2 are on verticals, he plays over the top of #2. Geronimo bails to the deep weakside one-half.

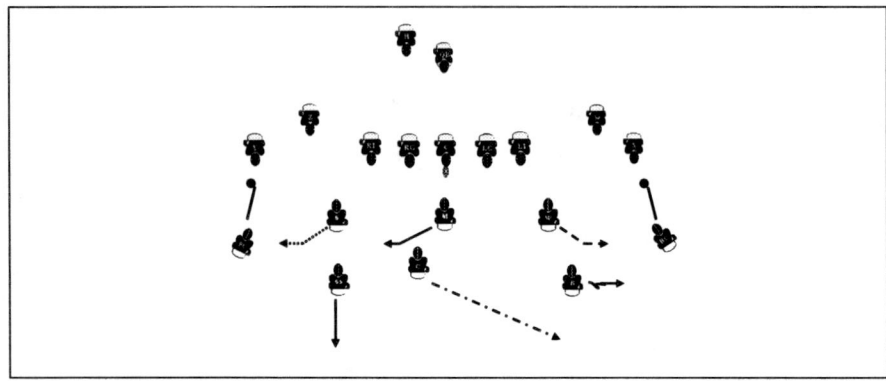

Figure 6-9. Cherokee cover 2 whip vs. a 22 set

Position	Pass responsibility
Sam	Uses his cover 2 rules and plays the strongside wall-curl-pull.
Mike	Uses his cover 2 rules and plays over the top of #3.
Will	Uses his cover 2 rules and plays the weakside wall-curl-pull.
Strong safety	Uses his cover 2 rules and plays the deep strongside half.
Rover	Plays over the top of any weakside vertical or first inside route. He has Geronimo help behind him, so he can play very aggressively on all verticals and inside routes.
Field corner	Uses his Cover 2 rules and re-routes #1 and plays the flats.
Boundary corner	Reads #2. If #2 is inside or vertical, he sinks with #1. If #2 is outside, he attacks him immediately.
Geronimo	Drops to the deep weakside half. He has vertical help by the Rover and corner, which allows him to concentrate on the quarterback in order to get a jump on the ball.

Figure 6-10. Position and pass responsibility for Cherokee cover 2 Whip vs. a 22 set

Cherokee Cover 2 Rhino (Figures 6-11 and 6-12)

Cherokee cover 2 rhino is a Crazy Horse front with cover 2 coverage. The purpose of this coverage is to move Rover into a position that allows him to blitz or defend a certain play or receiver. Everyone is playing cover 2 except Rover spins down to the low hole. Geronimo plays the deep weakside one-half.

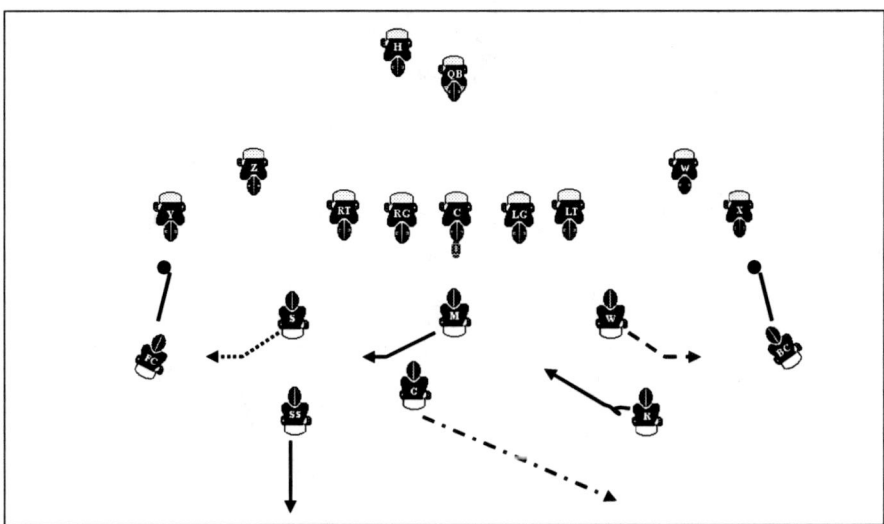

Figure 6-11. Cherokee cover 2 Rhino vs. a 22 set

Position	Pass responsibility
Sam	Uses his cover 2 rules and plays the strongside wall-curl-flats.
Mike	Uses his cover 2 rules and plays over the top of #3.
Will	Uses his cover 2 rules and plays the weakside wall-curl-flats.
Strong safety	Uses his cover 2 rules and plays the deep weakside half.
Rover	Spins down and plays the low hole area.
Field corner	Uses his cover 2 rules, reroutes #1, and plays the flats.
Boundary corner	Uses his cover 2 rules, reroutes #1, and plays the flats.
Geronimo	Drops to the deep weakside half.

Figure 6-12. Position and responsibility for Cherokee cover 2 Rhino vs a 22 set

Cherokee Cover 2 Snake (Figures 6-13 and 6-14)

Cherokee Cover 2 snake is a Crazy Horse front with cover 2 coverage. The purpose of this coverage is to move the strong safety into a position that allows him to blitz or defend a certain play or receiver. Everyone is playing cover 2 except the strong safety spins down to play the low hole. Geronimo plays the deep strongside one-half.

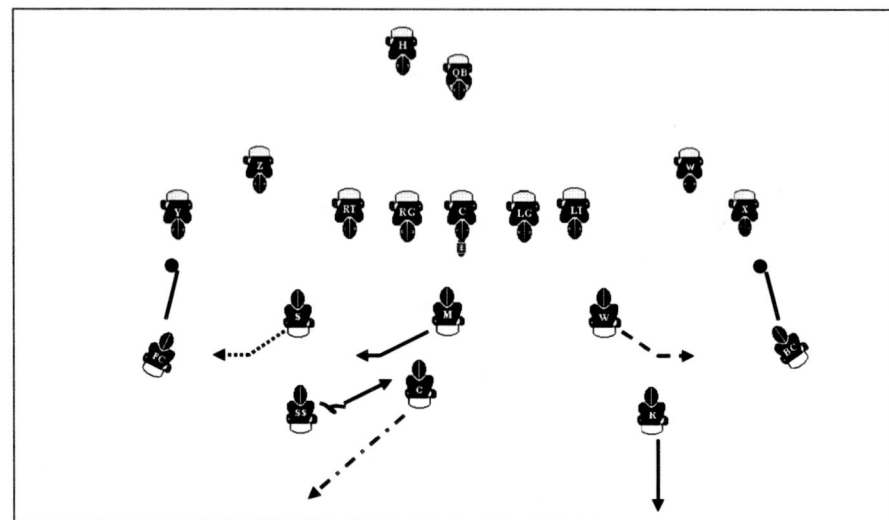

Figure 6-13. Cherokee cover 2 snake vs. a 22 set

Position	Pass responsibility
Sam	Uses his cover 2 rules and plays the strongside wall-curl-pull.
Mike	Uses his cover 2 rules and plays over the top of #3.
Will	Uses his cover 2 rules and plays the weakside wall-curl-flats.
Strong safety	Spins down and plays the low hole area.
Rover	Uses his cover 2 rules and plays the deep weakside half.
Field corner	Uses his cover 2 rules, reroutes #1, and plays the flats.
Boundary corner	Uses his cover 2 rules, reroutes #1, and plays the flats.
Geronimo	Drops to the deep strongside half.

Figure 6-14. Position and responsibility for Cherokee cover 2 snake vs. a 22 set

Cherokee Zippo (Figures 6-15 and 6-16)

Cherokee zippo is a Crazy Horse front with cover 3 coverage. The purpose of this coverage is to have man-to-man coverage on the H back and quarterback, allowing for better run support in the box. Everyone is playing cover 3 except the strong safety and Rover play man-to-man on either the H back or the quarterback, depending on who comes their way. Geronimo drops to the deep middle one-third.

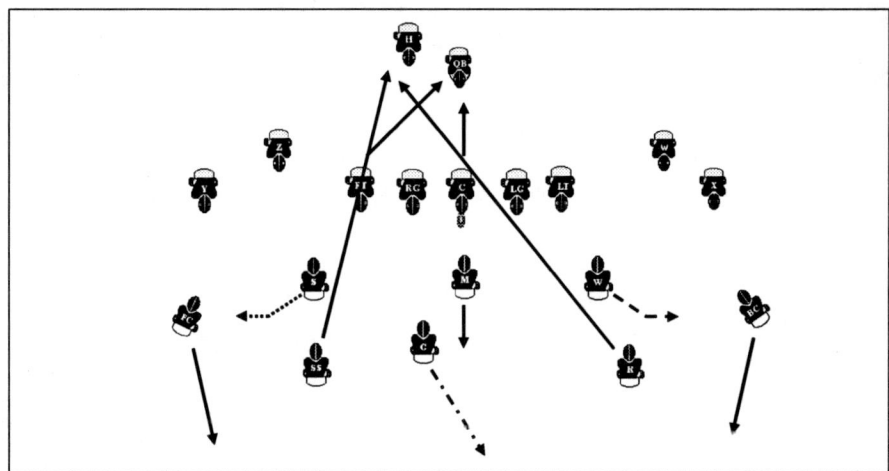

Figure 6-15. Cherokee zippo vs. a 22 set

Position	Pass responsibility
Sam	Plays the strongside wall-curl-flats.
Mike	Drops to the low hole.
Will	Plays the weakside wall-curl-flats.
Strong safety	Plays man-to-man on either the H back or quarterback, depending on who comes to the strongside. If neither comes to the strongside, he drops to the high hole and mirrors the quarterback.
Rover	Plays man-to-man on either the H back or quarterback, depending on who comes to the weakside. If neither comes to the weakside, he drops to the high hole and mirrors the quarterback.
Field corner	Uses his cover 3 rules and drops to the deep strongside one-third.
Boundary corner	Use his cover 3 rules and drops to the deep weakside one-third.
Geronimo	Drops to the deep middle one-third.

Figure 6-16. Position and pass responsibility for Cherokee zippo vs. a 22 set

Cherokee Cover 3 (Figures 6-17 and 6-18)

Cherokee cover 3 is a Crazy Horse front with cover 3 coverage. The purpose of this coverage is to confuse the quarterback's reads and to allow the linebackers to play the run more aggressively. Everyone is playing cover 3 except the strong safety and Rover drop to the curl-to-flats on their side. Geronimo drops the deep middle one-third.

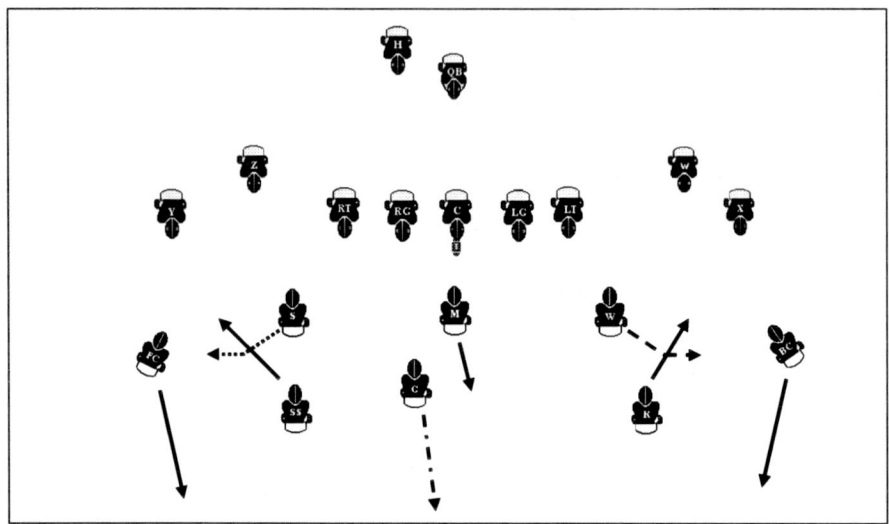

Figure 6-17. Cherokee cover 3 vs. a 22 set

Position	Pass responsibility
Sam	Plays the strongside hook/curl.
Mike	Plays the low hole.
Will	Plays the weakside hook/curl.
Strong safety	Plays the strongside curl-to-flats.
Rover	Plays the weakside curl-to-flats.
Field corner	Plays the strong deep outside one-third.
Boundary corner	Plays the weak deep outside one-third.
Geronimo	Drops to the deep middle one-third.

Figure 6-18. Position and responsibility for Cherokee cover 3 vs. a 22 set

Cherokee Cover 3 Press (Figures 6-19 and 6-20)

Cherokee cover 3 press is a Crazy Horse front with cover 3 and cover 2 coverage being used. The purpose of this coverage is to take away the short outside routes and to also give better run support defense. Everyone is playing cover 3 except the corners press the #1s and squat in the flats. Sam and Will drop to the wall-curl-pull. Mike drops to the low hole. The strong safety and Rover drop to the outside deep one-thirds. Geronimo drops into the middle deep one-third.

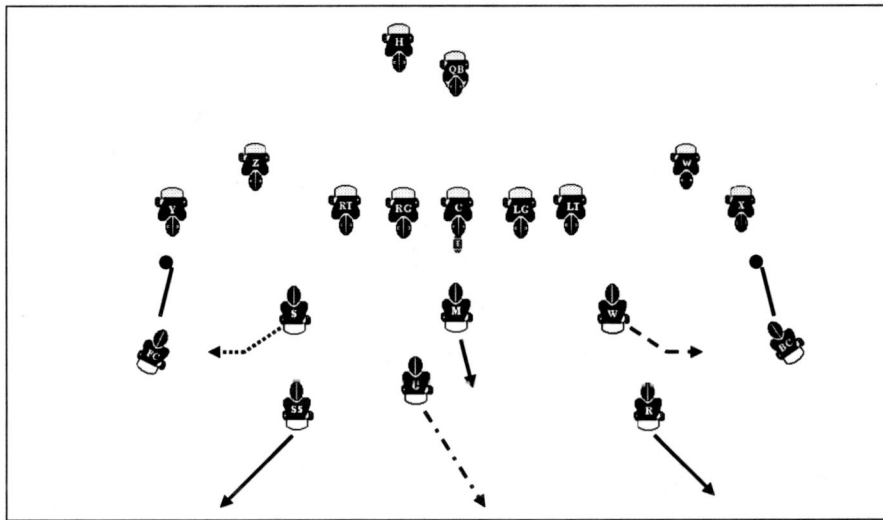

Figure 6-19. Cherokee Cover 3 press vs. a 22 set

Position	Pass responsibility
Sam	Uses his cover 3 rules and drops to the strongside wall-curl-pull.
Mike	Plays the low hole.
Will	Plays the weakside wall-curl-pull.
Strong safety	Plays the deep strong outside one-third.
Rover	Plays the deep weak outside one-third.
Field corner	Uses his cover 2 rules, reroutes #1, and squats in the flats. He will not pattern read as he does in cover 2, but remains in the flats.
Boundary corner	Uses his cover 2 rules, reroutes #1, and squats in the flats. He will not pattern read as he does in cover 2, but remains in the flats.
Geronimo	Drops to the deep middle one-third.

Figure 6-20. Position and pass responsibility for Cherokee cover 3 press vs a 22 set

Cherokee Cover 3 Man (Figures 6-21 and 6-22)

Cherokee cover 3 man is a Crazy Horse front with cover 3 and man-under coverage being used. The purpose of this coverage is to play man-to-man coverage, but, at the same time, have a safe three-deep zone coverage. The corners align in an Opie alignment on #1s. Sam and Will align in Marvin alignments on #2s.

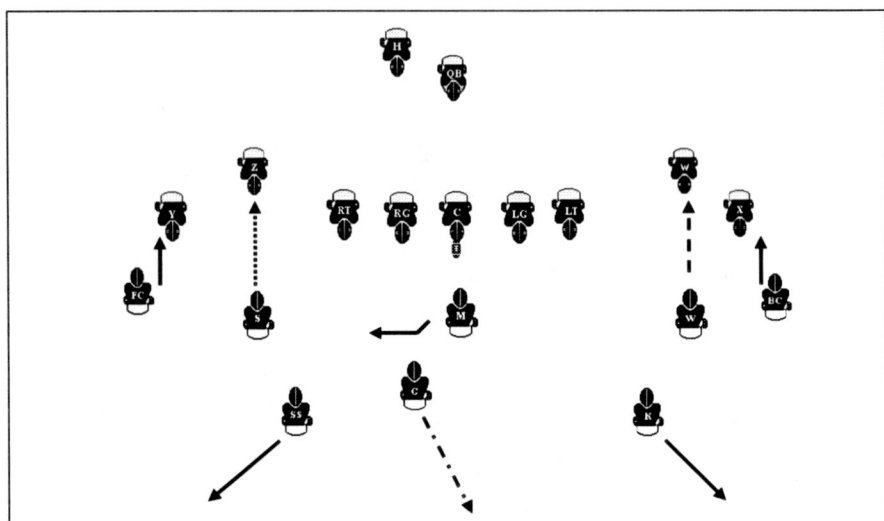

Figure 6-21. Cherokee cover 3 man vs. a 22 set

Position	Pass responsibility
Sam	Plays #2 man-to-man.
Mike	Stays over the top of #3.
Will	Plays #2 man-to-man.
Strong safety	Plays the deep strong outside one-third.
Rover	Plays the deep weak outside one-third.
Field corner	Plays #1 man-to-man.
Boundary corner	Plays #1 man-to-man.
Geronimo	Drops to the deep middle one-third.

Figure 6-22. Position and pass responsibility for Cherokee cover 3 man vs. a 22 set

Cherokee Cover 1 (Figures 6-23 and 6-24)

Cherokee cover 1 is a Crazy Horse front with man-free coverage. The purpose of this coverage is to play man-free and keep the linebackers more involved keying the H back and quarterback. The corners align in an Opie alignment on #1s. The strong safety and Rover align in Marvin alignments on #2s.

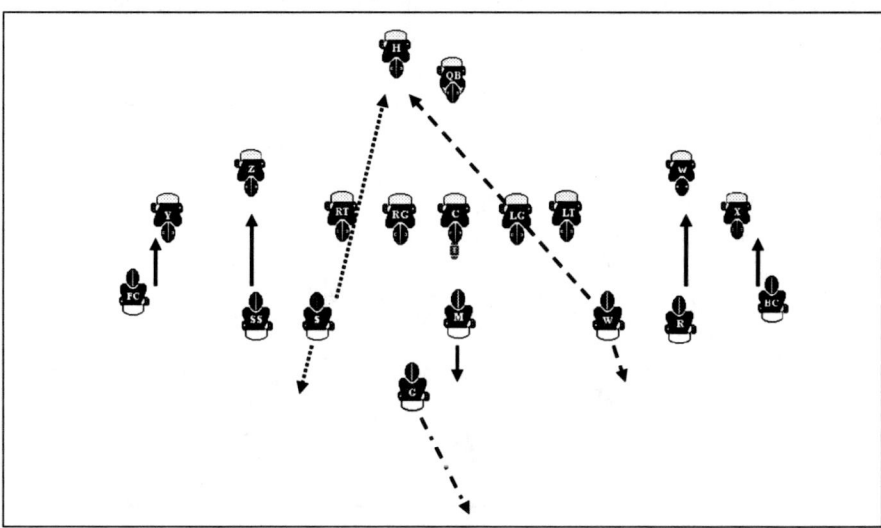

Figure 6-23. Cherokee cover 1 vs. a 22 set

Position	Pass responsibility
Sam	Plays the first back out to the strongside man-to-man or drops to the strongside hook.
Mike	Drops to the low hole and mirrors the quarterback.
Will	Plays the first back out to the weakside man-to-man or drops to the weakside hook.
Strong safety	Plays #2 strong man-to-man.
Rover	Plays #2 weak man-to-man.
Field corner	Plays #1 man-to-man.
Boundary corner	Plays #1 man-to-man.
Geronimo	Drops to the deep middle one-third.

Figure 6-24. Position and pass responsibility for Cherokee cover 1 vs. a 22 set

Cherokee Cover 0 (Figures 6-25 and 6-26)

Cherokee cover 0 is a Crazy Horse front with pure man-to-man coverage. The purpose of this coverage is to allow the linebackers to blitz without having pass coverage responsibilities. Geronimo aligns in a sky alignment on the H back. The strong safety and Rover align in Marvin or sky alignments on #2s. The corners align in Ike or sky alignments on #1s. All linebackers are free of pass coverage responsibility. Geronimo drops to the deep middle one-third.

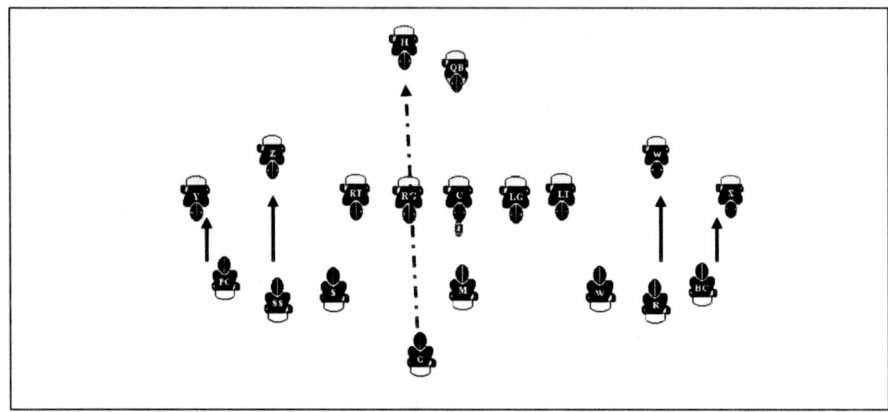

Figure 6-25. Cherokee cover 0 vs. a 22 set

Position	Pass responsibility
Sam	Executes the blitz that is called.
Mike	Executes the blitz that is called.
Will	Executes the blitz that is called.
Strong safety	Plays #2 man-to-man.
Rover	Plays #2 man-to-man.
Field corner	Plays #1 man-to-man.
Boundary corner	Plays #1 man-to-man.
Geronimo	Plays the H back man-to-man.

Figure 6-26. Position and pass responsibility for Cherokee cover 0 vs. a 22 set

Bracket Coverages

Bracket coverage is used to double cover specific receivers. Receivers are lettered A through E, from the strongside to the weakside. For instance, to double the #1 receiver in a 22 set, the coverage would be called with the letter A added to the call. Prowling and movement can be used to disguise who will be bracketed. In addition, who will play Ike and who will play sky alignments can be switched on the bracketed receiver. This section looks at Bracket and its various coverages vs. a 22 set.

Cover 0 "A" (Figures 6-27 and 6-28)

Cover 0 "A" is bracket coverage with the corner and strong safety bracketing the #1 receiver on the strongside. Sam aligns in a sky alignment on #2. Mike and Will slide to 30 techniques. Rover aligns in a sky alignment on #2. The boundary corner aligns in an Ike alignment on #1.

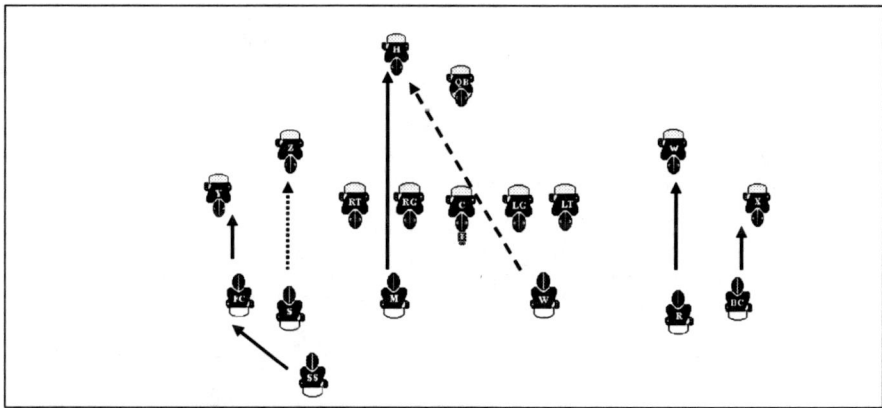

Figure 6-27. Cover 0 "A" vs. a 22 set

Position	Pass responsibility
Sam	Plays #2 man-to-man.
Mike	Plays man-to-man on the first back out to the strongside or drops to the low hole.
Will	Plays the first back out to the weakside man-to-man or drops to the weakside hook.
Strong safety	Brackets "A" man-to-man from a sky alignment.
Rover	Plays #2 man-to-man.
Field corner	Plays "A" man-to-man from an Ike alignment.
Boundary corner	Plays #1 man-to-man.

Figure 6-28. Position and pass responsibility for cover 0 "A" vs. a 22 set

Cover 0 "C" (Figures 6-29 and 6-30)

Cover 0 "C" is bracket coverage with the Geronimo and Rover bracketing the #2 receiver on the weakside. All linebackers align in the defense called. The corners align in Ike alignments. The strong safety aligns in a sky alignment.

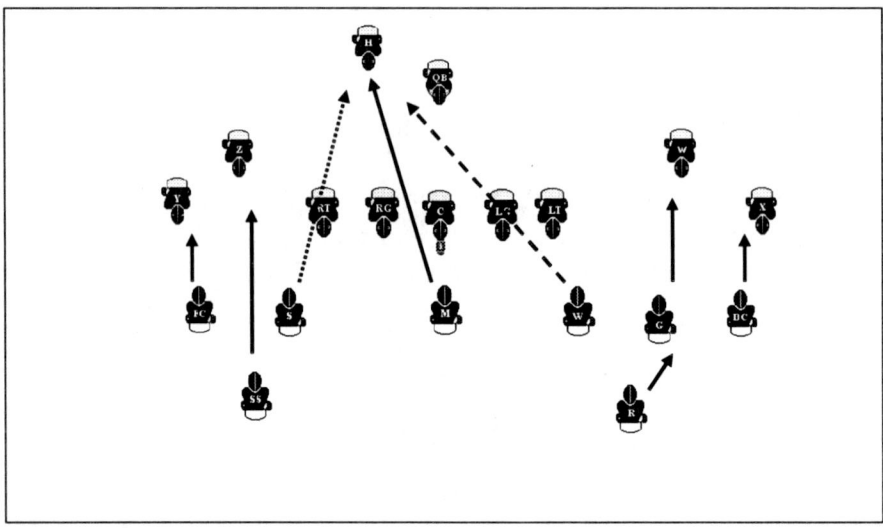

Figure 6-29. Cover 0 "C" vs. a 22 set

Position	Pass responsibility
Sam	Plays the first back out to the strongside man-to-man or drops to the strongside hook.
Mike	Drops to the low hole.
Will	Plays the first back out to the weakside man-to-man or drops to the weakside hook.
Strong safety	Plays #2 man-to-man.
Rover	Brackets "C" man-to-man from a sky alignment.
Field corner	Plays #1 man-to-man.
Boundary corner	Plays #1 man-to-man.
Geronimo	Brackets "C" man-to-man from an Ike alignment.

Figure 6-30. Position and pass responsibility for cover 0 "C" vs. a 22 set

Cover 0 "BC" (Figures 6-31 and 6-32)

Cover 0 "BC" is bracket coverage with the Tonto and the strong safety bracketing the #2 receiver on the strongside. Geronimo and Rover bracket #2 on the weakside. The linebackers align in the defense that is called. The corners align in Ike alignments. All other defenders play Cover 0.

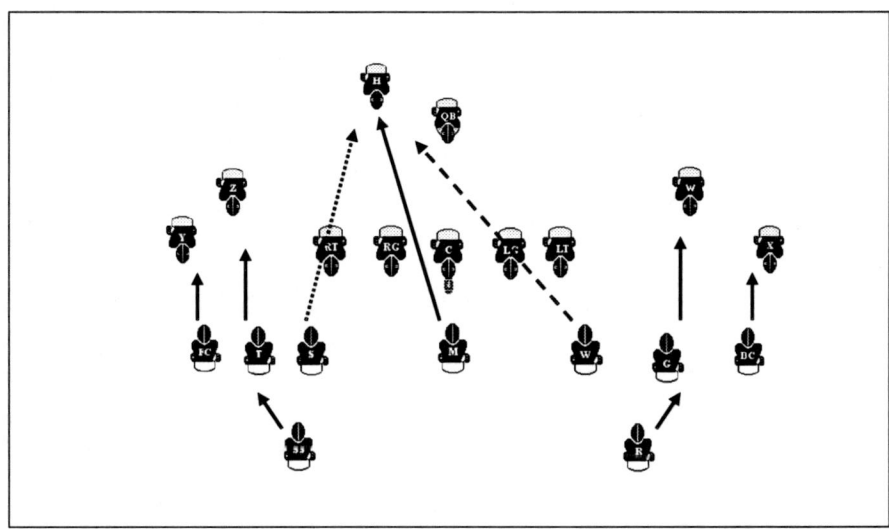

Figure 6-31. Cover 0 "BC" vs. a 22 set

Position	Pass responsibility
Sam	Plays the first back out to the strongside man-to-man or drops to the strongside hook.
Mike	Drops to the low hole and mirrors the quarterback.
Will	Plays the first back out to the weakside man-to-man or drops to the weakside hook.
Strong safety	Brackets "B" man-to-man from a sky alignment.
Rover	Brackets "C" man-to-man from a sky alignment.
Field corner	Plays #1 man-to-man.
Boundary corner	Plays #1 man-to-man.
Geronimo	Brackets "C" man-to-man from an Ike alignment.
Tonto	Brackets "B" man-to-man from an Ike alignment.

Figure 6-32. Position and pass responsibility for cover 0 "BC" vs. a 22 set

7

Special Considerations

Planning Coverages

The previous pages discussed several coverages. The coaching staff must decide the coverages that they will use. How many coverages they will use depends on the ability of the players and the offensive schemes that are being seen. The one area that cannot be confusing to coaches is the area of pass coverage. Confusion in pass coverage will lead to defensive mistakes and offensive touchdowns. It is important to keep it simple, but at the same time, add coverages as the season progresses.

Coverage Modifications

Color Calls (Figure 7-1)

Color calls are added to coverages in order to be able to check to certain coverages against one-back or no-back sets. Coaches may also want to use colors instead of numbers when they are communicating with the defense. Color calls are used to color code your coverages, which allows you to check to certain coverages against one-back and empty sets. For example, if in cover 2 you want to play cover 3 versus all one-back sets, you can call the coverage cover 2 red. If the offense comes out in a one-back or no-back set, you would check from cover 2 to cover 3, because cover 3 is also a red coverage.

Coverage	Color code
Cover 0	Black
Cover 1	Blue
Cover 2	Orange
Cover 3	Red
Cover 4	Green
Cover 5	Purple
Toro	White

Figure 7-1. Coverage color calls

Calling and Checking Coverages

Double digit calls are used to be able to run desired coverages against certain formations. For example, if in Cover 2 the play is to be cover 2 versus all pro sets (flanker on the tight end side), and at the same time use cover 5 versus all twins sets (flanker away from the tight end), the coverage cover 25 can be called. If the offense aligns in a pro set, run cover 2, and if the offensive comes out in a twin set, check to cover 5.

Adjusting to Motion

Certain types of motion will cause changes to certain coverages. When cross motion (motion that crosses the center) occurs, you can check to your second digit rules. If you align in your second digit rule and get cross motion, you go back to your first digit rule.   You need to game plan your motion rules. Single digit calls allow you to stay in the same defense when motion occurs.

- *Speed motion*: Quick motion that does not allow the defense time to adjust
- *Cross motion*: Motion that crosses the center and requires strength declaration change and adjustments
- *Zip-zap motion*: Motion that starts one way, and goes back the other way. It may or may not require adjustment.
- *Zap motion*: Motion that does not cross the center and requires no adjustment.

Special Man-to-Man Techniques

Bump Technique

Bump is a technique that is used when man-to-man coverage is called and motion occurs. If a defender's man goes in motion, the defender can swap man coverage with another defender. Basically, "you take my man and I will take your man."

Combo Technique

Combo is a technique that is used when two receivers align closer than five yards apart. When man coverage is used, the defenders play an inside-outside zone. The defenders can pick up their man after reading the release of the receivers.

Identifying Offensive Personnel

Most defensive coaches like to match defensive personnel to offensive personnel. If the offense has no tight end, coaches may want to think about bringing in their Arizona personnel, which can mean the nickel package or the dime package. The following number system can be used to identify offensive personnel who are in the game (this numbering should not be confused with the numbering of receivers):

- 10 personnel: One back and no tight end
- 11 personnel: One back and one tight end
- 12 personnel: One back and two tight ends
- 20 personnel: Two backs and no tight end
- 21 personnel: Two backs and one tight end
- 22 personnel: Two backs and two tight ends
- 23 personnel: Two backs and three tight ends
- 30 personnel: Three backs and no tight end
- 31 personnel: Three backs and one tight end
- 32 personnel: Three backs and two tight ends

About the Author

Denny M. Burdine has 30 years of football coaching experience at the high school level. Before retiring, he spent the last 17 years of his coaching career at Arkansas High School in Texarkana, Arkansas, where he served as a defensive coordinator, head football coach, athletic director, and history teacher.

His love for defensive football helped to establish him as one of the best defensive coaches in the state of Arkansas, with his defensive teams being ranked as one of the best in the state year in and year out. Some of his players have gone on to play at the Division I level, as well as in the NFL. During his career, he coached three NFL football players: Rod Smith of the Denver Broncos, Eric Warfield of the Kansas City Chiefs, and Mike Cherry of the New York Giants.

Burdine is a graduate of Southern Arkansas University. A strong believer in teaching character, leadership, and work ethics to players and students, he is listed in *Who's Who Among America's Teachers.*

Burdine and his wife, Judy, have two children, Jennifer and Lori, and four grandchildren.